ALSO BY DENIS MACK SMITH

Cavour and Garibaldi

Garibaldi (editor)

Italy: A Modern History

Medieval Sicily

The Making of Italy, 1796–1870

Mussolini's Roman Empire

Mussolini

CAVOUR

CAVOUR

Denis Mack Smith

Alfred A. Knopf　New York 1985

THIS IS A BORZOI BOOK
PUBLISHED BY ALFRED A. KNOPF, INC.

Copyright © 1985 by Denis Mack Smith

All rights reserved under International and Pan-American Copyright Conventions.
Published in the United States by Alfred A. Knopf, Inc., New York, and
simultaneously in Canada by Random House of Canada Limited, Toronto.
Distributed by Random House, Inc., New York. Originally published in Great
Britain by George Weidenfeld & Nicolson Ltd, London.

Library of Congress Cataloging in Publication Data

Mack Smith, Denis, 1920– Cavour.

Bibliography: p.
Includes index.
1. Cavour, Camillo Benso, conte di, 1810–1861.
2. Italy—History—1849-1870.   3. Statesmen—Italy—
Biography.   I. Title.
DG552.8.C3M17   1985   945′.08′0924 [B]   84-48815
ISBN 0-394-53885-4

Manufactured in the United States of America
First American Edition

Contents

Maps

SWITZERLAND

AUSTRIA

Savoy

Lombardy

Venetia

ISTRIA

OTTOMAN EMPIRE

Piedmont

Parma

NCE

Liguria

Modena

Romagna

DALMATIA

Nice

Monaco

Tuscany

Marche

ADRIATIC SEA

CORSICA

Papal States

Umbria

Abruzzi

Naples

TYRRHENIAN SEA

Sardinia

Calabria

Sicily

The Main Regions of Italy

Principal Places Mentioned

Preface

The most notable achievement in the life of Count Camille de Cavour was to preside over the unification of Italy. In March 1861, a few weeks before his death, the existence of a new united kingdom was officially proclaimed after many centuries in which the Italian peninsula had been divided into separate states. The joining together of these independent republics, duchies and kingdoms was something that very few people thought possible until it took place, so that nationhood had to be imposed by a small minority of patriots on a population that was barely ready for such a major change. This made the success of the national movement all the more remarkable. Lord Palmerston spoke for many contemporaries when he called it a miraculous ending to one of the most extraordinary and romantic stories in the whole of history.

One measure by which Cavour's accomplishment can be judged is the fact that he died at the early age of fifty. He can be compared to Gladstone, who was an older man yet had almost forty more years to live. These two politicians have been linked together as the most illustrious European liberals of their generation, but whereas Gladstone had achieved relatively little before 1861, Cavour by the age of fifty had earned a reputation from credible judges for being the ablest politician in Italian history. Nor was this opinion held merely by his fellow countrymen. Fifty years later the English historian George Trevelyan, despite his admiration for the more democratic Garibaldi, looked back on Cavour as the wisest and most beneficent statesman of his century 'if not of all time'.

His biography is chiefly interesting for the contribution he made to the political and economic history of Europe, because he was a superlative practitioner of the many arts that go towards the making of a successful politician. More than anyone else he developed the parliamentary system in Italy, as he laid down the basic traditions that governed political behaviour thereafter. During his last years he had to fight off domestic enemies to right and left, and also survived several attempts by King Victor Emanuel to find a more amenable and obedient Prime Minister. To the right of him were conservative opponents who wanted Italy to stay divided; to the left were Garibaldi and Mazzini whose vision of a united nation was far more radical and idealistic than his own. To succeed against such opponents, Cavour had to follow a difficult and sometimes labyrinthine path, enlisting alternately the support of both extremes against each other, and finally carrying into effect that pre-eminently difficult and almost paradoxical operation, a conservative revolution.

The successive stages in his career are more or less clearly marked. Until he reached the age of thirty-seven, his life was outwardly uneventful and is chiefly interesting for the development of his character and beliefs. He became an active politician only in 1847; it took him only five years before he was appointed Prime Minister of his native region of Piedmont-Sardinia. A third stage in his life found him working to make this region into the most prominent and progressive state in Italy. Then in the years 1855–9 he set himself with careful deliberation to precipitate a major European war, in the hope of dismembering the Austrian empire and unifying northern and central Italy. This war, when it took place in 1859, was a great disappointment, but the following year he used diplomacy where military means had only partially succeeded. After Garibaldi's revolutionary army of volunteers conquered Sicily and Naples, Cavour intervened to halt their radical revolution and annex these southern provinces. In the final months of his life he defied excommunication and declared war on the Pope. The last and perhaps the most considerable achievement of Italy's *risorgimento* was to destroy the temporal sovereignty of the Pope which had survived intact over so many centuries.

These victories were won against all the odds, and were the more astonishing in that Cavour's own province of Piedmont was small and possessed little natural leverage in the Italian peninsula. Not only had he to overcome opposition inside Piedmont, but all the other Italian states, despite the fact that a minority of their populations was sometimes prepared to help him, strongly opposed what he was doing. As a result the *risorgimento* had to be not merely a struggle against foreign oppression but a series of civil wars, and this inevitably opened wounds that were not easily healed. Cavour was very successful in rallying support for the new kingdom, but some internal divisions remained intractable – not merely the division between conservatives and political radicals, but between Church and State, between rich landowners and poor peasants, between the wealthier northern regions and the impoverished south.

The unification of Italy was in the end a great success story, but some incidental mishaps along the way are an essential part of the picture and throw into relief the full extent of the ultimate triumph. Sometimes Cavour appeared to be at the edge of total failure; sometimes he made what by his own admission were serious mistakes of judgement and employed methods that he knew would be thought discreditable; often he appeared to be the plaything of circumstance as events seemed to conspire against him. Cavour's ability can be appreciated only after tracing not only his successes, but the difficulties, the uncertainties, the errors, and what he himself referred to as the less admirable side of his handiwork. His capacity to recover from mistakes and exploit adverse conditions was an essential ingredient in what was empirical states-manship of the very highest order. No politician of the century – certainly not Bismarck – made so much out of so little. It was a thousand pities that he did not live long enough to apply his skill and intelligence to the initial problems of the kingdom that he did so much to create.

CAVOUR

CHAPTER 1

Childhood and Youth
1810 – 34

Camille de Cavour was born in 1810, the second son of the Marquis Michel Benso de Cavour. Their home town was Turin, the capital city of Piedmont in the extreme north-west of Italy, but the family was as much Swiss and French as Piedmontese because Michel's mother came from Savoy, north of the Alps, and Camille's mother Adèle was from Switzerland. The aristocracy of Turin belonged to a closed society in which pigtails and powdered wigs survived longer than elsewhere, where serfs and private feudal prisons could be found, and the 'King of Sardinia, Cyprus and Jerusalem' reigned as an absolute monarch. This narrow and provincial world survived even the great revolution of 1789 and invasion by the armies of Napoleon Bonaparte; but the monarchy was temporarily abolished, the Cavour family lost most of its inherited wealth, and Piedmont for a few years became a small outlying department of Napoleon's empire.

The future Prime Minister of Italy was thus born a subject of imperial France. His father, despite family traditions of reactionary conservatism and devoted loyalty to the Piedmontese monarchy, was sufficiently shrewd and calculating to rally more quickly than other aristocrats to the more emancipated Napoleonic régime, and rose to the rank of Chamberlain at court. So well did he adapt that Napoleon's sister, Pauline Borghese, became godmother to his son Camille. The fact that the Marquis de Cavour was a Catholic did not stop him using his position to speculate in purchasing Church properties confiscated by the godless French, and eventually this financial skill was employed along with his wife's substantial dowry to rescue the family fortunes.

Equal dexterity was shown after Napoleon's defeat. When the House of Savoy returned to the throne of Piedmont in 1814, the marquis momentarily lost his privileged position and even thought of emigrating, but opportunely changed sides again and was soon back in favour as a loyal servant of the restored monarchy. Liberal attitudes quickly disappeared after 1814 when pre-revolutionary laws were reintroduced in Turin and the nobility regained their monopoly of jobs in government. Schoolmasters and professors who had been appointed under Napoleon were dismissed when education was handed back to the Jesuits. Jews were forced to return into the ghetto and deprived of civil rights along with non-Catholics in general. No other government in Italy showed quite such a degree of unenlightenment. Even the Bourbon Kings of Naples, to say nothing of the Grand Duke of Tuscany and the Austrian administration in Lombardy and Venice, seemed almost progressive by comparison, and there was nothing to suggest that fifty years later Piedmont would become the nucleus of a liberal, unified Italian nation.

The name Piedmont is used for convenience to denote what should strictly be called the Kingdom of Sardinia. This kingdom was a composite state that, as well as its central region of Piedmont, included Savoy, Nice and the island of Sardinia; and by the treaty settlement of 1815 it was enlarged with the acquisition of the coastal territory of Liguria that had constituted the independent republic of Genoa. It was a small state with a population of not much over four million, less than a fifth of that in the whole Italian peninsula, and its component provinces still differed greatly one from another. Separate dialects and languages were spoken in the various regions; there were still differing systems of weights and measures; internal communication by sea and over mountain passes was not easy; and in the island of Sardinia, where the influence of the French Revolution and Napoleon never penetrated, there was still a feudal society that had changed little since the Middle Ages.

Camille de Cavour grew up in a restricted circle of titled and privileged families. Piedmontese dialect and French were the languages he learnt to speak. By his own account he was spoilt and coddled at home and received a defective education. For a time he disliked study and found reading difficult; indeed, all his life he was casual about spelling and grammar. Those who knew him as a boy described him as high-spirited and vivacious as well as obstinate, noisy, often bad tempered and undisciplined, yet almost always he was full of fun and looking for amusement. In extreme youth he already showed signs of possessing a strong and even bossy character; he was frequently disobedient, petulant and inconsiderate of other people, but essentially entertaining and likeable.

The practice of the time dictated that the family estates and title of marquis were entailed on the elder brother Gustave, so Camille knew he would have to find a career for himself: it was customary for younger sons of the nobility to become army officers or bishops. From the age of nine to sixteen he therefore attended the military academy as a boarder. This provided a harsh education. There were no holidays at the academy, and only Camille's privileged position as an aristocrat enabled him to see his family from time to time. For weeks at a stretch he might be away on military exercises and living in the open. Otherwise there was chapel twice a day, with long periods for prayer and meditation. Silence was obligatory except during recreation. Whether at work or play, a severe military discipline was used to curb any feeling of independence and to inculcate piety and absolute loyalty to the King.

The academy was an important though not happy experience for Cavour. With his sharp tongue, imperious manner and unconcealed sense of superiority he made few close friends there. One older boy to whom he became greatly attached had the reputation of being a liberal, possibly a republican, and eventually the two were forbidden to speak to each other. The young count was occasionally punished for slackness and bad discipline on parade; sometimes for impertinence and refusing to apologise. Once he had to live on bread and water for three days when found guilty of disobedience. On another occasion he was put under arrest for ten days after forbidden books were found in his possession. He always remembered his annoyance at fellow students who tried to curry favour with their superiors or who lessened a punishment by cringing to authority.

From reports on his behaviour it seems that he survived his schooldays reasonably well, though some scars must have remained. He was recalled as being somewhat aloof, often burying himself in newspapers and books on politics and history. He could be idle in class, and had especially poor marks for Italian language and literature. But he was exceptionally proficient at mathematics and mechanics. By his own account he had no talent for anything that needed imagination, although mathematics he found easy, exciting, and an excellent training in logic and clarity of thought. Later in life he said that he liked to reduce political and moral problems to imaginary graphs on which he would plot relevant factors before reaching a decision.

One privilege that he was granted in the last two years at school was the much sought-after appointment as page to a royal prince, the future King Charles Albert. The position of page conferred not merely economic advantages of free education, but priority in promotion irrespective of merit or examination results, and the Marquis Michel exerted himself to obtain this appointment, knowing from experience the advantages of preferment at court. Charles Albert was attracted and intrigued by the charm and intelligence of his fourteen-year-old page, but Cavour had too much self-respect to abide the demeaning duties of attendance at court functions. His pride of caste was offended by the scarlet uniform that looked to him like the livery of a domestic servant, and he was rash enough to say so in public. This insubordinate attitude eventually lost him the patronage of Charles Albert, and Cavour later admitted that he had been imprudent and ungrateful. His parents were keenly disappointed at his repeated questioning of rules and flouting of the accepted conventions of aristocratic society.

Just before his fifteenth birthday he was gazetted sub-lieutenant in the engineers, and after a further year at the academy was sent to assist in supervising the construction of fortifications near the French border. France, rather than the Austrian Habsburgs, was still regarded as the main potential enemy of Piedmont. The frontier fortresses were in lonely, isolated places without access by proper roads. They afforded few leisure-time distractions, and in his boredom the young soldier developed a taste for cards, billiards and gambling. By the end of 1828 he was beginning to wonder if he could endure his military career much longer.

But boredom gave him the incentive to read, and he filled notebooks with long passages copied from French, English and Scottish historians. Among these he especially admired Guizot for giving history some of the logic of mathematics and the physical sciences. The many transcriptions he made are an indication of his developing interests. From Gibbon he copied many pieces in the original English dealing with religion: on Julian the Apostate; on differences between medieval heresies; on the harm done by religious fanaticism 'insensibly corroding the vital principles of virtue and veracity'. The longest passage was a dozen pages from Dean Milman's *History of the Jews*.

Another, on the Jesuits, came from William Robertson's *History of Charles v.* Others, taken from David Hume's *History of England*, included paragraphs on the heretic Wycliffe, the struggle between King Henry and St Thomas Becket, and King Charles 1's arbitrary treatment of Parliament; and this Piedmontese aristocrat was struck by the fact that an Anglo-Saxon merchant might be promoted to the rank of Thane.

A very important influence on Cavour was that of his Swiss relatives. He had little in common with his cousins in Turin, but as a boy he travelled to Geneva almost every year – sometimes more than once. He used to stay with Jean-Jacques de Sellon, his mother's brother, and regularly visited his cousin Auguste de la Rive, both of whom provided a great intellectual stimulus. The de Sellons were strict Calvinists, while the de la Rives were Protestants of a more rationalist persuasion. Jean-Jacques was a dedicated pacifist who spent much of his life working to abolish the death penalty. On this and other unconventional topics there were discussions in Geneva which sometimes continued until dawn. Cavour agreed with his uncle that human life should ideally be inviolable, just as the morality of the gospels ought to apply in politics as well as in private behaviour; but on empirical grounds he accepted that the death penalty might sometimes be needed as a deterrent. Universal peace was admirable as another ideal, but freedom had to be defended by force if necessary; nor was international arbitration acceptable so long as most of the potential arbiters shared with the Austrian politician Metternich an interest in enslaving other peoples.

Cavour's political opinions during his years in the army were described as being ultra-liberal, 'Jacobin' and 'very exaggerated'. He realized that such views were likely to bar him from any expectation of wealth or political position, given the social milieu of Turin; but he was insistent that he would never change his opinions for personal advantage. On one occasion his father, irked by his liberal predisposition and general recalcitrance, talked of sending him 'to die of hunger in America' for being a renegade to his class and ancestry. Yet this young army officer was sufficiently conventional or sensible to swear an oath to defend the King 'against any of his subjects attempting to overthrow the established order'.

Probably this flirtation with radical ideas was in part intended to shock his conservative family and brother officers into questioning their absolutist and obscurantist prejudices, but it is also true that the

Geneva of Voltaire and Rousseau left a lasting imprint on his mind: letter after letter testified to his firm belief in the future progress of human society and the triumph of reason and enlightenment. He told his uncle that he thought wars would become less frequent because of a gradual extension of education and civilized values; meanwhile, every honest person should try to contribute to the inevitable advance of mankind. In holding these beliefs he acknowledged his primary debt to Rousseau for having taught people about universal human dignity and the path towards 'progress and social emancipation'.

Cavour's politics were at their most radical in 1830 when he spent nine months with the military engineers in Genoa. This port was the home town of Giuseppe Mazzini, a man five years his senior, who was already formulating the ideas that developed into a lifelong dedication to the unification of Italy. Genoa was the mercantile capital of the Kingdom of Sardinia: more lively and busy than Turin, more bourgeois, more Italian in sentiment and outlook, as well as being more frequented by foreigners. Until 1797 it had been an independent republic, and long after 1830 still nurtured some resentment at annexation by monarchist and absolutist Piedmont. Here Cavour found a new and unusually sympathetic environment, particularly in the salon of the Marquise Anne Giustiniani. Anne was a French lady with three children who took the young officer as one of her lovers. As she shared Mazzini's republican views, it is possible that in her hospitable house these two lifelong opponents met, for the only time in their lives.

In July 1830, when a revolution in Paris dethroned the Bourbon dynasty, Cavour was seen running down the corridor of his barracks in Genoa waving a paper-knife and crying 'long live the republic, down with all tyrants!' Probably he was not being wholly serious, for such words would have been a flagrant betrayal of his military oath. Yet he certainly welcomed what he called this 'glorious revolution' of July and hoped that some members of the Piedmontese aristocracy would be inspired by it to champion the cause of much more radical reform.

Charles Albert shortly afterwards succeeded to the throne and became if anything more reactionary than his predecessor, as well as closer to the absolutist and oppressive régime in Austria. Cavour, on the other hand, was coming to realize that political and social reforms were an urgently needed prophylactic against a possible class war. For a short time he believed – and it was the nearest he ever came to the more advanced social opinions of Mazzini – that if moderate reforms were not granted soon, violence might be justified to secure them.

There can be little wonder that someone with such views was under secret official surveillance, and Cavour thought his letters were being intercepted and read by the police. Nor is it surprising that, as he told his father, he could no longer honourably remain in the army if other officers were beginning to regard him as a potential traitor. The marquis reluctantly concurred, but eight more months of virtual exile had to be passed in the remote fortress of Bard before an honourable discharge could be arranged. The official reasons given for leaving the army were bad health and poor eyesight. Cavour wrote that renouncing a military career was a great sacrifice since it ended any hope of celebrity or of being able to use his talents for King and country; but in private he was delighted to return to civilian life.

Having failed to make one career at court and another in the army he fell into an intellectual and moral lassitude of which he was soon much ashamed, and some of his radical convictions weakened or disappeared. An added ingredient was disillusionment with the July revolution in Paris when he discovered that violence led in practice not to improvements in government but rather to more violence. He watched with much misgiving Mazzini's first futile attempt at armed rebellion, because he thought it would lead either to anarchy or to socialism, or to a counter-revolution by the conservative aristocracy who held the levers of power. Any extreme position in politics, any interference with peaceful processes of change, might be dangerous. He remained proud of belonging to the aristocracy, and his friends continued to come from this same class, but on top of resentment at being a disadvantaged younger son he chafed at the exaggerated privileges that propped up the old families and fuelled the threat of revolution.

Before he left the army, Cavour's intellectual interests were turning in the direction of social and economic affairs. He read the radical *Westminster Review*, perhaps in the house of some diplomat or foreign visitor who could evade the censorship. His liking for mathematics convinced him that there would one day be an equally precise science of economics, the rules of which were already beginning to be formulated, chiefly in Scotland and England. His early commonplace books contain quotations from John McCulloch, Nassau William Senior, David Ricardo and 'the Reverend Malthus who has made some of the greatest recent discoveries in political philosophy'. As he told an English acquaintance, he learnt to read English by getting up at 4.00 a.m. to study Adam Smith. At a time when many cereal-growing landowners were clamouring for increased protection, he determined to master this subject so that he could use the arguments of Adam Smith to confute the 'absurd errors' of the protectionists.

His first English friend was William Brockedon, a Fellow of the Royal Society, whose hobby took him every year to the Alpine valleys to find which of forty possible routes Hannibal's army had taken into Italy. Travelling together on mountain pathways the two used to discuss politics and literature. Cavour's notebooks in the early 1830s show that his reading included Alexander Pope, the 'incomparable' Shakespeare, Walter Scott and, above all, the novels of Bulwer-Lytton. He told Brockedon that he thought Byron the supreme poet of the nineteenth century – as Voltaire had been of the eighteenth – Byron who would always remain 'the favourite of strong spirits and anyone with a too exquisite sensibility'.

But in fact Cavour's taste never ran much to poetry or romanticism. The contemporary Englishman he admired most of all, apart from Robert Peel, was Jeremy Bentham, 'that great enquirer into the secrets of the human heart'; and he once said he could find no conflict between Bentham's utilitarianism and the precepts of the gospel. Utilitarianism was a corrective to Jacobinism: individuals who followed their own interests would sometimes make mistakes, but the sum total of all such errors would be less than those committed by the most enlightened of governments.

Through Bentham his attention was drawn to English politics, which he found somewhat confusing. In 1832 he thought that the future of Italy might well depend on Lord Grey's Reform Bill which, by widening the parliamentary suffrage, might immunize society against the worst dangers of revolution. But while his first sympathies were with reforming English Whigs, his real heroes became the Tory pragmatists whose sense of justice and political morality was a bulwark against both revolution and reaction. Peel, and above all the younger Pitt, 'the greatest statesman of his century', received more of Cavour's admiration than any other politicians whether past or present and from whatever country.

8

Growing up in a French-speaking society, he found French culture more easily accessible than English. Where France goes, he once wrote, the rest of Europe is almost bound to follow; for this reason, events in France seemed far more important than what was happening in Italy. The Baron de Barante, who was French ambassador in Piedmont until 1835, and Barante's secretary Count d'Haussonville, were therefore plied with questions about everything French. Cavour developed a liking for French novels as well as French wine. His personal library later in life included Hugo, Balzac, de Musset, Gautier, Stendhal, de Staël, Comte, Chateaubriand and many lesser names, though when or if these authors were read is impossible to know. In this library there were eventually fifty books on engineering and technology, as well as about eighty biographies and three hundred other works of history. One of his favourite authors was Alexis de Tocqueville, whose study of democracy in the United States he on one occasion called the most remarkable book of modern times; here, in his opinion, was the most likely pointer to the direction that the world was about to take: a book full of hope but also of warning.

It should be added that he had no special affection for music and the other arts. When he confessed to an admiration for Verdi he did not enlarge or explain what he meant and may have been thinking more of politics. He heard Bellini's *I Puritani* in Paris and thought it incomparably finer than Mozart, but after sitting through *Guillaume Tell* his only comment was that he could not hear the words. By his own admission, an essentially positivist and pragmatic mentality left him with little ear for poetry; and on his travels he preferred to study factories and methods of agriculture, while never mentioning architecture or pictures. When questioned about matters of taste he disclaimed any understanding of art, and once said he would find it harder to write a sonnet than make Italy into a nation.

Italian literature was strangely unfamiliar to him. As a schoolboy he had had to learn something of Dante and Petrarch; yet he did not refer to them in later life, and it was said that he can never have read *The Divine Comedy*. Three or four references prove that he knew Manzoni's great novel, *The Betrothed*, but so far as we know he did not possess a copy, and was oddly silent about other Italian historical novelists much in vogue at the time. Some of Italy's troubles he used to blame on an excessively literary education which he himself had succeeded in avoiding. A lack of familiarity with the Italian language sometimes made him feel guilty, but when in 1832 a friend invited him to visit Tuscany and repair this deficiency he could not find the inclination to accept, even though he was bored and unemployed at the time. He was delighted to discover that many of the most distinguished scientists of modern times had been Italians, but was upset to find that their names were unknown to him.

One Italian writer he admired was Machiavelli, whom he called the greatest philosopher of the sixteenth century, and what he found particularly memorable was Machiavelli's tirade against the temporal power of the Popes. He himself gave up believing in papal infallibility after reading Guizot and Benjamin Constant. His other religious views are not so easy to identify, especially since his enquiring mind saw more than one side to any question and was impatient of dogma or authority. Always inquisitive about religious matters, his curiosity at first received greater stimulus from the Calvinist Geneva of his mother's family than from Catholic Turin; but although he was sometimes accused of being a Protestant, the background to his life was and remained that of a non-practising Catholic. He was proud of being related through his father's French ancestry to St Francis de Sales. His mother converted to Catholicism after she left Switzerland to live in Turin, perhaps at the same time that his father renounced his early involvement with freemasonry. Cavour used to read and meditate on the Bible during his lonely years in the army, but was sorry to find insufficient rational arguments for faith, and concluded that by temperament and cast of mind he would never reach any profound belief.

He was nevertheless practical or opportunist enough to accept that Catholicism was socially useful, especially for those unable to think for themselves who might find support in ritual observance and absolution. There might even be utility in pretending to believe so as to set a good example to the masses. This attitude was accompanied by a moderate degree of anticlericalism which was fixed in his mind when he chanced upon shocking examples of immoral behaviour among the rural clergy. He was hostile by instinct and reason to any kind of persecution, whether by the Church or of the Church, and experience taught him to be equally hostile towards clerical intervention in politics. From de Tocqueville, the *Westminster Review*, and practical observation in Switzerland, he began to learn about other societies where a free Church could exist in a free state to their mutual profit.

* * *

In 1833 Cavour began a diary, while spending several months with his Swiss relatives, in which one of the first entries described what seems to have been a pilgrimage to Voltaire's house at Ferney. At Geneva he continued to see a good deal of Auguste de la Rive, who had an English wife and owned several farms in England. The anglophile, rationalist and strongly conservative views of this family made a considerable impact. In addition to being a professor of physics, Auguste was an active politician in the canton, and his son William later went to study chemistry in Edinburgh. Cavour used to stay near Geneva with his own uncle de Sellon, not far from whom lived de Sellon's two sisters, Victoire and Henriette, who had both married into the French aristocracy. Their husbands, the Duke of Clermont-Tonnerre and the Count d'Auzers, were loyal to the deposed Bourbons and had fled to Geneva. Animated political discussions within this family group continued to be an important part of Cavour's political development, though listening to reactionary opinions sometimes made him aggressively angry and his diary made reference to cross words that he later regretted.

Both his Swiss aunts were childless and eventually transferred to live with their sister in Turin. Plenty of room was available in the large ancestral palazzo for a number of families. As well as the head of house, the Marquis Michel, there was the older son Gustave and his three children. Gustave had once been regarded by Camille as his best friend, but by the time the diary opened the two were less close. The elder brother was the favourite son, more studious, more obedient, who was increasingly preoccupied with religion and wrote several strong attacks against the 'false philosophy' of Bentham and Hume. Camille by contrast was more open and impetuous, more amusing, with far wider interests and more of a taste for brilliant conversation. There were quarrels: for example, over how large an apartment each could have. When Gustave's infant son Auguste became the centre of attention, Camille remonstrated, and was furious when accused by his mother of being jealous. The diary recorded that he could sometimes hardly bear to continue living in the middle of this extended family, where serious talk was drowned in the prattle of children; but being financially dependent on what he called a meagre pittance from his father, he had nowhere else to go.

The idea was taking shape in Michel's mind that, as Gustave was bent on a life of study, Camille would eventually take over the agricultural interests of the family. One of their estates was at Grinzane near Alba, where the Duke of Clermont-Tonnerre owned half the village, and to this tiny community of three hundred souls Cavour was sent as mayor at the age of twenty-two. No doubt this was intended as a first training in public affairs, and even more as a guardianship of the family interests. It was very much a part-time job but he held it for seventeen years, building roads and a church, negotiating with brigands, sometimes organizing squads of peasants to clear the woods of highwaymen, introducing vines from France to make the famous wine of Barolo, and in general learning the rudiments of accountancy and farm management.

The years 1833–4 were nevertheless the most desperate of his life because he felt useless and had so little to occupy his mind. Though fond of his mother, he did not feel necessary for her happiness; and his father too, though kind and full of good advice, remained upset by his contentiousness and refusal to conform. The one close remaining friend seemed bored by his company, while new friends were hard to make; and he dejectedly confessed that his earlier idea of friendship had been too much a selfish desire to feel a sense of superiority over acquaintances who would accept his leadership.

In later years, Cavour had less time for introspection, but his early diary betrays the morbid self-pity of a person who, without the vivacity and verve that struck other people both earlier and later, could sometimes be morose and lethargic. He admitted to having a melancholy disposition and to a fear of becoming cynical and icily cold in his affections. He was bad tempered: for example, when beaten at chess. As well as eating too much he would become drunk and gamble for high stakes. He was putting on weight, 'and in my social position there is nothing so much to be dreaded as obesity, for it will make me look ridiculous'. He felt sure that if he had been born in England a person with his talents would by now be someone of consequence, whereas in Piedmont the early illusions of future worldly success were quickly disappearing.

This was one of several moments in his life when he thought of suicide as he contemplated a future 'without purpose, without hope, without desire'. Rather than be an undistinguished younger son he would a hundred times rather be dead. Among the excerpts he copied out from *Hamlet*, *King John* and *Macbeth* were that life was 'weary, stale, flat and unprofitable'; it was 'as tedious as a twice-told tale', 'a tale told by an idiot, signifying nothing'. In Hamlet's speech on suicide he underlined the words 'conscience doth make cowards of us all', adding that he would copy Hamlet and not kill himself 'for the moment', yet he wished he knew how to catch some deadly disease that would cure for ever a life ruined by an excess of intelligence and vanity.

For several years he had heard nothing from Anne Giustiniani, but in 1834 their affair recommenced and restored some of his self-confidence. On her side, though she had other lovers, it was deeply felt; on his, the underlying emotion seems to have been more a desire to possess an admiring and disinterested friend at a time when he felt lonely and unfulfilled. Her husband was obviously bored with her and seems to have encouraged their relationship, as also did Cavour's own parents, who were perhaps worried by his morbid self-concern. In one moment of romantic abandon he promised that he would dedicate the rest of his life to her; but he quickly admitted that this would be impossible and, while blaming himself for causing her unhappiness, advised that she should return to her own family. Anne was more than a little unbalanced and hysterical in character, and some years later committed suicide. Cavour had other casual love affairs – some of them concurrently, one or two possibly more than casual – and was flattered to think that he possessed an exceptional skill in seduction; but he succeeded best with older married women with whom there was less risk of any permanent attachment. He noted with positive approval Byron's advice in courtship, to 'disguise even tenderness if thou art wise'.

CHAPTER 2

Lessons from Abroad
1834 – 41

At twenty-four, Cavour was worried to feel himself becoming prematurely old. Repeatedly he bewailed the 'morbid' vanity of his youth and the inability to find an outlet for his driving energy. He continued to hope that events might allow him to become a politician who could command others and earn sufficient independence to escape a humiliating reliance on his family, but he could never honourably compromise with the autocratic government of Charles Albert. In one letter he referred to an early and now discarded dream that he might wake up one day to find himself the chief minister of a Kingdom of Italy, only to mock his own presumption.

This is not the only time he referred to the concept of national identity that Mazzini was continuing to put into circulation. Unlike Mazzini he spoke of the existence of a Piedmontese nation and a Sicilian nation, but he also agreed that some kind of Italian nationality was waiting to be born, and hoped that Italians would not fall too far behind the other national movements of liberation that he observed in Greece, Poland and Germany. Italians had once been in the van of European civilization and he hoped they would be so again if only other peoples would help them fight for freedom. Crushed by Austrian rule in the north and by papal rule further south, they would one day recover their former vigour, as indeed they had begun to do in the short period after Napoleon crowned himself King of Italy in 1805.

Possibly Cavour's concept of an Italian nation did not comprise more than those regions in the north of the peninsula that made up Napoleon's 'Kingdom of Italy', and certainly he continued to show a singular lack of interest in either Naples or Sicily. Though he once said he would be ashamed to travel abroad until thoroughly acquainted with his own country, in practice he gave little evidence of wanting to see anything outside Piedmont, and never in his life visited even the island of Sardinia, which was an integral part of his own kingdom. In the 1830s he set himself to learn the Italian language more seriously, and yet to the end of his life spoke French much better and knew far more about the history and culture of nations north of the Alps.

A more immediate concern than nationality was the desirability of political reforms in Piedmont and the overriding need to avoid any revolutionary change in society. Cavour at one point expressed the view that the world was moving inevitably towards democracy and argued against those who said that the United States was too democratic; but he was not sure that he welcomed the process too close to home, and at least wanted it to be delayed. The aristocracies of Europe had in his opinion condemned themselves to eventual destruction because of their obstinate refusal to accept innovations of any kind, and yet preferably they should not renounce their privileges before other classes acquired, as in England, a vested interest in stability and social order. Radical political changes were best left for the longer term. The immediate and urgent requirement was for minor social reforms so that the working classes could acquire something of the patriotism and sense of personal dignity that he observed in Switzerland but not at home.

By 1833–4, after some hesitations and oscillations, Cavour was formulating what became his central idea of the political *juste milieu*, the happy middle path that avoided extreme positions of any kind. Nothing else would enable society to escape the two extremes of despotism and anarchy. By nature and intellectual conviction he now felt himself to be essentially a conservative, indeed strongly so, but however much he disliked Mazzini and the republicans, he said he would not wish them crushed if the price was a greater degree of autocratic government; nor had he any sympathy with those conservatives who rejected all change. Moderation, balance, reasonableness, tolerance, these were the qualities required for a healthy society, and amid the perturbations of contemporary Europe he discerned what he was looking for when he visited Switzerland, England, and the France of King Louis-Philippe: there he learnt that only by a continuous process of making concessions in good time could the orderly progress of society be secured. This was to be the chief regulating principle of his political life.

As one practical application of this theory he turned his attention to prison reform, after being appalled to hear of prisons where scores of convicts were thrown together in the utmost squalor by a cruel system that made no attempt at regeneration. His courage as well as his concern for the poor was also demonstrated during an epidemic of cholera, for which he was awarded a medal. Then in 1834 he was able to show his true quality in a different field, after a request was sent by the Foreign Office in London to obtain information needed for what became the Poor Law Amendment Act; in response to this, Cavour's father – now mayor of Turin – asked his son to draw up a memorandum about treatment of the poor in Piedmont.

This memorandum was published the next year in England and was Cavour's first piece of serious writing in print. It pointed out that his own country possessed no system of public workhouses like that in England, and no old people's homes. He produced some interesting if imprecise statistics about wages, which indicated that most day labourers in the countryside could make ends meet only with difficulty. In years of bad harvest many or most had to rely on private charity, and many were permanently in debt to their employers. Only rarely could he find families who ate meat more than twice or three times a year. This degree of deprivation, if not immoral, was at least dangerous, and was hence a reason why those with sufficient knowledge and leisure should address their minds to the study of social betterment.

Stimulated by this experience, the next year Cavour persuaded his father to let him accompany a family friend on a journey of exploration to France and England. Two months spent in Paris gave him an invaluable political education and greatly increased his admiration for the French, especially since this was his first experience of seeing a parliament at work and of studying the industrial revolution at first hand. His pleasure in the material delights of civilized existence in Paris was somewhat marred when he came across the subversive doctrines of the republican opposition; but the speeches of Guizot and Thiers in Parliament confirmed his faith in the *juste milieu* and convinced him that no sovereign in Europe was as safe on his throne as Louis-Philippe. He visited prisons, schools, and noted wage levels in factories and what food was served in hospitals. In the evenings he and his friend attended theatres, balls, salons, political clubs, and of course the best restaurants in town.

One reason for going to England was to consult the public records to check a large debt thought to be owing to the de Sellon family by the

East India Company; but though this particular search proved fruitless, there was plenty to do. Journeys were made to examine farms in Cheshire and Norfolk, to visit factories in Birmingham and Manchester, and to see the sights of Windsor and Stratford. At Oxford he found less interest in the colleges than in how the Poor Law was being applied, but in Cambridge he attended a service in King's College Chapel and dined in Trinity as a guest of the librarian.

London was the main attraction. The indecipherable procedures of the House of Commons astonished him and he was not too favourably impressed by the lax manners of honourable members, but he had the great satisfaction of hearing Peel speak. The Inns of Court he found equally archaic, and had to take on trust the claim that an absurd system produced excellent lawyers. Nor was he much impressed by University College, the creation of his admired Bentham, and he found it hard to comprehend how students could profitably be given freedom to choose their own courses of study.

Cavour's abundant curiosity on this visit shows the wide range of his interests. He attended the King's Bench and Exchequer Courts; he visited Harrow School; he went to the main gas works to inspect new methods of street lighting, and was surprised that the workers could afford meat and beer every day. The railway from Greenwich to London – sometimes carried high on arches – was an amazing sight, and he noted Mr Brunel's technique of reinforcing concrete with metal rods. Expeditions were made to a lunatic asylum, to the children's home in Covent Garden, to Bart's hospital and St Thomas's where he remarked that the practice of having only female nurses would not be acceptable in the stricter society of Piedmont.

The prisons, especially, impressed him with their efficiency, extra-ordinary cleanliness and concern for rehabilitation. Newgate was the best. At Milbank prison he attended a baptismal ceremony and was intrigued to observe hardened criminals moved to tears by a sermon from the Bishop of London. He was told, and apparently believed, that all prisoners learnt to write and read before being discharged. At Tothilfields he watched prisoners on the treadmill and was glad when the governor agreed with him that this device could be more profitably employed working some useful machine.

Among people in public life he met Edwin Chadwick, the social reformer and Poor Law Commissioner. De Tocqueville he saw twice, once at the house of Nassau William Senior and once with Charles

Babbage, the professor of mathematics at Cambridge who invented a famous calculating machine (both Babbage and Senior were later in correspondence with Cavour). Brockedon took him to the annual dinner of the Royal Geographical Society, where he was surprised into making what he called his 'maiden speech' in response to a toast, and was glad that his halting English just sufficed. Brockedon also went with him to call on the scientist Faraday and inspect some of the latest mechanical inventions. Lord Elphinstone accompanied him to see the Horse Guards Parade, which he thought the most beautiful sight in the world. On the Queen's birthday he watched the splendid carriages of the nobility arriving at Buckingham Palace, and reflected that he was perhaps observing the final moments of a gilded aristocracy before its inescapable decline.

Like most visitors to London he was also taken to the docks, to the waxworks, and to the famous beer factory of Barclay and Perkins. One of his most detailed descriptions was of a Quaker Meeting which touched him deeply. A member of the anti-slavery movement argued that abolition of slavery in the British colonies was bound to put pressure on the United States to follow suit: the sooner the better, was his comment, or else a revolution might split the American union in two.

One of Cavour's general conclusions was the immense difficulty of understanding England, since first impressions were deceptive and the more interesting truths seemed to lie deep under the surface. In some ways the country compared unfavourably with France, and in particular he missed the wit and sparkling conversation of the Paris salons. He was worried at first by what he took to be the excessive speed of political democratization in a society where the gap between social classes remained so wide. But it came as a surprise to find so little sign of popular discontent. Even the working classes appeared too desirous of social stability to contemplate revolution, while the emergent labour unions were far less fearsome than was generally believed by property-owners in the rest of Europe.

What chiefly struck him was the prosperity everywhere, the sense of security, the administrative efficiency, the desire for reform and the immense energy generated by a truly individualistic society. Although France could teach the world about greater equality, only in England could one appreciate real liberty. The former taught ideas; the latter taught their practical application. 'The English have learnt how to work together; they know how to discuss without altercation and to respect individual opinions; even the smallest minorities can expect to be heard with attention, and often a single voice will suffice to postpone a decision until clarification of an issue succeeds in producing a consensus.'

Cavour had to curtail his stay in England because his father was short of money and in any case wanted his son back home to help run the family estates. The Marquis de Cavour had recently refused an offer to become Viceroy in the island of Sardinia, but in 1835 was appointed *Vicario* of Turin, a position that for the next twelve years made him virtually a Minister of Police responsible only to the King and wielding very considerable power. The post also earned its incumbent the reputation – not entirely justified – of being a dedicated absolutist involved in the persecution of liberals, and there was a widespread but unconfirmed suspicion that he used his position to make money improperly. The whole family was eventually tainted with these suspicions. But the marquis also belonged to a new generation of entrepreneurs in Piedmont. He was a pioneer in starting a service of steamboats on Lake Maggiore. Over many years he had speculated profitably in land and commodities – and less profitably in government securities, when he gambled on the outcome of a revolution in Naples. On several occasions he was able to lend money to King Charles Albert.

The young Camille thus entered into a family tradition that combined financial speculation, entrepreneurship and public service. On his return to Italy he tried to secure a post in the bureaucracy, but was given only an unpaid position on the Commission of Statistics. Since his father was busy organizing the police, the farms at Leri were not doing as well as they might, and the son was glad to be offered their superintendence as a means of earning a more independent livelihood. Leri was twenty-five miles north-east of Turin. It had belonged to a Cistercian monastery for seven hundred years, but was secularized during the Napoleonic period and bought by the Cavours in 1818. Four farms were spread over some three thousand acres. The family had in effect what was a quasi-feudal lordship over this area of flat, fertile countryside, and was almost the only provider of jobs for its *sudditi* or 'subjects'.

Cavour found that he liked this kind of work enormously. His main achievements as an agricultural innovator came later, in the 1840s, but his immediate task in the years after 1835 was to make the estate profitable. This was well-watered country ideal for growing rice, one of Piedmont's few notable exports. He was soon clearing woodland and improving irrigation canals. To supplement their wages he encouraged the peasants to produce silk, giving them silkworms to cultivate. He made a study of sugar beet, but experiments with seed from Silesia convinced him that he could not undercut the price of colonial sugar. Finding that far too little attention was being paid to animal husbandry he used rice husks and beet for fattening cattle and pigs imported from England. He studied all he could discover about advances in plant and animal breeding made by Bakewell, Coke and 'Turnip Towns-hend', and himself experimented with Spanish merinos, Leicestershire sheep and shorthorn cattle.

His father was on one occasion given an order for eight hundred sheep by Mehemet Ali, the Pasha of Egypt, and a further demand from the same buyer forced the estate to import more animals from Hungary. For this purpose Cavour decided in 1836 to travel to Villach, giving himself the additional reason that he must get away from the gaming tables of Turin where his lack of self-control was making him look ridiculous. This journey lasted a month and was the one occasion until almost the end of his life when he ventured out of Piedmont with the intention of seeing a little of northern Italy.

At the Lombard frontier, after the conventional offer of small bribes to customs officials, he was harassed by the Austrian police as a suspected liberal. He was not much impressed by Milan; and at Verona, where 'out of deference to Shakespeare' he sought out the legendary tomb of Juliet, he was equally disappointed. At Udine he had to buy new horses and was furious at his own naïveté when tricked into buying a lame nag. Nor was he much more skilful at Villach when selecting the sheep he had come to buy. On the way home he stopped at Trieste and was surprised to find the Austrian officials more efficient and friendly than he expected. Moving on by boat he spent four days in Venice, where he apparently found little of much interest. He had originally hoped to cross into the Papal States and Tuscany, but quarantine regulations at the papal frontier forced him to turn back.

* * *

One task awaiting his return was to write a memorandum on the system of workhouses for the poor in England. From what he had seen in Manchester and Liverpool he was convinced that this kind of 'legal charity' was beneficial; the work given to able-bodied residents was not excessive, and those unable to work were far better treated than in the charitable Catholic organizations of Turin or Paris. But this piece of research was never completed. He had perhaps intended the article as the first of a number of publications on social problems, but was forced to admit that a faulty education made it hard for him to put his thoughts onto paper. In any case, other preoccupations took his mind off further writing for the next few years.

One of these preoccupations was more travel abroad. In Turin the cultural atmosphere was heavy; there was no bright talk, no new books of much note to discuss, and politics was almost a taboo subject. On the other hand, Cavour liked conversing with strangers – even those who might have been thought boring whom he encountered in the post-chaise to Savoy and Switzerland. He still journeyed almost every autumn to Geneva, which he called his second fatherland. Twice in 1837 he was in Paris, and once more the following year. His aunt Victoire had inherited vast estates in France, and also huge debts which her nephew was now called upon to investigate and settle. At her expense, and perhaps in part without her knowledge, he was able to enter the elegant world of Paris: eating well, staying at the better hotels, with an expensive tailor and a smart equipage for attending the races at Chantilly.

In Paris he also began a mild affair with Mélanie Waldor, a novelist some fifteen years his senior, who had been the mistress of the elder Dumas and was now separated from her husband. His family would have preferred him to settle down in Turin and marry one of a number of rich women whose parents had already made soundings in his direction. But Cavour defended himself by explaining that he was not a good match and a fundamental 'lassitude of the heart' underneath superficial gaiety made him someone who could never give a woman true happiness.

A more serious passion was gambling – and in very bad company. After losing a large sum in Turin he promised that he would try to control himself, but in desperation he discovered that he could not stop. He borrowed from his brother to pay one gambling debt in Paris, and immediately returned to the tables at the Jockey Club. Soon he was winning or losing ten times as much as he had just lost, and was doing so night after night, even staking more at a single session than his whole annual allowance.

This enduring and compulsive love of risk led him also to invest in cereal futures, and it became his regular practice to buy quantities of grain as soon as he could see that the harvest might fail. In 1839 he joined the board of directors of the Savoy Company, which was interested in a linking boat service and railway line between the Rhone valley and Geneva. With luck and better judgement this might have been a profitable speculation, but it proved quite outside his capacity and range of experience. Success depended on the influence he hoped he could exert at court, because he needed government guarantees of preferential treatment against possible competitors. This was a very strange expectation in view of his general political attitude. His father, who Cavour admitted was a better judge of investment and who was now close to the centres of power, warned him against too committed an involvement, but in vain.

Worse still, when the company was forced into liquidation, he decided to buy up the bankrupt stock at a discount after borrowing more money without his father's knowledge. He convinced some of his companions in Turin to back this venture, assuring them that it carried absolutely no risk of failure. But it was under-capitalized and unsupported by public confidence. He was also inveigled into placing undue reliance on inexperienced young engineers and a new type of steam engine which turned out to be a complete failure. When the company collapsed again, he tried to put the blame on other people; but his father pointed out that he ought rather to blame his own miscalculation and lack of serious preparation. He honourably tried to pay off some of the debts incurred by others at his instigation, but his own losses were larger than he could easily afford.

An even greater shock awaited him when, to recoup his losses, he broke an undertaking to his family and secretly recommenced gambling on the Paris bourse. In August 1840 there was a possibility that France would back Mehemet Ali in a middle-eastern war over Syria. When the stock exchanges panicked three times in quick succession as war seemed probable, he could not resist temptation. Convinced that France was strong enough to challenge England and the rest of Europe, he persuaded himself that Louis-Philippe would be forced to fight so as to win popularity and recover something of what the French had lost by

Napoleon's defeat. A major war would incidentally send up the price of timber on his aunt's forests in the Vosges, at the same time as cutting off supplies of grain from the Black Sea and so raising prices for his own produce at Leri. On a sudden impulse, relying on a completely inaccurate tip from a lady whose favours he shared with the British ambassador, he decided that England was about to declare war. Against his stockbroker's advice he therefore sold securities that he did not own, intending to buy them back when the stock market collapsed; but after the war scare ended, their price rose and he was left with a substantial bill to pay.

Pocketing his pride, Cavour threw himself on the generosity of his family, promising that he would reform his ways and devote himself entirely to farming. His father settled this very considerable debt, and in a splendidly magnanimous and sympathetic letter spelt out the consequences of vanity and conceit. His son must not assume that he could make himself rich and famous without more humility, more common sense and less extravagance with other people's money. If only he would come home and settle down to matrimony, he had the brains and strength of character to be useful in his own country, and might one day be of service in government.

CHAPTER 3

Apprenticeship in Public Life
1841 – 7

Few lessons in his life can have been more important in the development of Cavour's character than this financial disaster, and he never made such a mistake again, though a love of taking more carefully calculated risks informed all his later career. After another minor crisis of depression he continued his search for something more serious to do. Back in Turin he took a leading part in starting new infant schools, thereby alarming the clergy who feared that primary education outside their supervision would aid the spread of infidelity. In 1841 he helped to launch the Whist Club, which in fact was a social club for the aristocracy and visiting foreigners, with rooms where newspapers could be read and politics sometimes discussed. He remained an addict to whist – occasionally playing for high stakes but not normally more than he could afford – and earned the reputation of being one of the best players in town. 'To win at whist you must take care of the small cards', he told a friend, and 'you are never obliged to return your partner's lead if you have a strong suit of your own.' Such lessons, whether correct or wrong, were part of his education in politics.

He also helped in launching an Agricultural Association designed to spread the knowledge of new farming techniques. The King himself became a member, and the association was sufficiently progressive to admit women 'provided that they professed the Christian religion'. An annual general assembly became a great social and even quasi-political occasion. Local meetings used to be held in the various regions, one deliberate intention being to lessen the rivalries and distrust between neighbouring provinces of the kingdom. Prizes were offered and Cavour obtained one for his wine cellar. He was elected to some of its central committees: those dealing with agricultural statistics, the society's publications, and the study of animal diseases.

Abroad once more in 1841, and again for six months in 1842–3, he was present in Geneva when a minor revolution in that canton overthrew the oligarchy of his conservative friends. This came as a great surprise for he had failed to read some of the signs of the times. Another long stay in Paris followed, during which he met Dumas, Merimée, Ampère and Saint-Beuve, as well as attending courses on religion and philosophy at the Sorbonne. The experience made him more convinced than ever that Paris was the intellectual capital of the world. An enlightened but essentially conservative government was making France into the country where revolution was, in his opinion, least to be feared: this was a judgement that proved to be too hasty.

Many Italians were living in Paris, either as forced exiles or else voluntarily escaping to a freer society away from what Cavour once called the intellectual hell of Turin; but any suggestion that he should follow their example and leave Italy met a firm refusal. He described these expatriates as a hopeless collection of people, undignified, cowardly and bringing discredit on their home country: the autocratic Charles Albert 'is a hundred times more admirable'. Much though he preferred the intellectual excitement and social attractions of France, he was summoned back home by duty, self-respect and self-interest.

First he accompanied his cousin de la Rive on another quick visit to England which he hoped to finance out of winnings at whist. This time he was encouraged to discover that in some respects farming was less efficient in England than at Leri, but he was also fascinated to observe the development of subsoil drainage and a variety of new agricultural machines. In politics what interested him more than anything was that some leaders of the Tory party, against strong opposition from the landed interest which normally supported them, were being converted to free trade, and this confirmed him in the view that Peel was the most admirable and high-principled of contemporary politicians. Nothing, he thought, was more important for the future of humanity than the increase in international trade that would follow abolition of protective duties; and this one single reform would confirm the position of England as the 'avant-garde of civilization'.

Back home he received an invitation from de la Rive to write for a Swiss magazine and no doubt they had talked about this together. There was no periodical in Piedmont that would print the sort of article he might wish to publish, because the censorship was severe, harsher even than in Austrian Milan. Many topics could not be publicly raised at all in Turin. The very word 'constitution' was damned; so was 'liberty', unless held up for disapproval; so was the subject of railways, which was thought to carry political and indeed progressive overtones. To circumvent the censorship a generation of political writers – notably Vincenzo Gioberti, Cesare Balbo and Giacomo Durando – published for preference in Belgium or Switzerland, although this was technically illegal. No newspapers from England or Prussia were permitted to circulate freely in Piedmont for fear of Protestant contagion. Cavour sometimes used his father's influence to import forbidden books, and as an exceptional favour was permitted to receive official parliamentary documents published at Westminster.

The main obstacle to freedom of thought was what he called 'the exaggeration of religious principles', because the Jesuits were powerful at court and used their influence over education and politics to isolate the country from intellectual fashions current elsewhere. They strongly disliked Cavour's infant schools, and Archbishop Fransoni publicly deplored the spread of literacy among the common people because it carried potential danger to religion and social order. Such an intolerant attitude struck Cavour as more dangerous than communism and as a direct challenge to the liberal and secular values that he prized. When he now wrote, using a phrase that Lord Acton later made famous, that 'absolute power inevitably corrupts', he was thinking of the Jesuits. Fortunately the chief defenders of freedom were no longer merely unbelievers or latitudinarians; many were Catholics, and many even among the parish clergy were tending towards 'Christian democracy' and a conciliation between religion and liberalism. Charles Albert, however, resisted this tendency. The King still allowed the existence of separate law courts for any ecclesiastics who were accused of crime; he still permitted a right of asylum in churches for any criminal who sought refuge; he even asserted that his sole principle in government was to secure the greater glory of God. But such extreme and exclusive views were increasingly unacceptable to public opinion among educated laymen.

Cavour's political development in this period can be traced in a long essay of 1844 that he published in Geneva about the Irish question. Some of his basic ideas are here 'explicit: the *juste milieu*; the fear of revolution; the defence of private property. Some of the responsibility for Irish backwardness he blamed on those among the Catholic clergy who were fanatical in exploiting popular ignorance. But he mainly blamed the English for their oppression, because persecution was self-defeating and would inevitably strengthen national and religious opposition. Nevertheless, he refused to call the oppression of Ireland any worse than other examples of intolerance which had been commonly admitted in many other countries and which the morality of former times had condoned. Though he was ready to sympathize with the motives of Daniel O'Connell in criticizing the union between Ireland and England, he could not share them, despite their general acceptance on the Continent. On the contrary, the injustice suffered by the Irish was in his view social rather than political, and the union was politically as necessary to them as to the English. What was chiefly wrong in Ireland was absentee landlordism and the Protestant supremacy. The best solution would be land reform; especially he advocated legislation against entails and primogeniture, which would reduce the big estates and put much more of the land into possession of those who in fact worked it.

This article on Ireland brought Cavour some notoriety and was soon being quoted even at Westminster. More interesting and more important was an article on railways published two years later in a small Paris magazine. He had himself continued to invest on a limited scale in French railways, and had been hoping that his father could persuade Charles Albert to allow private companies to build railways in Piedmont. But the government, though it accepted the idea in principle, was unwilling to allow private capitalists to manage a public service that had strategic and military implications. Cavour's article had a carefully designed practical purpose: to persuade the King and other reactionary Italian rulers that there might be a positive advantage for them in favouring a means of communication that was bound to come before long.

One of his arguments was that a nationwide railway system would make Italy a link on the routes between Europe and Africa and between London and the far east. Turin might thereby become a nodal point on a main highway between the 'German and the Latin races', and this would be helped by the fact that the 'Piedmontese nation' alone possessed the better qualities of both Latins and Germans. Inside Italy a well-designed railway network would weaken the provincial and municipal rivalries that were such an obstacle to progress, and by consolidating a common sentiment among Italians would contribute to the development of national consciousness. Cavour shied away from what he called an 'excessive sentiment of nationality'; yet Italy was much more than the geographical expression that Metternich liked to pretend. The country would become richer with railways, but also more 'Europeanized', and would thus share the moral and intellectual advantages that northern nations had recently been experiencing. In Naples, Tuscany and Lombardy some railroads were already either built or projected, so Charles Albert would have to decide quickly if there was to be much chance of Piedmontese pre-eminence in the peninsula.

Cavour found writing hard and much preferred his other occupations as a man of affairs, even though his investments in industry were not proving particularly successful. The country had a slender basis for an industrial revolution, since not only was the potential market small, but wood was the only fuel available in quantity and the forests of the Alps were becoming exhausted. There were still some internal customs barriers, notably between the island of Sardinia and the mainland. Moreover, rich people preferred to invest in land and in the security and status that went with it. Nor did the authorities encourage industrial development, which they seemed to identify with liberalism and free thought. Cavour's own involvement was mainly in a chemical plant at Turin from which he had high hopes, but it was too ambitiously conceived and after a few years went into liquidation.

From his father he inherited a close connection with Émile and Hippolyte de la Rüe, two members of a Protestant Swiss family whose banking and commercial house operated in Genoa and had close family links with similar firms in London and Liverpool. Through them he transacted most of his international business and with their help acquired a useful familiarity with the money markets of Europe. When Émile recommended that the government permit the establishment of a bank in Genoa the proposal was strongly supported by Cavour, and the bank opened in 1845. Much prejudice had to be overcome before banknotes circulated freely or bank credits became customary in agriculture and industry. But three years later another bank was established in Turin, partly at Cavour's instigation and with himself on its governing council. These two institutions developed into what eventually became the Bank of Italy, and the shareholdings he possessed in them made a considerable profit.

Setting up these banks brought him into closer touch with the world of government, and on one occasion he now acknowledged that he would like nothing better than to be a minister if only he could avoid publicly renouncing his principles or grovelling to the throne. He was confident that he possessed as much ability and knowledge of affairs as existing ministers of the Crown, some of whom indeed tried to persuade Charles Albert that he should receive an appointment. But the King, no doubt remembering earlier disagreements with his former page, refused. It is also fairly clear that Cavour would not have accepted a junior post.

By now there were few relics remaining of his early flirtation with radicalism, and Henry Layard, a visiting friend from England, was somewhat surprised to note that he did not attend meetings of the younger progressive aristocrats in Turin. Instead he had reached the conviction that 'the only real progress is slow and wisely ordered'. Not by force, not by insurrection or conspiracy could lasting improvements be achieved; any worthwhile change should if possible be won by means of legitimate authority rooted in a country's traditions. He was sure that Mazzini's friends could never succeed, because by affronting tradition and established institutions these extremist patriots would offend the basically conservative instincts of every class in society. Cavour was aware by now that he was no more of a liberal than others who had already accepted posts in government. Indeed he was surprised to discover that he was accused of being a timid conservative and even reactionary. Disliked by the real extremists of right and left, he felt himself more than ever to be a useless member of society who was better known abroad than at home. It was sad to think that he had squandered his youth to so little effect.

Some of the hostility to him can be gauged from a contested election in 1846 for the presidency of the Agricultural Association. This body, with a membership of almost three thousand members, was very gradually becoming politicized, especially by Lorenzo Valerio at the head of a bourgeois and democratic faction opposed to the aristocratic monopoly of its official directorate. Cavour strongly backed the aristocrats and opposed Valerio's attempt to give the Association a more liberal voice. Nor was he too scrupulous about the means he used. At the annual meeting in 1846 he arrived with a noisy rabble of nobles who succeeded in electing the Count de Salmour as president. But when his friends carelessly went off to celebrate their victory, the democrats remained behind and quite properly voted their own representatives on to the committee. Cavour, who had a quick temper, was with difficulty restrained on this occasion from physically assaulting his bourgeois opponents. What was much worse, he then went to his father, the powerful chief of police, to have the new committee suspended for being politically subversive. This was a very strange episode, and the fact that the King subsequently decided to back Valerio suggests that Cavour had entirely misjudged the situation. The incident made him even more unpopular by further identifying him with class prejudice and the much-hated activity of his father's secret police.

CHAPTER 4

The Revolutionary Years
1847 – 9

In 1847–8 the various autocratic régimes of Italy began to lose ground
as revolutionary ideas gained acceptance through the peninsula. The
election of Pius IX as Pope, followed by his introduction of political
reforms in Rome and his proposal to unite the peninsula in a customs
union, awoke great enthusiasm among some Italians who so far had
possessed no voice in politics. In Turin there also seemed a possibility,
accepted by conservatives and liberals alike, that a concerted move
might be attempted to liberate Lombardy and Venice from the
Austrians. As late as September 1847, Cavour was so much preoccupied with his farms that he had little time to think about such
things. He welcomed the signs of hatred against foreign rule and saw
them as a stimulus to patriotic feeling, but was accused by Valerio's
friends of not wanting to risk his reputation by publicly associating
himself with any demand for constitutional change. Then in October a
series of popular demonstrations put pressure on Charles Albert, who
suddenly decided to introduce a few reforms similar to those already
adopted in Rome and Tuscany. As soon as the publication of political
newspapers was permitted, Valerio launched the *Concordia*, and the
liberal conservatives supported Count Balbo in starting another paper
whose title, the *Risorgimento*, symbolized their hopes for a resurgence or
renaissance of Italy.

Balbo was particularly anxious to have Cavour as assistant director
and leader writer. This was a brave move because of the latter's current
unpopularity, and at a meeting called to discuss the editorial policy of
the *Risorgimento*, those present began to walk out when Cavour started
to speak. Even so, the journal was an immediate success with a limited
audience. Its programme was to champion liberal conservatism and
moderate reforms. It admitted that Charles Albert's 'wise and

moderate' government had increased the country's prosperity, but the history of England demonstrated that only with much more extensive political freedoms could a nation become powerful and rich. One objective must be the removal of protectionist restrictions on trade, but only in stages so as to allow the economy to adjust. Equally important was to assist the lower classes who composed the great bulk of the population, and who must be helped to become 'more moral, more religious, and better educated'. A longer-term aim would be to achieve 'an economic unity of the Italian peninsula', after which the country 'would perhaps quickly take its place among the richest nations in the world'.

Cavour soon learnt that slight distortions and exagerations were needed in journalism to strike the imagination of readers. To gain a sympathetic hearing from ministers he bestowed excessive and presumably not altogether sincere praise on Charles Albert. In his articles he was conciliatory towards the Church, because only if the parish clergy were prised loose from the two extremes of radicalism and traditional authoritarianism would moderates have much chance of winning broad popular support. His special responsibility on the paper was foreign policy, and here he argued against all interference by foreign governments in Italian affairs. Yet in private he explained that he saw danger in the growing popular excitement against Austria, because the extremists – and this included or perhaps meant Mazzini – might exploit it for their own revolutionary purposes. He admitted that he was 'obliged to be over-patriotic and cry out against Austria along with everyone else', but was anxious not to take patriotism to excess.

To win its small audience the *Risorgimento* had to be sold under cost price, and the loss was carried in good part by Cavour himself, especially after he took over the chief editorship from Balbo in the spring of 1848. The paper suffered under the further handicap of seeming to be a purely aristocratic journal that was not sufficiently 'Italian' and was thought to be merely cloaking itself with a superficial liberalism. This supposition may have been unfair, but it was an understandable reaction among the public because Cavour made no pretence about fearing that liberal reforms could go too far and too fast. He maintained that no further substantial concessions were required from 'those who perhaps wrongly are called the privileged classes', and he especially decried the mistake made by the French Revolution of

1789 when a necessary political revolt turned into a disastrous social revolution. Piedmont in his opinion did not need social revolution. Nor should the country risk too much political experimentation, because innovations always carried some danger of going wrong, and as a general principle it was best to stick to traditional procedures that were known to work adequately.

The experience of journalism was invaluable to Cavour. His knowledge of the Italian language, though he had been practising, was still only moderate, and he had to use the dictionary a great deal, as well as relying on collaborators to revise what he wrote. But the effort of having to translate mentally from the French helped to give him a terse and clear style that avoided abstractions and circumlocution. He later recalled how he had found writing for a newspaper an excellent political training. A journalist learnt by everyday practice what could be said and what concealed; he learnt to write clearly, quickly and on many different subjects; and in his own case he thought that without first becoming a journalist he might never have become a politician. Another instructive aspect of journalism was the teamwork involved and the constant discussions out of which the policy of a paper was formed. Furthermore the *Risorgimento* provided an outlet for his love of a fight and was soon engaged in active polemics with all the other newspapers of Turin.

Already by December 1847 it was beginning to appear that the modest reforms conceded by Charles Albert were insufficient; there was even pressure on him to grant a parliamentary constitution, which was something he had solemnly promised that he would never permit. In January 1848 a meeting between four editors of the principal Turin newspapers discussed drawing up an appeal to make the King change his mind on this point. Cavour here found himself in agreement with Angelo Brofferio, a prominent lawyer and journalist well over to the left. On the other hand, Valerio distrusted this apparent conversion of the aristocratic party to liberal sentiments, and also was afraid that such a radical demand for a constitution might so alarm the government that the reform movement would be brought to a halt.

A decisive factor at the end of January was that King Ferdinando of Naples, hitherto one of the more reactionary monarchs, followed the example of institutional reforms already conceded in Rome and

Tuscany and granted a constitution. This raised expectations in Turin, and Cavour was able to repeat more forcibly that if Piedmont remained aloof she might lose any possibility of leadership in Italy. Moreover, only a constitutional government would be able to stop the growing demand for ever more revolutionary change. He appealed to Charles Albert to take his earlier concessions to their logical conclusion. There was no time for further delay, because in Genoa people were already taking to the streets in popular demonstrations. The King's ministers gave the same advice: that if a constitution was inevitable, it was better to concede with grace and not wait until popular insurrections compelled them to grant something far more radical and democratic.

Charles Albert reluctantly gave way and early in February approved the *statuto* which became the basic constitution of Italy until the time of Mussolini. The editors of the *Risorgimento* boasted that Piedmont had secured by peaceful means what in England had cost 'centuries of civil war'. In festivities to celebrate the event, Cavour, Valerio and Brofferio marched with other journalists in a procession through the streets singing what became the national hymn, 'Fratelli d'Italia'. After being appointed to a commission to draw up an electoral law, he spent some busy weeks studying the practices of Belgium, France and England so as to profit from the experience of other countries. The commission agreed to have single-member constituencies as in England. They briefly considered universal suffrage but rejected it as something that would perpetuate what Cavour called the fallacy of thinking that citizens had a natural right to participate in government. No people should be electors unless their income and intelligence indicated that they probably had a vested interest in social order. Ideally the electorate should be the mercantile classes, the professions, and especially owners of land. Fortunately the middle classes in Piedmont were mostly property-owners with too much to lose from revolution.

In the middle of the discussions on this point, the alarming news arrived of barricades going up in the streets of Paris when a popular uprising led to the abdication of Louis-Philippe, and this persuaded the commission to adopt a wider suffrage than it had at first thought advisable. Cavour was greatly shocked by these events in Paris, since he had been convinced that no state in Europe was as socially stable as France or less exposed to the danger of a republican revolution. Caught unawares, he feared that the result would be to set back the cause of gradual reform everywhere in Europe, especially when he learnt that a similar insurrection seemed imminent in Genoa. But he had to admit that the government of Louis-Philippe must have been more ineffective and corrupt than he had imagined, and that just possibly the new republican régime in France would be an improvement. He had no unalterable objection to republicanism, so long as it would help Europe to withstand the more serious danger from socialism and communism that was appearing in Germany.

The threat of social revolution became more real when a few weeks later a body of French republicans tried to invade Chambéry, the chief town of Savoy. Further acts of much more savage mob violence also took place in the streets of Paris. On the other hand, the huge Chartist assembly in London showed that working-class demonstrations could sometimes be peaceful, and the English example suggested that the basic political freedoms of speech and assembly could be useful in defusing social unrest, provided at least that action was simultaneously taken to relieve poverty and unemployment. Cavour drew his own conclusions after closely observing these events. He was convinced that private property must remain sacred and intangible, yet here was evidence that the English might be right in adopting the concept of 'legal charity': in other words taxing the rich so as to help the more deprived members of society.

Charles Albert's first Prime Minister under the new *statuto* was Count Balbo, and the other ministers were all chosen from the titled nobility. Some people thought that Cavour might be given the department of agriculture, and he was upset not to be asked. But he was too much disliked and mistrusted by both right and left. A very serious test for Balbo came on 18 March when a popular insurrection against the Austrians broke out in Lombardy and, after five days of street fighting in Milan, ended with Marshal Radetzky's army in full retreat. Charles Albert hesitated, weighing up the undesirability of aiding what was manifestly a popular revolution, but also recognizing that the Piedmontese monarchy would suffer in reputation if it stood aside during a war for Italian independence. On 21 March one journalist on the *Risorgimento* called for an immediate declaration of war against Austria, and Cavour supported this demand strongly in a signed editorial two days later. Even if the army was unready, almost anything would be better than allowing Lombardy to become an independent republic, and it was vitally important to stop the dangerous infection of radical republicanism spreading from Milan into Piedmont. He was overheard saying that, rather than accept further delay, Balbo should ignore the King and assume dictatorial powers.

Charles Albert took his ministers' advice and agreed to support the insurgent Milanese. As an earnest of good will he adopted the tricolour of revolutionary Italy to replace the blue flag of his own dynasty of Savoy. Not that he had any vision of a united Italy: faithful to the traditions of his predecessors, he rather envisaged the acquisition of Lombardy and Venice as a legitimate dynastic ambition, and obviously such a success would give him an unchallenged primacy over his fellow sovereigns in Italy. Cavour shared this same ambition, but now went further in speculating that a new Kingdom of Northern Italy might be created which, along with the other independent regions of the peninsula, might one day be federated in what he called 'a great republican-monarchic state'.

Charles Albert took for granted that royal dignity compelled him to be Commander-in-Chief, a position to which he was entitled by the constitution but for which he had absolutely no talent or experience. Nor, as was soon apparent, did the rest of the general staff possess more than a theoretical knowledge of how to fight a war. Cavour's favourite nephew Auguste wrote home from the war zone that the incompetence of the senior Piedmontese officers passed all belief. Neither did the rank and file have much enthusiasm for fighting such a war of liberation. Cavour was bold enough in the pages of the *Risorgimento* to comment on these grave and surprising military deficiencies. At the end of May his nephew was killed at the battle of Goito, a loss that would remain in his memory as the greatest personal tragedy of his life: one of his co-editors found him distraught and rolling on the floor in grief.

The Austrians had their own serious military problems and soon declared their readiness to accept mediation on the basis of allowing the Lombards their freedom. This suggestion was given substance when a plebiscite in Lombardy showed a large majority wanting to form a unified state with Piedmont, though the plebiscite also laid down the condition that a constituent assembly be summoned to discuss the possibility of a new constitution. This proviso created a problem, because many people in Piedmont were unwilling to accept the risk that a constituent assembly might choose Milan rather than Turin as the capital city. Cavour was unenthusiastic about changing the constitution, but agreed that concessions to Milan might be a price worth paying. What he had not expected was the mutual execration that now broke out between Lombards and Piedmontese, between Turin and Genoa, between federalists and 'fusionists', between republicans and monarchists. A serious military defeat at Custoza in July was the worst and most astonishing event of all. In desperation he offered to rejoin the army in his capacity as an ex-officer, which some people thought he should have done sooner. Early in August, however, Charles Albert suddenly abandoned Milan and astonished nearly everyone by arranging an armistice, making the additional mistake of publicly blaming the Milanese for his defeat; after which, Cavour began to think that perhaps only if the King abdicated could the monarchy be saved as an institution.

Hopes had run too high and the disillusionment and recriminations which followed were bound to be all the more bitter. Cavour called for an enquiry into why the war had gone badly. Another personal disappointment was that his confident expectation of being elected to Parliament was dashed when the first elections were held in April. The other leading journalists, including Valerio, Brofferio and Durando, were successful; but among the electorate there was much dislike and suspicion of the aristocratic classes with whom Cavour was identified, and he himself was especially singled out for attack, not least because of his sarcastic insinuations in the *Risorgimento* against the honesty and good faith of his bourgeois opponents. Although there was a notable lack of experienced and public-spirited candidates, Cavour failed in all four of the constituencies where he stood for election; in one he obtained twelve votes, and even in Turin only eleven people voted for him after an election address that was rendered almost inaudible by chatter and heckling.

He was so upset by this reverse that he talked of giving up politics and journalism. He confessed to a friend that he once again renounced all ambition in public life. No doubt the experience taught him to be less disdainful of others and of public opinion. At all events, his self-confidence returned when supplementary elections in June gave him a seat by a convincing majority. On arrival in Parliament he chose to sit well over to the right as part of what he called the 'conservative party', well away from any unwelcome confusion with the 'democrats' and 'liberals'; nor did he object too strenuously when some people labelled him with the appellation of *codino* or 'pigtail' that was reserved for the more extreme reactionaries.

During July he spoke in most parliamentary debates and with a persistence and aggressiveness lacking elsewhere on the government benches. In a Europe that seemed to be moving to the left, his policy was to champion 'the sacrosanct principles of family life and private property that are being threatened by socialism'. Proudly but with some exaggeration he defended the aristocratic classes whose sons had died on the battlefield at a time when most lawyers and journalists of the 'democratic party' were frequenting the cafés of Turin. The democrats were criticized by him for being vulgar, dishonest and inept. When Genoese politicians blamed the Piedmontese army for arriving too late and losing a war that had been already won by the common people of Milan, he angrily replied that the Genoese were cowards and ten times less courageous than the Piedmontese. These were some of the remarks that reinforced his reputation for being the spokesman of his home province and class rather than a sincere Italian. Sometimes with his light voice he could hardly make himself heard in Parliament over the hubbub that his sharp criticisms aroused.

Such was the bewilderment at the news of military defeat that the *Risorgimento* joined other papers in calling for a denunciation of the armistice and a renewal of hostilities, on the grounds that to defeat Austria and obtain a more independent Italy must take precedence over preserving the internal liberties of Piedmont. When rioting broke out again in Genoa, Cavour wrote that continuance of the war would be 'the best if not the only method of restoring order'. He agreed that a successful military campaign might be beyond the country's capacity if she fought alone, but there were good chances of a major European war from which Piedmont might emerge with profit if she played her hand well. Even England, though preferring peace, was friendly to Italy and might be provoked to take arms by her jealousy of Germany's growing power. Most likely of all was 'a terrible racial war between Slavism and Germanism', and he thought that a well-organized rebellion of the Slavs and Hungarians could well succeed in capturing Vienna. The French could surely be prevailed on to join such a war because it would be in their national interest to back Piedmont and limit the influence of Austria in Italy.

Successive governments throughout the autumn did not share his optimism, but Cavour became further convinced in October that the Austrian empire was on the verge of total collapse. Though he told his man of affairs, de la Rüe, that the time had not yet come to speculate financially on the likelihood of war, he deluded himself that the army needed only a few more days of training. He assumed that the King and most of the deputies in Parliament were eager to avenge Custoza, and his first oratorical success was a frankly demagogic speech asserting that another war was now certain and the chances of winning were good. The alternative would be to sign a humiliating peace that would probably mean the collapse of the monarchy; and Genoa might even break free to turn the province of Liguria once again into an independent republic. This must be prevented at all costs.

Towards the end of 1848, Cavour was sufficiently alarmed to become involved in plans for a military coup in Turin, especially after General Lamarmora privately told him that the army could be relied upon to put down any internal resistance. This idea came to nothing, and in the January elections, to his surprise and chagrin, he lost his parliamentary seat when the new Prime Minister, the *abbé* Gioberti, preferred to support a democratic nonentity against him. Cavour had violently attacked Gioberti as a renegade priest and unbridled demagogue, but by February 1849 came round to praising him as perhaps the last hope for the defence of Piedmont against revolution. Gioberti was commended in particular for his plan to use Piedmontese troops to put down revolutions in central Italy by supporting the Grand Duke Leopold in Tuscany and Pope Pius ix in Rome. Pius fled into exile when Mazzini and Garibaldi led a revolution to set up a Roman republic, and Cavour had no doubt that this democratic republic must be defeated so that the Pope's temporal authority could be restored.

He was ready once again to accept a military dictatorship – even under Gioberti if that were the only way to overturn the radical majority that had been elected in the Turin Parliament. For the same reason he remained personally convinced that another war against Austria might be necessary to re-establish governmental authority in Turin. Only by fighting would Piedmont counter the 'infamous calumnies' being spread by the republicans in denigration of the army and King Charles Albert. A war and even a lost war would be less ruinous than the consequences if the democrats in Parliament had their way and won power. In any case he optimistically thought that the chances of victory were good. A Polish general, Chrzanowski, had been hired as commander so as to avoid the incompetent royal leadership of the previous year, and under such a man Cavour was hopeful that the army, with what he quite wrongly assumed to be greatly superior numbers, would quickly re-enter Milan in triumph. If the Lombards had lost confidence in Piedmont and did not want to help, so much the worse for them; and he angrily commented that anyone in Milan who hinted at wanting a republic ought to be shot without compunction. The Venetians, who by now had set up their own separate republic under Daniele Manin, could surely be made to change their minds and surrender their independence to a victorious Piedmontese monarchy.

In March 1849 a new Prime Minister, General Chiodo, finally denounced the armistice and ordered the army to attack, but by some inexplicable mischance the government's order never reached the Commander-in-Chief. Three days later all was over, when the Austrians recovered the initiative and inflicted a crushing defeat on the Piedmontese at Novara. The government, like Cavour himself, had made a huge miscalculation. He could not understand this defeat but insisted that, had he himself been in power, he would somehow have found a way to chase the Austrians back over the Alps. In his anger he found plenty of other people to blame. He criticized the Polish general in whom he had shown so much confidence a few days earlier; he blamed the incompetence of the King and the stupidity of the government for having wanted a war that he himself had been fiercely advocating; he blamed the soldiers, three-quarters of whom he now said had been opposed to the war and some of whom had been treasonous in simply refusing to fight. Above all, while omitting to remember his own irresponsible optimism, he blamed the 'ultra-democratic' party in power for having decided upon war before mobilizing what he extravagantly called the 'immense resources' of the country.

CHAPTER 5

Parliamentary Politics
1849 – 50

Charles Albert honourably accepted responsibility for this second military defeat, abdicating and leaving for exile in Portugal. His son, Victor Emanuel, succeeded him and a conservative administration was appointed under General de Launay, to whom Cavour pledged his personal support. In private talk with the Austrians the new King tried to make out that he had personally opposed the war, and called the Lombards contemptible *canaille* who were unworthy of him; nor did he stop short of criticizing his father for making concessions to the democrats. He even reached the point of promising the national enemy that he would use force to crush the radical majority in Parliament if only he was granted a generous peace. Radetzky in reply assured the young King that Austrian soldiers were at his disposal for restoring monarchic authority in Turin. Fortunately, their assistance was not needed.

These two unsuccessful wars against Austria cost a great deal, and not only in financial terms. They shook confidence in the armed forces, in the monarchy and in the constitution itself. Lowered morale was evident in a naval mutiny and another serious insurrection in Genoa: this city had to be bombarded by government order and was then partially sacked by indignant and undisciplined troops. In an attempt to restore confidence a commission of enquiry spent months trying to find out why an apparent victory in the spring of 1848 had turned so quickly into a double defeat, but Cavour agreed with the government that the final verdict was too wounding to be made public. Perhaps he was right. Even though some useful lessons might have been learnt for the future, he thought that every politician – including himself – would emerge from the enquiry diminished, and that quite possibly this would so damage popular confidence that the continued existence of parliamentary institutions would be endangered.

Another blow to morale was that, whereas the Piedmontese now withdrew from the fight for national liberation, Manin and his republican friends continued to defy the Austrians in Venice, while Mazzini and Garibaldi astonished the whole of Europe by holding out against a much larger French army in Rome. These republicans, wrote Cavour, might possibly be honest and disinterested, but in practice they were dragging the good name of Italy into the mud by fighting a lost cause. He called Mazzini a traitor to the cause of Italian independence, a man of 'pompous and useless words' who was too much lacking in physical and moral courage to make an effective patriotic leader; anyone who tried to build up such men into heroes was misguided. He thought it ridiculous when Valerio praised Garibaldi for saving the honour of Italian arms. Cavour's newspaper preferred to praise the French troops who eventually defeated Garibaldi and restored papal government, after which the French remained for most of the next twenty years as a garrison in Rome. The defeat of Mazzini and Manin left Piedmont as the one Italian state not dependent on foreign help, the only one governed by a constitution. In Tuscany, Leopold was restored by Austrian arms; in Naples, the Bourbon King Ferdinando, backed by Russia and Austria, revoked the constitution that he had sworn to maintain; in Venice, Manin was forced into exile and the Austrians reimposed their direct rule.

Cavour felt frustrated in being out of Parliament at this critical moment, and his conservative friends, even those who already thought him the best financial brain in the country, did nothing to help him find useful employment. He pretended once more that he was glad to stand aside from political difficulties, especially since he would not have known how to tackle them without increasing his own unpopularity; but he was clearly hurt. In April 1849, at one of the lowest moments in his political fortunes, he drew up a will. Most of his estate would go to his brother's family, but a substantial sum was left to found two more infant schools in Turin. He expressed the hope that Gustave would have a hundred masses said for his soul and take care of the poor families in the ricefields of Leri.

In May 1849, frustrated in his political ambitions, Cavour again thought he might give up the 'dismal profession' of journalism and return to the more useful study of economics. His newspaper was not selling well and continued to lose a good deal of his money. In any case he had never intended to continue as editor for more than a few months; he wondered briefly whether his resignation, by making the paper seem less an organ of the aristocracy, might confer a wider acceptability on what he felt to be the one journal in Italy that was a consistent champion of moderation and liberal conservatism.

This period of depression ended in July when he was again elected to Parliament. The young King had dissolved the previous legislature in the hope of securing another that was more conservative, and Cavour wrote that if this failed there might once again be no alternative but to resort to a *coup d'état*. Unfortunately most of the new deputies represented once again what he variously termed the 'so-called democrats', the 'liberals', the 'ultra-liberals' or the 'party of lawyers'. Against this leftist majority the Marquis Massimo d'Azeglio as Prime Minister tried to muster conservative support and received Cavour's enthusiastic backing. Azeglio was a well-known novelist and painter who had been badly wounded in the war of 1848 and whose patriotic credentials were impeccable. Cavour again pretended that he was glad not to be given a post in the government. Instead he was offered the job of ambassador in London and was tempted to accept, but on second thoughts, fortunately for Italy, he decided that he ought to stay as a deputy so long as the co-existence of a right-wing government and a strongly left-wing Parliament put the future of the constitution at risk.

Almost at once there was another clash between Parliament and government over negotiations for the treaty of peace with Austria. Cavour was asked to join a delegation to conduct these negotiations but was presumptuous enough to refuse when he was not allowed to lead it; or perhaps he simply felt that it would add to his unpopularity. The Austrians in fact showed considerable generosity and asked only for financial reparations which were well short of what Piedmontese aggressiveness must have cost them. But the treaty was presented to the Turin Parliament as a *fait accompli* by the government, and the deputies were strictly correct in maintaining that their consent was necessary and was improperly being taken for granted. This created a constitutional impasse.

One political move with great significance for Piedmont's future was Azeglio's generous insistence on welcoming many Lombards and Venetians who had been compromised in the fighting against Austria and who preferred exile rather than return to Austrian rule. Possibly as many as fifty thousand exiles received hospitality at one time or another. Those without financial resources were given help by the government. Others were people of education and experience who eventually secured jobs in teaching, journalism or administration. Some Piedmontese strongly resented this influx, but Cavour, although he successfully objected to most of them being given full civil and political rights, agreed with Azeglio in realizing how useful they might be. Even some who were politically to the left brought with them money, great intelligence and the sense of belonging to a wider Italian community. Since Cavour knew little about other regions of Italy, their presence would be an invaluable part of his education in *italianità*.

Generosity, however, had its limits, and he was strongly against allowing Garibaldi and Mazzini back into their native country. Garibaldi was in fact arrested at Genoa when he tried to land after his tragic and heroic defeat at the hands of the French in Rome. Parliament condemned the government by a large majority for arresting a fellow-citizen without trial, because this was a clear violation of the *statuto* with its guarantees about due process of law. In particular it was argued that Garibaldi had become the symbol of national independence and brought Italy's cause to the attention of the whole world. But the government in Turin was strongly supported by Cavour in refusing to agree with such an assessment and claimed that Garibaldi had forfeited his citizenship by fighting against the Pope: the time might come when he could be allowed back home, but for the moment he must abandon his family and accept a life far away from Italy.

In a Parliament where few other deputies knew much about constitutional government, Cavour had the great advantage of having attended other legislatures and of having carefully studied Erskine May's treatise on parliamentary practice. He asked for and received further information from James Abercromby, who had been Speaker of the House of Commons in London. Yet he suffered from being no orator, and continued to find difficulty with the Italian language. His voice was said to lack masculinity and was as metallic in sound as it was jerky in delivery, while listeners were irritated by its monotony and the tiresome mannerism of a nervous cough as he struggled to find the right word. Nevertheless, what he lacked in eloquence and elegance he more than made up for in clarity and precision. His speeches were always to the point and wasted no time on irrelevancies or declamation, which was a welcome change from the fluent rhetorical extravaganzas of Brofferio and the lawyers.

Already in August 1849 he was confident enough to tell Parliament that its procedural regulations were among the worst in Europe. He never liked the continual 'interpellations' and 'orders of the day', nor the cumbersome committee system and other subtleties of procedure that made the process of legislation unduly slow. Often he caused offence to other deputies by drawing attention to the more effective practices in England and elsewhere. The original *statuto* of 1848 laid down that the constitution was unalterable, but Cavour made clear that if given the chance he would try to change it. For instance he resented the fact that catholicism was declared in the constitution to be the official religion whereas other religious beliefs were merely tolerated. He would also have preferred some element of election to the senate, instead of appointment by the King. But such changes were too substantial to be considered so late in the day.

Another objection he raised was that, perhaps because of the haste in which the original constitution had been drawn up, Piedmont had adopted the French system of prefects or intendants. These provincial intendants were appointed by the central government, as were mayors of towns, and their powers were such that there was a built-in tendency to over-centralization. Cavour was convinced that Belgium and the Anglo-Saxon countries had a better and more representative system of local self-government, whereas in Piedmont the excessive concentration of power was a root cause of much that was wrong in society. Centralization was expensive; it needed too many officials; and in general it hindered the growth of a truly free society. Governments in Piedmont and France often seemed to be trying to control everything, which in practice resulted in inefficiency as well as depriving ordinary citizens of self-respect and a sense of personal responsibility.

The first eighteen months of constitutional government had not been an unqualified success. Azeglio was the eighth Prime Minister in this short period, and still the relation of ministers to the Crown was far from clearly defined. Sometimes the King refused to accept their advice, and sometimes even appointed another minister without consulting them. Victor Emanuel had sworn to abide by the provisions of the constitution, yet he criticized his father for conceding too much to

45

popular wishes and for what he called telling lies to the public; he himself, so he shamelessly insisted, would always speak the truth. In private he said he was prepared to fall back on martial law if necessary to curb the opposition. He told both the Austrian and French ambassadors towards the end of 1849 that he disapproved of parliamentary liberties and a free press, and that with a couple of regiments he could at any moment bring the opposition to heel. To the papal nuncio he confirmed that he was only awaiting a convenient moment before revoking the constitution altogether.

Nor were these just isolated remarks. The King was confronted by a constitutional obstruction in that the parliamentary majority refused to sanction the treaty he had already signed with Austria. Cavour was still a strong champion of royal prerogative, believing in constitutional government but not yet in parliamentary government. He tried in November to convince the deputies of the centre-left that the treaty was unavoidable even if unwelcome. When they refused to co-operate, Azeglio dissolved Parliament for the third time in a year and persuaded Victor Emanuel to issue to the electorate a personal appeal that was virtually an ultimatum. In this 'Proclamation of Moncalieri' the King reproached the outgoing deputies for their opposition, explaining that he intended to save the country from 'the tyranny of parties' and if necessary would govern without parliament.

Cavour was subsequently praised for having opposed this royal proclamation, but in fact his attitude was not so clear-cut. Many people argued that a King should never enter into party politics, if for no other reason than that he might have to abdicate if his party was too weak to govern. Cavour later explained that he had been consulted about the proclamation, and though he preferred not to commit himself too openly, he in fact sanctioned Azeglio's decision to involve the monarch and even believed that this may have saved the constitution from complete collapse. In normal times the 'Proclamation of Moncalieri' would perhaps have been wrong, but he knew that constitutional governments must sometimes employ exceptional means: where necessary they should not hesitate to use force, or to confiscate property, or to resort to repression and even terrorism – with the one proviso that the end must be good enough to justify the means adopted.

Fortunately the elections of December 1849 at last returned a substantial majority of moderates. The King told Archbishop Charvaz that he was still ready to suspend the constitution if need be; but when

Parliament met he realized that there was no longer any danger of revolution and hence no need for counter-revolution. This fourth Legislature survived until 1853 and permitted Azeglio to govern through a vitally important period during which the operation of parliamentary government was consolidated.

Cavour took his seat again and was given a position on the Finance Committee, where he soon proved that he knew far more about finance and economics than any of the ministers. His pugnacious interventions in debate were authoritative, sometimes decisive and often provocative. In April he challenged another member of Parliament to a duel by pistols, in which fortunately neither was injured. This was a strange episode, because the point at issue seems to have been completely unimportant and no question of personal honour was involved; in addition, duels were a criminal offence punishable by imprisonment. The government, to Cavour's annoyance, asked leave of Parliament to bring both himself and his adversary before the courts, but a majority of deputies refused permission and the matter was allowed to drop. Cavour remained convinced that duels were a proper method of conducting such private quarrels. He would not admit that he had set a bad example in defying the law, nor that the virtual immunity from prosecution given to a deputy was a bad precedent for the future.

Another of his settled convictions was that members of Parliament should be men of property and receive no salary, because it was important not to attract the wrong type of person into politics. He was luckier than most of his opponents in being rich enough to devote most of his time to parliamentary duties, and this gave him a great advantage over Brofferio and the professional lawyers. Soon he emerged as leader of a small group of moderate conservatives on the centre-right who, while not always agreeing with official policy, generally backed the government. Almost every day he intervened in debates, usually in support of Azeglio's search for a middle course between the extremes of right and left. He advocated administrative decentralization. He wanted freer trade and a reduction in customs duties; but he also threatened to move a vote of censure if Giovanni Nigra, the Minister of Finance, failed to explain how the government intended to balance the budget in the next financial year. Such a balance, he optimistically imagined, could be easily achieved – though it was something that in later years he himself never succeeded in obtaining.

His firm conviction was that the country could afford considerably higher taxes. If customs revenue was reduced, and if poorer people were helped by lower taxes on food, the consequent reduction in revenue could be made up elsewhere without difficulty. There was still no direct tax on buildings, or on non-landed property, or on incomes from commerce and industry, or on the professions. In England a general tax on incomes had recently been re-introduced, and he agreed that such a tax was in theory excellent though it might be impossible to adopt in Piedmont. He was opposed to any progressive element in taxation because by threatening to penalize the rich it would drive money out of the country, and already far too much capital was being quietly exported to England and elsewhere. Capitalist enterprise, whether local or foreign, must not be frightened away or else the whole economy would suffer, and among the chief losers would be 'the poorer classes, the most interesting members of society'.

One major reform which Cavour supported was a series of laws introduced by Count Siccardi restricting those ecclesiastical privileges that were incompatible with various articles of the *statuto*. One 'Siccardi law' abolished the separate law-courts for ecclesiastics, because they violated the principle of equal justice for all. Another abolished the right of criminals to seek asylum in churches. A third reduced the number of feast days when people were forbidden to work. Cavour argued that the working classes neither wanted so much free time nor knew how to use it decorously; in addition, the Protestant Swiss, who were permitted to work fifteen more days a year than the Piedmontese, thereby had an unfair advantage for their exports. Another Siccardi law forbade monasteries to acquire property in mortmain without permission. His own contribution to the debate was greeted on the left with applause because it was a clear sign that he was moving away from Balbo and his more conservative friends. He argued that these were reforms demanded urgently by public opinion as a test of the effectiveness of constitutional government, and the Church must learn to adapt to the *statuto*, otherwise both religion and the constitution would suffer.

The Siccardi laws were a major landmark in the modernization of Piedmont. Yet Cavour was far from being an extreme anticlerical. The clergy had supported his own election in 1849, and although he was coming round to accept the long-term aim of separating Church and

State so that neither would encroach on the other, he was anxious to move slowly and not prematurely antagonize anyone who might disagree. Preferably such changes should be made by mutual consent with the Vatican, but failing such consent he was already reconciled to overriding the existing concordat and defying Rome by unilateral action. He had observed that the peasants at Leri, although very religious, had little notion of papal authority and would be unimpressed by the medieval weapon of excommunication. This observation enabled him to look with some equanimity on the breach that now opened with Rome: he could not know that the quarrel would last well into the next century and exert a severely distorting influence on Italy's political and constitutional development.

In protest at the Siccardi laws the papal nuncio left the country and the Archbishop of Turin instructed his clergy to refuse obedience to summons before a secular court. In May 1850 the Archbishop was therefore arrested. A few months later another scandal was created when the Minister of Agriculture, the very pious Count di Santarosa, was refused the last rites of the Church on his death-bed merely because he could not in conscience disavow what had happened. Cavour arrived at Santarosa's house a few moments after his death and had to be held back from coming to blows with the priest responsible for this uncharitable decision. When, in retaliation, the Archbishop was expelled from the country and his property seized, the Pope refused to appoint a successor and the breach became official. The Archbishop was still in exile when he died a dozen years later.

CHAPTER 6

Minister for Economic Affairs
1850 – 51

In October 1850, Cavour was at last rewarded for his work in Parliament by becoming Minister for Trade and Agriculture. Azeglio made the appointment with mixed feelings, because as a good judge of character he knew he was choosing an ambitious, headstrong and difficult colleague. The King warned the other ministers, using language that was apparently too vulgar to be reported, that they might live to regret their choice. Cavour thought twice before accepting and briefly wondered if it might not suit him better to bring the government down. His eventual decision was, he explained, a personal sacrifice undertaken from a sense of duty: joining the government might possibly ruin his own reputation by committing him to a subordinate position in a short-lived administration, yet the country would suffer grave damage if the government collapsed and the King appointed other ministers who were clerical and reactionary.

As a member of the Cabinet he immediately made his presence felt by insisting on the resignation of the Minister of Education who was known to be lukewarm about the Siccardi laws. An opposition newspaper announced his appointment as that of an excessively anglophile 'Lord Cavour', and others assumed that he had been forced upon Azeglio by the English government which had selfish reasons for wanting more free trade in Piedmont. According to the Austrian ambassador, the new minister was an ambitious intriguer who would be as perfidious an ally as he was dangerous an enemy; a man with few friends and many critics; a trouble-maker with a reputation for being none too high-principled in his personal financial dealings. In reporting to London, the English ambassador agreed that Cavour possessed a difficult and 'overbearing' temperament, yet his readiness in debate and knowledge of finance would be a great strength to the government:

the one disadvantage for England, it was thought, was that he might be too favourable to France.

By the age of forty, when he at last won political power, Cavour's personality was fully shaped. In physical presence the new minister was well under medium height, thick-set in build, with broad shoulders, a slight stoop, and stumpy legs that seemed too short for this body. Caricatures make clear that his most prominent feature was corpulence, and visitors noted that to hold this in check he kept various medicines in his room. His thinning hair was fair, almost red, but beginning to turn grey. Lively, pale-blue eyes were set in a face whose roundness was accentuated by a light beard running under his chin from ear to ear. Short sight forced him always to wear spectacles. He had a large forehead, and a rosy or sanguine complexion which became highly coloured in moments of anger. He dressed with what might have been studied negligence, usually in dark brown tail coat, black stockings, black silk tie, brown satin waistcoat and grey, rumpled trousers.

Now that he had begun to achieve political success he was more sure of himself, less anxious, less acrimonious, and as a result less unpopular. High among the salient aspects of his temperament in middle life were affability and joviality, and though he continued to be often distrusted, few people failed to like him whatever their political views. His young cousin William de la Rive, despite being much more of an unrelenting conservative than Cavour, singled out for praise the fact that he shared many qualities with the admirable Charles James Fox. He and Fox loved social occasions, were both great gamblers, had the same powerful intellect, the same rashness and vivacity, with an exuberant wit and manifest liberality of mind.

Others among his close collaborators commented on his easy-going temperament and genuine interest in meeting new acquaintances from whatever walk of life. His talk moved easily from the serious to the jocular and, on rare occasions, the bawdy. Good nature and a complete lack of solemnity were noted by almost everyone, and de la Rive, himself perhaps over-serious, called him the most amusing person he had ever met. Some people wondered if he had too much brain for too little heart, and Cavour himself was worried that he might be too cold and calculating; but a friendly smile and unaffected laughter came easily and often. One critic described him as possessing 'the terrible gift of familiarity' and an infallible charm that captivated even most of his political enemies.

While some of these qualities of character became more noticeable after 1850, Cavour's intellectual gifts had always included a formidable memory, to which in time was added an exceptional propensity for hard work. He had an unusual ability for close study of the minutiae, at the same time quickly seizing the essentials of any argument. He remained sometimes inconsiderate of others, as he had been in youth, and to the end of his life had a tendency to be sardonic, even caustic. He was impetuous and, on occasion, tactless. His mother had reproached him for making hurtful remarks that offended other people's self-respect, and more than one colleague used of him the phrase a *mauvais coucheur*; in other words he could be quarrelsome and not always easy to work with. Quick to lose his temper, he sometimes became so angry that he seems to have lost any memory of what he said, but he was almost always the first to make up a quarrel and never bore resentment for long. His secretary remarked enigmatically that he had 'the delicate sensibility of a woman'. He hated unreasoning prejudice as he hated any kind of intolerance, but though he disliked Charles Albert and despised the golden-tongued Brofferio, he perhaps never truly hated anyone – except possibly Mazzini, and that may well have been less a visceral dislike than a finely judged sense of political tactics.

When Cavour wrote that he lacked personal ambition he was not being truthful. Friends as well as enemies remarked on his love of power, though few could deny that he was truly and unostentatiously generous: this generosity was shown in gifts of money to the poor of Turin, in throwing lavish parties and in secretly paying the fines imposed by the courts on those who insulted him in print. Pius ix compared him favourably in this respect with his brother Gustave, who was far more of an orthodox and practising Christian but far less charitable. Camille was not indifferent to money and worked hard for what he earned, though he took no immoderate pleasure in luxurious living. His main indulgences were food and good wine: he sent his chef to be trained in Paris; he was fond of strong wine which he considered to be a specific against the obesity that he disliked so much, and imported great quantities of champagne, burgundy, rum and Dutch liqueurs.

Despite his early fears about never having a sufficient income, by now he was rich: one exaggerated rumour called him the richest person in the kingdom. No longer was he embittered by the anxiety of feeling dependent on his father. At her death in 1846, his mother left most of her estate to the elder son, Gustave, whose own heir Auguste thought this unfair; Auguste tried to compensate on his death in 1848 by leaving his uncle a large fortune. Camille renounced this legacy, keeping only the bloodstained uniform of his nephew under a glass case by his bedside; the money he turned over to Gustave in settlement of an earlier gambling debt. His own personal wealth, apart from speculations which were not notably successful, came mostly from two other legacies: one from his aunt Victoire in 1849, the other from his father a year later.

Azeglio's first impressions of the new minister were more favourable than expected. It was extremely useful to have a *coq de combat* on the government's side in Parliament, and for some months there was little sign of the arrogance and bad temper that other colleagues had been fearing. For his part Cavour admired Azeglio as a person, though not as a politician; by now he had ample evidence that the Prime Minister had no natural inclination for the rough and tumble of parliamentary politics. Azeglio acknowledged his own lack of talent as an orator and administrator, frankly confessing that he did not enjoy the exercise of power, nor the pretences and dissembling of accepted political practice, nor the double morality in public life which Cavour and other successful politicians adopted so easily. Though unswervingly loyal to the constitution, the Prime Minister disliked debates and spoke in them as little as possible. The crippling leg-wound received at Vicenza had never healed, and in 1852 he was still threatened with an amputation, so that for weeks at a time he could not leave his bed; this left the path to supreme power wide open for any ambitious rival.

Cavour, in addition to the Department of Trade and Agriculture, soon took the Shipping Ministry as well. Government policy specified that the Piedmontese navy ought if possible to catch up with that of Naples and become as strong as any other fleet in Italy, but morale was low after the mutiny in 1849, and senior officers were still entrenched in a world of aristocratic privilege that rendered them autocratic, thoroughly disobedient and not too keen about switching to the new practice of steam navigation. To restore discipline, Cavour summoned two naval captains before a court martial for insubordination and corruption, only to discover that they enjoyed very powerful protection close to the throne. Captain Persano twice ran his ship aground, once with the King himself and the whole royal family on board, but this did not prevent his eventual rise to the senior post in the navy, where his incompetence became legendary. Lesser examples of incapability were kept secret. As well as continuing the switch from sail to steam, Cavour encouraged the change from paddle steamers to screw propulsion, and for this purpose ordered the building of a new frigate in England as a model to copy. He was fascinated by altogether new and hypothetical ideas about power generation in marine engines. Among other technical innovations, he changed the calibre of naval guns to the metric system. He also began hesitantly to implement a proposal by his predecessor to construct a naval base at La Spezia so as to leave the narrow port of Genoa for merchant vessels.

Azeglio remained Prime Minister until 1852, during which period his moderation and good sense made an indispensable contribution by keeping politics on an even keel, encouraging the practice of parliamentary government and winning favourable opinions abroad. Cavour helped this process, quickly making himself the second most prominent member of the administration. In one week of January 1851 he intervened fifty times in debates on many different subjects. If other ministers were absent from the *camera* (or lower house of Parliament) he was always ready to speak impromptu on their behalf, and was particularly useful in coming to the rescue of Giovanni Nigra at the Ministry of Finance. When opposition deputies read speeches of carefully prepared and technical criticism, he did not even need to take notes before intervening to confute them. Several commentators remarked that he would make an excellent Prime Minister before long. But his sights were set immediately on the vital Ministry of Finance where the worthy but not very competent Senator Nigra was obviously out of his depth, and in April 1851, after threatening resignation, he was given the post for which he was best equipped.

In this new job Cavour set himself to put the disorganized finances of the country into some kind of order. The first task was to examine the ledgers of the various departments, which he found in such a hopeless muddle that it was hard to make even a rough estimate of the national debt. After a thorough study of all sources of revenue he calculated that he had been too optimistic in his hope of bringing the budget into balance during 1851–2, yet still thought it ought to be possible in a year's time. For this purpose a series of eight new taxes was devised. He was fortunate in that recent years had seen an expansion of the economy, and he set himself to encourage this still further so as to increase the taxable revenue of the state.

He relied in particular on the prospect that a balanced budget would make it easier to borrow, whether at home or abroad. The Paris house of Rothschild, the chief banker of the Austrian empire, was the principal source of international loans, and Nigra had used it to begin paying off the war reparations to Austria. Cavour continued to use Rothschild, though he insisted on introducing an element of competition from other foreign banks. His first loan was obtained in 1851 through the small Hambro bank of London, and though Rothschild countered by trying to depress the price of Piedmontese securities in Paris, the operation was carried out successfully. The man Cavour chose to conduct the negotiations in London was someone who later became a strong political opponent, the conservative Count Thaon de Revel.

Cavour remained convinced that economics were gradually approaching the point of becoming an exact science whose principles could be demonstrated by logic and practical results. One such demonstrable principle was that people should be free to conduct their affairs as market forces dictated. Any law interfering with their freedom to work or save or own property might damage society, whereas enlightened self-interest by individuals could usually be relied upon to contribute to the general good. Government-sponsored enterprises were almost always uneconomical, whereas Switzerland and England had proved that the greater the economic freedom, the greater the prosperity and the less the strife between classes. Governmental intervention would sooner or later mean socialism, and although he agreed that the socialist aim of greater fairness in distribution would theoretically attract anyone with a social conscience, in practical application it would reduce wealth and consequently hurt poor as well as rich.

Cavour had already shown impatience with those who could not comprehend the logic behind greater freedom of trade. He acknowledged that Charles Albert's government should be given much of the credit for reducing protective duties, but far more was required. In agriculture, by artificially raising the cost of cereals and wine, protection had resulted in unsuitable land being brought into cultivation, at the same time as it damaged consumers through higher basic food prices and rents. In industry, the high protection given to excavation of iron ore kept more than a hundred small mines in being, but again immobilized capital in inefficient and non-economic enterprises, thereby doubling the price of a wide range of goods. An over-protected industry had little incentive to search for new and cheaper methods of production. He had himself visited textile factories to investigate the possibilities of a different policy, and the experience persuaded him that a great deal of Piedmontese industry was quite capable of standing on its own feet despite all the feigned outcries of distress at any hint of change.

As Minister of Trade and then of Finance he extended the range of this argument, but he recognized that the change to freer trade would be damaging if it happened too fast. He also admitted that some customs duties were necessary purely for revenue purposes, and in practice did not go so far in reducing tariffs as did the grand-ducal government of Tuscany. Access to official statistics nevertheless showed him that smuggling of highly protected commodities some-times accounted for up to ninety per cent of goods traded, and this could only be stopped if lower duties made contraband unprofitable. On the other hand there were special cases – for instance soap, where considerations of hygiene and social welfare justified some protection of an industry in difficulties. But these were exceptions, and in general it was wrong to impose an extra burden on consumers so as to profit a few producers, whether farmers or industrialists. He pointed to instances where lower duties were already forcing textile factories to modernize and reduce costs, with excellent results in increased exports. To lower the protection on iron would, of course, drive many inefficient mines out of production, but would cheapen a vital raw material of agriculture as well as industry.

Time would show that there were some good arguments on the other side of this debate, but Cavour believed that facts and logic pointed in a single direction. One unfair criticism of his policy was that personal financial involvements made him an interested party, and some of his parliamentary critics argued that by adjusting the duties on phos-phorus and sulphur he was helping his own chemical factory. Cavour disdained to reply except to exclaim in a fury that his accusers were lying, at which he was called to order for using unparliamentary language. He repeatedly insisted that he had sold off the whole of his investment portfolio on becoming a minister; yet, quite apart from his remaining agricultural interests, he was still joint owner of what he thought must be the largest chemical plant in Italy, and this inevitably exposed him to criticism.

The long debates over tariff changes were exhausting, but his command of the subject and resilience in discussion carried through what was a major reform, so that by the end of 1851 commercial treaties were already signed with France, England, Portugal, Greece, Switzerland, Belgium and certain smaller states in Germany. He took care to point out that politics as well as economics were involved, since these countries were desirable allies and the help of other liberal states might be needed to ensure the survival of the Piedmontese constitution. It was important to persuade France and England that Piedmont would be a useful ally and a profitable outlet for capital investment. The treaty with France was the most troublesome in Parliament, since after four months of discussion the French continued to offer less than the full reciprocity that other countries had agreed to; and in the end he won a vote of approval only by once more threatening resignation.

As soon as politics became a full-time occupation, Cavour no longer had time for direct supervision over the family estates, but an excellent manager was discovered in Giacinto Corio, to whom he and his brother handed over the day-to-day administration as a full partner. The letters that arrived almost every week from Corio were among his chief private pleasures. Farming became no longer a profession but a hobby. He liked to study the accounts, to discuss a new rotation of crops, to plan next year's production and to compile comparative statistics on the effect of using different fertilizers from year to year. Leri was one of the first estates in Piedmont to import guano from Peru and North Africa, and he earned considerable profit by selling it to neighbouring farmers. Other experiments were conducted with various artificial fertilizers made with or mixed with chemical products from his factory, but he became somewhat disillusioned with these and Corio was sceptical about their utility.

Leri remained Cavour's favourite residence when he could find the odd week or weekend of holiday, and it was no doubt at Leri that he caught the malaria that ten years later proved fatal. Ever since 1842, if not earlier, he had suffered from occasional 'tertian fevers', as did Corio and many of their employees. He was confined to bed for a week in October 1851 with a mysterious intermittent fever, again for two weeks in November 1852, for another two weeks in February 1853, and once more the following August; contemporary medicine, however, was unable to diagnose what was wrong. The symptoms that became familiar to his close friends included violent abdominal pains, copious sweating, and sometimes 'mental disorientation'.

He was well aware that the paddy fields from which his family derived much of its income were dangerous to the health of those who worked there. Most landowners were only moderately troubled by this danger because they personally spent most or all of their time in town, and their country houses were often well away from the irrigated fields. Nevertheless, the risks from this mysterious illness were so well known that many laws since the seventeenth century had tried to stop the planting of new rice fields and to encourage the more salubrious cultivation of other cereals; but rice was a cheaply propagated and profitable crop. Consequently, laws were disregarded and the extent of land under rice doubled in the forty years before 1854. Half the region round Leri was said to be growing rice illegally.

Cavour admitted that the law was being openly flouted, he himself being as guilty as the rest, but he tried to convince himself and Parliament that the ill health prevalent in the area had other causes such as poor housing and bad diet. He knew that most medical experts disagreed with him and hence that some restrictions ought to be enforced so as to minimize any possible danger; but he had a dogmatic conviction that interference with individual enterprise was in theory misguided, and hence he not only failed to enforce existing laws but overrode parliamentary opposition in order to make possible a further extension of irrigated land. Too many vested interests were involved, as well as the prosperity of a large area, and a host of casual labourers needed the work and the wages. Cavour said that a full parliamentary discussion on the medical aspect of this subject would take too long and be too acrimonious. Instead he would encourage landowners, for reasons of humanity as well as of hard economic sense, to follow his example and improve the housing and material circumstances of their workers. The duty payable on imported quinine was reduced but not abolished, and many sufferers were hence unable to afford the one available remedy for this terrible un-named scourge.

CHAPTER 7

A Move to the Left
1851 – 2

In 1851 in Paris, the philosopher-politician Gioberti wrote a book entitled *The Revival of Italy* that obtained a wide circulation, its main theme being that Piedmont should work towards establishing her hegemony throughout the Italian peninsula. In the last pages of this long treatise the author mentioned Cavour as a man of great talent on whom much might depend, but who was unfortunately less interested in the rest of Italy than were Balbo, Azeglio or followers of the ideologue Mazzini. Seen from the vantage-point of Paris, the new minister appeared to be too much of an inward-looking Piedmontese in politics, too French in language, too English in his ideas. Yet Gioberti concluded that there was time for him to learn: one day he might become less concerned with the expansion of Piedmont and more with bringing to birth a new Italian nationality.

Cavour's feelings for the rest of Italy were not strong and if anything seem to have become weaker after the early 1830s, but they received a new impetus from the wars of 1848–9 and from his association with the patriotic Azeglio. Though he could still speak of the existence of a 'Ligurian nation' and a 'Piedmontese nation', he came to agree with Gioberti that Turin might one day constitute a nucleus round which other members of the Italian family might gather. Elsewhere in Italy he was well enough known by reputation to be offered membership in July 1851 of the famous Florentine society, the *Georgofili*; and his note of acceptance expressed the hope that, as Piedmont learnt economic lessons from Tuscany, so Tuscans would one day learn from Turin that some Italians were mature enough for self-government.

If other people could regard Cavour as much more Piedmontese than Italian, one good reason was his ignorance of other regions. But a more important reason in his own mind was that the cause of Italian patriotism had been partly pre-empted by Mazzini and the revolutionaries, so that any patriotic movement carried some danger of confusion with democratic ideas and even with republicanism. Nationality held no attraction for the conservatives if it implied too great an element of social or political revolution. Fortunately this danger receded when, in December 1851, Louis Napoleon's *coup d'état* in Paris represented a major defeat for republican and socialist ideas in Europe; after which more than one message came from Paris that French national interests might be served by a strengthening of Piedmont as a counter to Austrian influence in Italy. Early in 1852 a hint was dropped by the French that their two countries might one day ally against Austria, the aim being for Piedmont to obtain Lombardy and the Duchies of Parma and Modena, while France would be compensated with Nice and Savoy. This was a proposal that the Piedmontese government took up very effectively some six years later.

Cavour was not as interested in foreign policy as he became later, but he felt keenly the humiliation of the defeat of Novara and was sure that one day Piedmont would resume her attempt to drive the Austrians out of Northern Italy. As Finance Minister he refused a request for reduced expenditure on the army, but was in no hurry to pick a quarrel with Vienna until he could be sure of French or English help. After he had negotiated agreements in favour of freer trade with other countries, in January 1852 some of the patriots were offended when he proposed a further treaty giving 'most favoured nation' privileges to the Austrians, and he had to point out to Parliament that, of all his trade agreements, this with Austria offered the most practical advantages, and political differences should not stand in its way.

King Victor Emanuel often liked to impress his entourage by telling them how peacetime inactivity bored him and he was counting the days until he could jump into the saddle and lead his army to war. As he was simultaneously head of State, head of the executive, and Commander-in-Chief of the army, this kind of remark was disconcerting enough, but more ominous was that he could speak on different occasions about Austria being either the enemy or his ally in such a war. For the benefit of the patriots – those whom Azeglio called the *italianissimi* – the King talked of fighting against Austria, whereas to the Austrians he privately repeated that he was rather on their side against the Italian revolutionaries. He added that if his ministers refused to agree to join an anti-revolutionary war he would dismiss them, and that anyone who stood in his way would risk execution. He again informed the Austrians that he agreed with them in hating the Lombards. Such remarks were not generally known, or else he would quickly have lost the reputation that Azeglio had painstakingly built up for him as the *re galantuomo*, the patriotic gentleman-King; but ministers were of course aware that such a monarch was not completely trustworthy as a guardian of the constitution or a champion of the national interest.

It was the more worrying that Azeglio's apparent victory in the elections of December 1849 turned out to be far from completely secure, especially as the Prime Minister paid so little attention to the arts of political management and most deputies had no strict party allegiance. Azeglio's technique was what he called a 'see-saw', moving now slightly to the right, now to the left, with a floating and almost casual majority adapted to each issue in turn. He and Cavour both called themselves conservatives, yet their economic and anticlerical policies were increasingly liberal. This left them with little or no support from the extreme right round the clerical Count Solaro della Margherita, whose loyalty to the constitution was suspect. Moreover some of the more moderate conservatives were not much more reliable. A former colleague, Balbo, led about twenty-five deputies who opposed the Siccardi laws, and Thaon de Revel was the spokesman for some who had doubts about free trade on grounds of theory and practice. Balbo and Revel briefly considered organising a separate party of their own, and though they decided to stay part of Azeglio's majority on most other issues, their votes were evidently undependable.

Ever since 1849, Cavour had speculated about a possible realignment in politics, because he wanted more solid backing for a policy of reforms that were at once liberal and conservative. Initially he hoped that most deputies in Parliament would not form into parties, since etymologically the word 'party' implied divisiveness and separate factions. In practice, however, he soon realized the need for a more disciplined majority, because experience showed how easy it was for a casual coalition to come into being over an individual issue and even win a surprise vote against government policy.

Another politician with the same preoccupation was a prominent lawyer, Urbano Rattazzi, who sat with a group of about thirty deputies on the centre-left of Parliament. This group, ill at ease in the more

extreme company of Valerio and Brofferio further over to the left, had
made overtures to Azeglio and Cavour in August 1849 for a possible
parliamentary alliance. Cavour's own view at the time was that these
men were insufficiently reliable and that Rattazzi in particular was 'the
very incarnation of sophistry', so that it would be a real 'crime' to
accept such an offer. They for their part became less interested after the
royal Proclamation of Moncalieri which they thought unconstitutional,
and they had good reasons for sharing Gioberti's fear that Cavour might
not be a genuine patriot or sufficiently liberal in outlook.

The Siccardi laws in 1850 went some way towards reassuring them,
and prepared the way for a closer alliance between centre-right and
centre-left. Cavour remarked that he as a conservative would have
expected to feel more at home in the company of Revel and Menabrea
who sat near him on the right, but during 1851 the two centre groupings
found that they had common enemies at the two extremes. In
December 1851, Revel announced to the chamber, in what some
thought a bid for power, that he and his friends might desert the
government majority unless Azeglio introduced more press controls
and a more restrictive electoral law. This minor ultimatum came in the
same week that the *coup* of Louis Napoleon convinced Cavour that the
major danger in Europe was no longer from the left. If there was any
risk of an illiberal right-wing administration coming to power in
Piedmont, a more formal arrangement with Rattazzi might be needed,
and perhaps quickly.

Cavour never described in detail the events leading to his very
important decision to consummate the *connubio* or marriage between
centre-right and centre-left. One of the sub-editors of the *Risorgimento*,
Michelangelo Castelli, a friend of both men, had for some time been
working for a fusion between what he called the aristocratic party of
Cavour and the bourgeois party of Rattazzi. Castelli arranged a
meeting between them in which the general principle of a parliamentary alliance was settled. Cavour claimed that he then tried to
persuade Azeglio to accept this alliance, but there can be little doubt
that one secret intention was nothing less than to displace his leader. In
January 1852 he forced a minor change in policy after threatening the
Cabinet with his resignation, and according to other ministers he
increasingly interfered in their departments and took controversial
decisions without waiting for a collective discussion on policy. Three
ministers had already resigned because they found him to be too

ambitious and domineering as a colleague.

One preliminary hurdle was the need to win parliamentary approval for the De Foresta law, so called after the minister who introduced it. This law was designed to deprive juries of competence in legal actions where heads of other states were libelled in the press, and it was a restrictive measure that required support from both moderate and extreme conservatives. Cavour told Parliament that the government was under no foreign pressure to introduce such a law, but in private he explained to Rattazzi that the secret intention was to meet the express wishes of Louis Napoleon and obtain his good will. Rattazzi accepted this argument, and though he would be obliged on libertarian grounds to speak against the law, he promised to do so with moderation.

The law was duly passed, backed by the right and centre-right and also by some individual deputies of the left and centre-left. Such a confused vote helps to explain why the absence of disciplined parties made it advisable to seek a more cohesive alliance in the centre of politics. Although Cavour was strongly in favour of this law, he knew it was widely unpopular with those who treasured the jury system as a defence of individual liberties, and after the vote he put pressure on De Foresta to resign and take upon himself most of the consequent odium and unpopularity.

In February 1852 the moment arrived for publicly announcing the existence of the *connubio*. Since Cavour was still a member of the Cabinet and could count on only one other minister to support him, he chose to act secretly and hope that some of the others might accept it as an accomplished fact; he also tried to allay suspicions by privately assuring them that he still distrusted Rattazzi. Several days later he let drop a remark that he intended to make a provocative speech against Revel's group of moderate conservatives. After delivering this alarming news he was requested at least to make clear that he was making no statement of government policy; but when his turn came to address Parliament, he said that he spoke for the whole Cabinet who had agreed to renounce in future any support from Balbo, Revel and Menabrea. The Prime Minister was not present and learnt of this astonishing statement only after all was over.

Cavour had acted with careful deliberation for he calculated that the other ministers could hardly continue long in office if deprived of his parliamentary skills; nor would they dare to repudiate him at a moment of great political tension. A few weeks later he forced the pace and persuaded the *camera* to elect Rattazzi as their Speaker. Once again he chose not to raise this question formally in Cabinet because he would have been defeated; instead he allowed the inaccurate rumour to circulate that the other ministers supported him in wanting Rattazzi's appointment. At a lunch given by Azeglio, after friendly talk on other subjects, the Prime Minister said he would like Boncompagni as Speaker, at which Cavour became so beside himself with anger that he hurled his plate on to the floor and rushed from the room shouting that his host must be mad. This outburst of uncontrollable anger seems to have been spontaneous and not contrived; similar scenes occurred at other critical moments in his life.

Once Rattazzi was chosen, Azeglio tried to accommodate himself to what had happened so as not to provoke a ministerial crisis by making public these divisions inside the Cabinet, but when foreign newspapers called the *connubio* a change in government policy he was obliged to issue a public denial. Cavour reacted to this reproof by stating that he could no longer continue carrying the main burden of parliamentary business in a subordinate capacity. Victor Emanuel spent some days trying to patch up these differences: as well as being annoyed at such an underhand piece of intrigue on the part of a junior minister, the King pointed out that the constitution would be in danger if one member of the Cabinet broke ranks and ignored collective responsibility over so controversial an issue.

Feeling himself undermined, Azeglio offered to resign, and after Cavour made another angry scene the rest of the Cabinet resigned as well. But the King asked the Prime Minister to stay, in particular because he was the one member of the government who was known and respected abroad. As Gioberti commented, Cavour might be the abler and more energetic of the two, but Azeglio was seen to be more straightforward, more credible and more 'Italian'. So it was Cavour who had to go, after explaining his conviction that the government could not last long without him. Nor was he alone in believing that only his energy, parliamentary ability and knowledge of economics could bring the country's finances back into balance.

Azeglio returned unwillingly to the premiership. As well as being a self-confessed amateur in politics he was still very much an invalid, and in any case the task he had set himself was nearly complete. He had restored confidence in the monarchy after Charles Albert's disastrous defeats at Custoza and Novara, and had done his best to persuade

Victor Emanuel that parliamentary government might not only be the best defence against revolution, but would certainly win Piedmont a position of leadership throughout Italy among all those who wanted enlightened and efficient government. These were achievements of fundamental importance. Azeglio's private comments show that he had the sense and generosity to appreciate that Cavour was still trying to live down the disadvantage of having grown up an *enfant gâté* in the house of an autocratic Minister of Police; yet the Prime Minister also recognized that this younger and more energetic man, if only he could curb his tendency to play the tyrant and run everyone else's job for them, might have a great future.

After a year and a half as a minister, Cavour in May 1852 returned to private life for five months. Most of this time he spent abroad, giving the excuse that to stay in Turin would embarrass the government, though a more genuine motive was to avoid embarrassing himself. After toying once again with the idea of a tour through Italy, he decided that he would derive more intellectual and political profit from a visit to England and France. The previous year he had exhibited some of his own wines at the Great Exhibition in the Crystal Palace, and he wanted to take a closer look at English farms and factories.

As a tourist he showed the same fascinated inquisitiveness as on earlier journeys. In London he visited Woolwich Arsenal and the docks. In addition to buying four cases of books, he met the leaders of the main political parties, and also went, accompanied by a policeman, to inspect the 'lowest dens of infamy and vice' in the slums. He journeyed to Newcastle where the naval frigate he had ordered was being built. After being enchanted by Edinburgh, he took a volume of Walter Scott on a search for 'romantic emotions' in the Highlands. In letters home he wrote that he was becoming more of an anglomaniac than ever, and might stay through the winter if Azeglio's government should survive that long; or indeed, if the 'clerical-reactionary faction' won power in Turin, he thought of emigrating to live in London.

Moving to Paris, this time he did not find 'the new Babylon' quite as sympathetic as London, but politically France could be exploited to much better effect. Several times he met Daniele Manin in Paris and tried without avail to persuade this Venetian republican to return from exile and accept the monarchy along with a safe seat in the Turin

Parliament. He saw many French political leaders. Rattazzi, no doubt by design, came to meet him in Paris and an invitation was obtained for them both to dine with Louis Napoleon so as to obtain French approval for the new political alliance. The two guests were given another broad hint that the prince-president had it in mind to restore the empire of his uncle, Napoleon *le Grand*. They therefore saw it as important to convince this would-be Emperor that he could count on the Piedmontese help that he again asked for, and especially they needed to persuade him that a new centre alliance in Turin might usefully serve the interests of Napoleonic imperialism.

One disappointment for Cavour on his travels was to find that, in England at least, very few people had heard of him, whereas everyone knew the name of Azeglio. Lord Malmesbury, the Foreign Secretary, advised him to rejoin Azeglio's government, a piece of advice echoed by friendly politicians in Turin who thought that the *connubio* had been altogether too abrupt and provocative; but Cavour was already telling others in Switzerland and France that he would soon be back as Prime Minister. A false rumour was even spread by him to convince people in Turin that the French and British Foreign Ministers were positively asking for his own appointment: he was fully aware that support from either London or Paris or both might be a crucial factor in his and his country's success.

During this journey through Europe, Cavour kept in touch with his political allies at home, notably with General Lamarmora who had remained a minister in Azeglio's government. His three closest advisers, Lamarmora, Rattazzi and Castelli, recommended that he patch up his differences with the Prime Minister, if only because there was a danger that otherwise the government could possibly be supplanted by reactionaries who might overturn the constitution. Azeglio was another who begged him to return to the Cabinet. But Cavour was playing for higher stakes and was prepared to take the risk of a counter-revolution. He promised he would avoid attacking ministers in public and confirmed that he had no personal or even serious political differences with them. He also agreed that the existing government probably had the support of a majority of deputies. Nevertheless, since the country needed more forceful leadership, he would not actively cooperate to keep them in office.

As Cavour wrote to a friend in the summer of 1852, his main hopes were centred on the monarchy and the possibility that the King was looking for a new premier, especially as a controversial issue had arisen over the royal prerogative and the legalization of civil marriage. The proposal to allow a secular marriage ceremony had been approved by a large majority in the chamber, but Victor Emanuel, who at first did not demur, changed his mind when reminded by the Vatican that marriage was a Christian sacrament and civil marriage meant legalized concubinage – which his own irregular private life made a sensitive point. In October, under papal pressure, he refused his signature to the bill, at which Azeglio, despite not being very enthusiastic about this particular measure, resigned on the grounds that a royal veto flouted the conventions of parliamentary government and could not be accepted with honour. No doubt the Prime Minister knew that Cavour would be more pliable on this point, for he recommended to the King to invite his rival to take the vacant post of Premier.

Victor Emanuel did not particulary like Cavour and seems to have been a little afraid of him, but took this advice after laying down a condition that the bill on civil marriage be withdrawn. Cavour had personally avoided voting on the bill so as to remain uncommitted, and he now put out feelers to discover if the Vatican would agree to some kind of compromise. When the Pope proved obdurate, Victor Emanuel turned to Balbo and Revel, who both replied that they could not command a majority in Parliament and that a new election was out of the question as it would be won by the left. Cavour was therefore summoned again early in November and this time agreed to make a concession: he could not withdraw a bill already passed by the lower house, but would not exert pressure to get it through the senate. This put him in an ambiguous position: his enemies could accuse him of damaging the authority of Parliament and conniving at a royal veto in order to win power; whereas his supporters preferred to think that he was saving the spirit of the constitution by reconciling monarchy and legislature.

The Marquis d'Azeglio was only fifty-four years old on leaving office for the last time, and it was a pity that a man of his good sense and experience was not consulted more often by the King over the next decade. He returned to his previous career as an artist and spent some time in London painting and selling his pictures. In politics he remained a qualified supporter of his successor, and the fact that his own ministerial colleagues remained in the new Cabinet was an indication that this was more a change of personalities than policy. Rattazzi was asked to join the government, but tactfully refused so as not to create additional difficulties for the new Prime Minister too soon.

CHAPTER 8

Prime Minister
1852 – 5

Cavour's first major test as Prime Minister came in December 1852 when the bill on civil marriage came before the senate. He now spoke in favour, asserting that public opinion wanted this reform more than any other, and stressing that the Church permitted civil marriage in other Catholic countries. Piedmont's legal system could not be allowed to fall behind that of other Italian states, otherwise her claim to primacy in Italy would be called in question. He also emphasized that if the Pope failed to permit such a moderate reform, there would be a dangerous increase in anti-clericalism and possibly a counter-attack on excessive ecclesiastical wealth. Some listeners, however, thought that he advanced these arguments without much enthusiasm and was pleased when the vote went against him.

The King wrote personally to tell leaders of the senate that he expected them to defeat the bill, and since senators owed their appointment to the monarchy they were not insensible to this unparliamentary expression of his wishes. Indeed a few months earlier he had hinted that he was ready to nominate another sixty senators to be sure of getting a loyal majority for the policies he wanted. The bill was duly rejected by a small minority. Cavour explained that he thought civil marriage a necessary law for any civilized state, but was prepared to wait; and in fact he never reintroduced it.

This was a characteristic illustration of his common-sense belief that reforms should never be rushed if they were too controversial. As he told Parliament early in 1853, theoretically he preferred clear decisions that avoided fudging and ambiguity, and yet a slow process of change with broad agreement was generally more effective than drastic changes that aroused conscientious opposition. One example in his mind was the modernization of England that had proceeded through the centuries by a series of compromises in a continuous search for a *juste milieu*; another example was the United States, which was beginning to compromise over slavery even if it had not gone far enough. Not that he would wish to follow Anglo-Saxon examples too abruptly: it was not necessary, at least not yet, to make the senate subordinate to the chamber, nor need the royal prerogative be so reduced that the King became merely a figurehead.

Cavour was much aware of the fact that he had come into politics with little experience of administration except as mayor of a small village; and this remained one of the charges against him – that he was less good as an administrator than as a politician. Nonetheless he knew that some improvement in the bureaucratic system was an essential preliminary to political success. Many provincial intendants, like many magistrates and bureaucrats in Turin, were resistant to change since they had learnt their jobs under the autocratic government of Charles Albert. Azeglio had gone some way towards reform by dismissing a few senior civil servants and aristocratic army officers; now Cavour, despite being himself an aristocrat, followed suit by easing a few other nobles out of various sinecures and ambassadorships. Privilege had to give way to efficiency, and he issued further instructions about punctuality and the precise keeping of office hours. Especially in the Ministry of Finance, which he took care to supervise himself, the amount of work greatly increased while the number of employees fell.

To help with reorganizing the administration, Rattazzi joined the Cabinet in October 1853. Some who knew them both were astonished to see Cavour's growing infatuation – this was the word used – with someone so different from himself. But Rattazzi was the ablest member of the lower house after Cavour, an excellent extempore speaker and debater, and the leader of the centre-left deputies whose support was absolutely necessary after the breach with Revel and Menabrea. Such a man, as Minister of Justice, could be relied on to modernize the penal code and, possibly by threatening their statutory security of tenure, to bring judges more into conformity with the principles and practice of constitutional government. By assuming responsibility for further anticlerical measures, Rattazzi would also take on his own shoulders some of the unpopularity engendered by government policy.

The two departments that Cavour considered most important were those of finance and foreign affairs. In foreign policy he inherited from Azeglio and Balbo the idea of a mission to free Italy from Austrian predominance by means of what he usually called 'the aggrandisement of Piedmont'. Here too he wanted to feel his way and find a middle path. He could accept neither Mazzini's exaggerated and utopian notions about Italian nationality nor the other extreme view held by Solaro della Margherita that Piedmont, as a self-sufficient nation already, might in a sense be diminished by becoming more Italian. In Solaro's opinion, Austria was a necessary bulwark of conservatism in Europe, whereas Cavour thought that the harsh policy of Vienna towards her Lombard subjects was morally offensive and a dangerous encouragement to anti-conservative and revolutionary forces in Italy.

Another inheritance from Azeglio was the conviction that Piedmont, instead to trying to go it alone as she had in 1848–9, must at the very least secure either French or English help, and preferably both. After December 1852, when Louis Napoleon changed his title to the Emperor Napleon III, there was talk once again of Piedmont reaching some secret agreement with the French by which she might acquire Lombardy and Venice in return for giving up Savoy and Nice to the new French empire. Already Cavour was wondering if another European war could be utilized for some such alteration of frontiers, and with this in mind a modest programme of rearmament had secretly begun. In fact he started to fortify the garrison town of Casale without waiting for parliamentary consent. Such an action was strictly unconstitutional, but he considered it necessary and threatened resignation if Parliament refused to condone what he had done.

Of course he had no intention of provoking Austria prematurely or by a direct confrontation. On the contrary, when in February 1853 he learnt that a republican uprising under Mazzini's inspiration was about to break out in Milan, he tried to warn the Austrians and ordered the frontier guards to prevent anyone leaving Piedmont to lend assistance. Victor Emanuel congratulated the Emperor Franz Joseph on brutally putting down this insurrection and gave his word, for what it was worth, that Piedmont would never support any revolution in Italy.

At this point, in the first of a series of grave miscalculations, the Austrians over-reacted; in reprisal against Mazzini but also against Turin they sequestered the property of a number of Lombards living as refugees in Piedmont, some of whom had by now taken local citizenship. Cavour was privately delighted and publicly indignant. International law made it hard for him to denounce the executions of rebels by the Austrian administration, but law was on his side when he made a vigorous public protest at this violation of property rights, and Parliament was persuaded to vote a sum of money to compensate some of the innocent victims. He would have liked a counter-reprisal to confiscate the property of Austrian citizens living in Piedmont, but was dissuaded from this excessive reaction by Azeglio. The King went much further and talked about setting the whole of Europe ablaze in a war of liberation; and if his government refused to support him in this, he boasted, not for the last time, that the royal prerogative would be employed to appoint a more subservient Prime Minister.

Cavour had other ideas. He realized more quickly than most that the failed insurrection in Milan would fortunately weaken Mazzini's influence by demonstrating the lack of popular support for these disorganized movements, and would surely convince some patriotic republicans that the best hope for Italy lay in rallying behind Piedmont and its monarchy. He seized the occasion to imprison the editor of a Mazzinian newspaper in Genoa and confiscate its printing press. After consulting the United States' representative in Turin, he sent two naval vessels to America carrying into enforced exile a hundred of the more extreme among the refugees who had made their home in Piedmont.

In the course of 1853, Cavour came to realize that the alliance between the two centre parties should be consolidated by new elections. Not that he had much opposition to fear in the lower house; yet there remained a fear that the reactionaries might still use the aristocratic senate to block further reforms or even to overturn government and constitution. In November the upper house was bold enough to challenge him by rejecting an important finance bill. His own preference in response to this would have been for more of his supporters to be appointed to the senate, but this time the King was reluctant to agree because a conservative majority in the senate was always a useful brake on the chamber and a defence of the monarch's residual authority. Here was another reason why ministers wanted an election, so as to bring pressure on the monarchy by proving that their policies had widespread support.

Another calculation was that electoral success would be easier for the government before the full burden of new taxes began to be felt. Already there was serious unrest among the poorer classes after a bad harvest had caused a food shortage and price increases. Because of his belief in free trade, Cavour did not want to use the traditional emergency measures of price control and prohibition of cereal exports. Once again, therefore, he was exposed to the unfair accusation of callous profiteering at the expense of the poor: an accusation that arose understandably from his regular practice at Leri, where he continued to buy grain on his own account whenever he realized that the harvest might be bad and prices would rise. On at least one occasion he had to be given a police guard on his way to Parliament; and after his house was assaulted by an angry mob, a visiting Englishman, Bayle St John, reported that no one else in Piedmont was now so unpopular.

But the poor had no say in an election, whereas the threat of lower-class unrest helped to win Cavour the support of the one per cent of the population who voted. In one constituency a deputy was returned to Parliament by the votes of only seven electors. By the judicious use of government influence, the elections in December turned out to be strongly in his favour, and this must have persuaded the King and some of the conservatives that, despite all their reservations, Cavour was still the best available politician to run the government. Both right and left emerged from this election much weaker. Out of two hundred and four deputies, about a hundred and twenty would usually support his centre coalition (this compared with perhaps ninety in the previous Parliament), while the independent left were down to under fifty and the independent conservatives to under twenty. The latter had their main stronghold in Savoy, north of the Alps; the left had theirs in Genoa and Liguria; and this underlines the fact that both groups represented in part a regional protest vote against the predominant authority of Turin. But from now onwards Cavour could rely on a fairly safe majority, quite apart from the fact that there were individuals on right and left who would break ranks on occasion to support him.

Throughout 1854 his unassailable position can be observed in what was called his virtually autocratic authority over the lower house. Hardly ever did he miss a debate, and on some days might intervene ten times or more. The opposition used to complain that so great was his personal ascendency that this was quite unlike parliamentary government as the term was understood in other countries, while even some of his own supporters were worried by his evident dislike of sharing power or of allowing other than mediocrities into his immediate entourage.

Valerio on the left remonstrated that many important issues of policy were decided outside Parliament, and in particular that ministers continued to be appointed or to resign quite irrespective of votes in the chamber. Revel, speaking for the moderate right, warned that Parliament would take root in Piedmont only if it were treated in a less cavalier fashion and not merely expected to sanction decisions already being put into effect. But these were minority voices, and most deputies were evidently content to let ministers run things as they wished.

Foreign policy, for instance, was always decided with little reference to Parliament. To some extent it remained part of the royal prerogative, and the King regularly used private emissaries to conduct a parallel foreign policy behind the back of his ministers. There was inevitably much secret diplomacy over Piedmont's attitude to what developed into the Crimean War. In June 1853 the Russians, hoping to extend their empire to the Danube and beyond by profiting from a possible dissolution of the Ottoman Empire, invaded the Turkish principalities of Moldavia and Wallachia. Cavour had already been shrewd enough to consider the hypothesis of a war in eastern Europe that he might turn to good account, and Victor Emanuel, thrilled at the chance of intervening on the field of battle, privately assured the French ambassador that France could count on his personal help to bring this about.

Cavour used to joke about the sovereign's outbursts of verbal belligerence each winter as soon as the campaign season could be seen approaching. The Prime Minister's own enthusiasm was somewhat muted on this occasion because any war involving Russia would cut off very necessary imports of wheat from the Black Sea. In any case he correctly feared that the King wanted war as an excuse for reasserting his personal authority and shaking off constitutional shackles. Nevertheless Cavour was on record as opposing Tsarist autocracy and what he condemned as the dangerous incursion of Russian influence into Europe. He may also have known that Palmerston and Napoleon thought of giving Moldavia and Wallachia to Austria as part of a bargain that ceded Lombardy and Venetia to the Piedmontese. Best of all would be if Austria were to side with Russia in this war, because there would then be good chances for a more heroic aggrandisement of Piedmont by alliance with the two western powers.

Unfortunately the Emperor of Austria, Franz Joseph, showed signs of likewise preferring to join the western allies, and to help persuade him to do so the French offered to guarantee Austria in keeping her Italian possessions. This was very unpleasant news for Cavour, who briefly thought that the French offer might compel him to resign in favour of a more conservative and pro-Austrian government under Revel. One alternative would be to join this grand anti-Russian alliance on the same side as the Austrians. But the other ministers were not enthusiastic about joining Austria, especially as it might involve a costly campaign in a distant area where Italian interests were not conspicuously involved. The King was almost alone in excitement at the prospect of a war which, though far from the patriotic anti-Austrian battles demanded by Mazzini, might help to recover the prestige of the monarchy and cancel the psychological trauma of the defeat at Novara. Victor Emanuel repeated to the French ambassador that it was upon himself, the monarch, not on the Prime Minister, that France should rely if Piedmontese help was required.

While discussion of these possibilities continued, there were further minor shocks created by real or suspected Mazzinian insurrections in Italy. After an outbreak of violence at Sarzana in September 1853, Cavour took the opportunity to send more potential trouble-makers into exile, until the Americans began to fear that he was treating their country as a kind of Botany Bay for undesirables. At the same time he continued trying to win over Mazzini's disillusioned adherents. In April 1854, Garibaldi was allowed to return after five years of wandering around the world, but only after assurances that this revolutionary general had broken with the republicans. Manin was sent another cordial invitation to return from Paris: this Venetian exile was almost ready to renounce republicanism, but only if he could be sure that Cavour did not have in mind merely another move for the aggrandisement of Piedmont. Manin's opinion, almost as much as that of Mazzini, was that Piedmontese ambitions might well endanger a movement of national liberation, just as they had done in 1848–9 when other Italian countries were alienated by Charles Albert's attempt to impose the interests of this one Italian state on everyone else.

Meanwhile Cavour continued to prepare for possible hostilities in eastern Europe, and the chances became much more interesting in March 1854 when France and England finally joined the Turks in their war against Russia. He again spoke in the *camera* against a proposal to decrease expenditure on the army, and in fact started secretly building further fortifications between Turin and the Austrian frontier. He tried to arrange a new loan in England, only to find that, since he had already over-stretched the supply of credit in order to stimulate productive capacity, foreigners were unwilling to lend without better security than he could offer. He therefore floated a loan for thirty-five million *lire* on the domestic market. It was a resounding success, especially among smaller investors – a fact that testified to the increased prosperity of many people in the country and his personal backing from a growing middle class.

As the war against Russia gathered momentum he became more inclined to disregard the natural fear of finding himself on the same side as Austria, and in October suggested to the western allies that Piedmont might join them in the hope of being able to participate in redrawing the frontiers of Europe. In particular he tried to persuade the British minister in Turin, Sir James Hudson, that if some tangible inducements were offered, the Piedmontese could be counted on to act as supporters of England at the peace settlement and as a guarantee against any preponderant influence of France in Europe. He probably knew that the British were trying to obtain auxiliary troops in Spain, Portugal, Sweden, Switzerland and Germany; he was ready to offer fifteen thousand Piedmontese so long as these soldiers were treated as allies and not mercenaries. As an ally, he could expect to take part in the peace conference.

Cavour's decision to enter the Crimean War has been described as a masterpiece of subtle diplomacy, and certainly it shows his remarkable ability to surmount difficult circumstances. He had to act against the wishes of all his ministerial colleagues, and against what he admitted to be almost universal disapprobation of the war by public opinion. The possible gains were remote and incalculable. All he could be fairly certain of winning was the good opinion of France and England. These two countries wanted his alliance but mainly so as to be able to reassure their more important ally, Austria, that he would not start any trouble in northern Italy, and their eagerness for Austrian help was another reason why they could promise him nothing in the way of territorial compensations.

The crucial decision to fight was taken almost by accident in January 1855 when he discovered that Victor Emanuel, acting like any unparliamentary autocrat, was privately negotiating with the French.

The King had already told the French ambassador that he was about to appoint a new conservative government which would join the war against Russia, and indeed Revel had already privately signified his readiness to become Prime Minister. Cavour received positive proof of this intrigue by information leaked from the French embassy, and a few hours later astonished the Cabinet by proposing that they should forestall the King and themselves agree to declare war. He found no enthusiasm among the other ministers, but told them that it might be the only chance of averting a return to monarchical autocracy.

Only one member of the Cabinet, General Dabormida, resigned rather than accept this logic. Dabormida's argument was that they had no interest in fighting against Russia unless the western allies guaranteed specific gains for Piedmont. He knew, in his capacity as Foreign Minister, what Cavour perhaps did not fully appreciate: that France and England were coming round towards the idea that such guarantees might be offered. But in these hurried hours of crisis Cavour overruled him – thus devaluing an important bargaining counter – and did so in order to cover up a discreditable palace intrigue. The other ministers were persuaded not to resign but to support the Prime Minister against the King's private machinations, and Cavour was then empowered to assure England and France that Piedmontese participation would be entirely disinterested: they would ask for no increase in territory and not even for a financial subsidy.

Despite the unpopularity of the war, and in part because parliament was called on to confirm the decision to fight only after a commitment had been made from which they could hardly back down with honour, both houses gave their approval. From the benches on the left came the criticism that such a distant war was a waste of resources that were needed at home for the inevitable *terza riscossa* against Austria. From the right came the objection that it was wrong to launch the country into hostilities to meet the convenience of Paris and London without any prospect of territorial acquisitions.

Against such views Cavour used all his dialectical skill, arguing that a military victory was needed to raise Piedmont's reputation in the outside world and demonstrate the valour of her army. In private he once said that war on the same side as Russia would be preferable to neutrality. But in public he stressed that fighting against Russia would make Piedmont the champion of western civilized values against an autocratic and anti-national empire, whose triumph would be fatal to

77

the cause of liberty and patriotism everywhere. This was a plausible argument – though it should be noted that a year later he reversed it with equal plausibility when he needed to justify a close alliance with illiberal Tsarist Russia.

At the same time as this political crisis over the war, another constitutional conflict opened over a project to dissolve the monasteries and confiscate their property. Cavour had, until recently, been a strong defender of the right to form associations and of the sanctity of private property, but he was now moving away from a doctrinaire liberalism towards believing that the state had a prior right to supervise ecclesiastical institutions and the management of Church land. One motive was that further anticlerical measures would consolidate his alliance with Rattazzi's more radical followers in Parliament. Sometimes he was prepared to acknowledge that a further dose of anticlericalism might be unpopular among the masses, yet he was equally sure that it would strongly appeal to the small minority of the population represented in Parliament. As he explained to a friend, the papacy was 'the chief cause of the misfortunes of Italy'; and by taking a firm line with Rome he might win broad liberal backing at a highly dangerous moment when the King was undermining the principles of responsible parliamentary government.

Another motive was the materialistic calculation that an excessive number of monks and priests were unprofitably absorbing too much of the national wealth. There were ten thousand priests in Piedmont and almost as many monks and friars, one for every two hundred of the population; in the island of Sardinia the ratio was one to 127, and only some six per cent of the clergy were registered as literate. Yet all ecclesiastics claimed exemption from military service, and Cavour was sure that this exemption was the chief reason why their number was so high. The bishops were among the richest anywhere in Europe, earning salaries sometimes a thousand times as much as the stipends of parish priests, and this was an imbalance that the government thought it had a duty to redress. Some ten thousand pious foundations owned a vast extent of landed property, and yet the State at a time of great financial stringency was contributing nearly a million *lire* a year to supplement clerical incomes. Not only did Cavour want to use some of the monastic buildings as prisons and military barracks, but he intended to reallocate expenditure by reducing the number of dioceses; he also wanted to abolish this annual subsidy of a million *lire*, and in addition hoped to obtain five million *lire* from sales of Church property to meet part of the deficit in the State budget.

Negotiations with the Vatican had been continuing for some time on these proposals, but the Pope understandably objected that the Church was being asked to make substantial sacrifices with nothing appreciable offered in return. It was pointed out, by liberals as well as ecclesiastics, that the constitution expressly guaranteed the inviolate rights of private property, and Cavour was among the most vociferous defenders of property rights for the laity. But now he was proposing to deprive one class of people of what had been legally guaranteed by a concordat as well as by the constitution. As he informed Parliament, the Church was evidently not prepared to give way, so the State would have to act unilaterally.

In January and February 1855 a bill came before Parliament for the abolition of any monastic orders not devoted to education or charity. Cavour argued in the debate that many monasteries had misappropriated legacies given to them over the centuries and many habitually left their land uncultivated while the peasants living on it were hungry and underemployed. On a higher level of general principle he called the monasteries 'useless', even positively harmful and 'an impediment to social progress'. Land held in mortmain should, in his view, be put back into circulation so that it could be properly exploited, and of course this argument strongly appealed to lay landowners anxious to extend their estates. Other countries offered proof that prosperity and public morality were in inverse proportion to the extent of monasticism, and he himself had found religion to be most flourishing in countries where the proportion of regular clergy to the rest of the population was lowest. The mendicant orders in particular set a bad example of begging and idleness in a society that ought to be based on the ethic of hard work; hence they should disappear. Without wanting to make the monastic life illegal, he saw overwhelming arguments for abolishing privileges that were unjustified and out of date.

The King at first agreed to support this proposed legislation, but the deaths in quick succession of his wife, his mother and his brother aroused a superstitious fear of supernatural retribution, especially when Pope Pius explained to him that these afflictions were clear evidence of divine punishment. After the lower house of Parliament had voted by a large majority for the bill, Victor Emanuel therefore sent word to Rome that his conscience would prevent him signing it; anything would be preferable, even having Mazzini as Prime Minister. He reminded the Vatican that he had once dismissed Azeglio rather than sign a bill on civil marriage, and was now prepared to force Cavour's resignation rather than agree to the confiscation of Church property.

Cavour knew something of this private correspondence between the royal palace and Rome. He also had to admit that his proposed legislation, as well as being unpopular, was likely to be defeated when it came before the King's friends in the senate. In April Senator Calabiana, the Bishop of Casale, put to the upper house a counter-proposal already privately agreed between Pope and King, namely that the bishops should make a voluntary annual payment of a million *lire* so as to meet Cavour's basic demand and render the new law unnecessary. On this issue the ministers resigned so as to force Victor Emanuel to clarify and justify his use of the royal prerogative. They did not even wait for a parliamentary vote before resigning, knowing that a vote in the senate was likely to support Calabiana and make their own return to office more problematic by the rules of the constitution. The King thereupon opened discussions with the conservatives in the hope of appointing a pro-clerical minority government, but had to be told – he apparently had forgotten – that the one likely candidate on the right was opposed to the war against Russia which he was so anxious to fight. In some desperation he even hinted to Brofferio's small group of deputies, who were well over to the left, that he would prefer to have them in power rather than allow Cavour and Rattazzi back.

Calabiana's proposal brought the implications of this fundamental disagreement to public attention, and persuaded some observers that the future of parliamentary government was at stake. Even Azeglio, who had not liked the bill and who thought Cavour less than trustworthy, braved the royal displeasure and wrote to warn his sovereign against bringing the monarchy into the political arena: if the King clashed with his ministers he might ruin the country at the same time as destroying his own reputation as a constitutional monarch. General Lamarmora, the Minister of War, reinforced this warning with the decisive argument that only if Cavour returned to office would Victor Emanuel get the war he so much wanted.

The crisis ended when Cavour agreed to a compromise that would allow all dispossessed friars and monks to receive lodging and a pension for life; his earlier proposal had been less generous. The financial gains from the bill thus turned out to be less than he had hoped, but his reappointment was none the less a great political victory. No longer was there a danger that an alliance between King, bishops and conservatives would upset the supremacy of the lower house. Some loyalists protested against the idea that the monarchy should be outside party politics; they thought that there was nothing wrong if the King overrode a vote in the elected house. But most politicians no doubt were pleased that a headstrong and not very intelligent sovereign had lost this battle. Though Victor Emanuel had said that on grounds of conscience he would abdicate before signing such a measure, he soon changed his mind, and Cavour made a somewhat threatening speech recalling how Charles I had been deposed in England for resisting the trend of his times. The Pope issued a major excommunication against anyone who signed or voted for the bill, but in practice this had little impact except to split clericals from royalists and make the government's task that much easier.

CHAPTER 9

War and Peace
1855 – 6

In the early months of 1855 these two extended crises, over foreign policy and religion, left Cavour tired but triumphant. After Dabormida's resignation he personally held the two most important and demanding Cabinet posts – foreign affairs and finance – as well as the office of Prime Minister; and in Lamarmora's absence he had to take additional responsibility for the army and navy. He had to be continuously and ubiquitously present because in his absence work often came to a halt, and in every department a force of inertia seemed to operate against any changes that he aimed to introduce. Only in June did Senator Cibrario take over the Foreign Office: and this was a purely nominal appointment of someone who could be relied on to take no initiative of his own, so that the work-load was redistributed only in part.

In April a small expeditionary force commanded by General Alfonso Lamarmora left Genoa for Balaklava. There had been some delay because Cavour was still hoping (and continued to hope until June) that Austria would enter the war on the Russian side, in which case the Piedmontese army might be needed at home for an attack on Lombardy. At the same time the Prime Minister took the precaution of pretending to the Austrians that his principal desire was for friendly relations with them and for a reconciliation between Vienna and the Lombards. Naturally he wanted to be prepared for any possible development.

Victor Emanuel, flattered by his courtiers into imagining that he was a talented general, was eager to go in person to the Crimea, and confidently assumed that the French and British would want him to take command of the combined allied forces. However, he made the impossible condition that another two hundred thousand troops should in that case be sent so as to make the war 'more serious'. When his offer was politely rejected, he blamed the British refusal on their jealousy that he might succeed too well and win too many laurels in battle. Lamarmora when he left for the Crimea was still unsure whether the Piedmontese force was expected to work with the British contingent or the French. Contradictory promises on this point had been made in London and Paris by Cavour, who needed to keep his options open and postpone as long as possible a political choice between these two countries. Lamarmora was merely instructed to use his imagination once he arrived, and said later that he would have resigned had he known of the embarrassment this equivocation would cause.

As the summer of 1855 passed, Cavour became more and more worried that the war might end before the Piedmontese troops had time to distinguish themselves, while in the meantime they were being decimated by cholera. The tension was such that he spoke again of leaving politics. Fortunately, on 16 August a Russian attack on the River Tchernaya provided the opportunity for a glorious feat of arms, and he was seen weeping with joy over a victory that he hoped would wipe out memories of Novara. The claim was sometimes made in later years that the Piedmontese on this single day won the Crimean War for the allies. This was an exaggeration but, although only fourteen soldiers were killed, their one serious participation in the war was undoubtedly a moral success of which the country could be proud.

In November, Cavour accompanied the King on a visit to Paris and London. Napoleon III had recently sent further information to Turin about his longer-term plans to extend the frontiers of France and incidentally to 'alter the map of Italy'. Though the French Emperor was not enthusiastic about Cavour's liberal ideas in domestic politics, he based his foreign policy on the hope that an enlarged Piedmont would effectively replace Austrian by French influence in the Italian peninsula. Hence Cavour urgently needed to talk with the Emperor, and also wished for a preliminary discussion in England about what could be hoped for from a peace congress when the Russian war came to an end. He had initially agreed that there would be no territorial changes as a result of the fighting, but circumstances were changing and Piedmont might just possibly be able to alter the rules and to claim some tangible reward for her sacrifices.

On the journey to Paris, he persuaded a presumably reluctant Victor Emanuel to make himself more presentable by trimming four inches off his enormous moustache. But there was no chance of being able to control the latter's coarse barrack-room language, which was soon delighting and shocking the Parisian salons. Among the King's more repeatable remarks to Queen Victoria and other public figures were statements about wanting to execute Mazzini, shoot the priests *en masse*, and 'exterminate' the Austrians. His unsubtle attempts at diplomacy included trying to turn the Queen against both Napoleon and her own ministers; and then creating trouble with the French by trying to make them believe that Palmerston in private spoke of Napoleon as a coward and adventurer. At one point Cavour, in protest against such mischievous gossip, threatened to return home.

Since the difficult relations between these two men would before long become a factor of considerable importance – in particular over the task of finding the King another wife – it should be added that the sovereign, apparently without telling Cavour, had sent word to England that he might consider marriage to Queen Victoria's cousin. On arriving in London his offer was rebuffed, but he covered up by pretending to his courtiers that the Queen's eldest daughter had fallen in love with him at Windsor and he had turned her down as being too much of an intellectual. Cavour used his visit to London more profitably: once again meeting the more important politicians, ingratiating himself with flattering remarks about how he trusted England but distrusted the French, visiting Spithead for a naval review and discussing a further loan with Hambro; but he very quickly discovered that his wish for a political alliance against Austria met with no enthusiasm at all.

It is significant that Cavour chose to avoid Manin when passing through Paris on this occasion. Manin and his chief political supporter in Turin, the Marquis Pallavicino, had already in 1854 sounded the Prime Minister about a possible movement for the unification of the whole of Italy, and Cavour had expressed only a guarded interest. Then in September 1855 Manin publicly announced that Cavour, by backing Italian unity, would make many republicans desert Mazzini, but such a challenging programme received a bad press in all the newspapers in Turin which supported the government. Manin and Pallavicino assumed from this and from the apparent ambiguity in Cavour's public attitude towards Austria that their earlier view was probably correct: in other words that he was still essentially a Piedmontese who, interested primarily in the expansion of his own province, might well be an enemy of true Italian patriotism.

Cavour was rarely doctrinaire on major issues, and in fact had no thought at all of Italian unity unless and until he could discover whether the idea was practicable and well supported. Furthermore his brief stay in Paris convinced him that the French, while they would strongly support an expansion of Piedmont in northern Italy, were decidedly not in favour of building up too big and strong a neighbour on their south-eastern frontier. His first and superficial task, therefore, was to convince them that he was not over-ambitious, nor the 'anglomaniac' that they supposed, nor aiming at substantial territorial gains, but was nevertheless ready to support Napoleon's imperial ambitions in Europe. His underlying objective however, as he now privately informed Victor Emanuel, was 'to extend the boundaries of the royal domain and ensure its predominance over the rest of Italy'.

In December 1855 the Austrians threatened Russia that they were on the point of allying with the western powers, and this ultimatum persuaded the Tsar to bring the Crimean War to a close. For Cavour the news was deplorable: he had been hoping for a much longer war and further glorious military victories with more casualties that would give Piedmont title to greater consideration. Quite as bad was that Austria earned herself a greatly strengthened position in Europe and a decisive say in the peace settlement by her last-minute intervention. The sacrifices of men and money by Piedmont had still brought no prospect of material compensation, but on the contrary a great increase in the authority of her chief enemy who had contributed absolutely nothing. The one remaining hope was to retrieve by skilful diplomacy some of what had been lost. Since both France and England indicated that they were concerned to promote Italy's interests, he therefore decided to ignore his earlier undertaking about not asking in the peace congress for territorial acquisitions.

One possibility which Palmerston was ready to consider was reviving the idea of Piedmontese annexation of Lombardy, and in exchange to let Austria take either part of central Italy or else the principalities of Moldavia and Wallachia in eastern Europe. Another idea was to give these two Danubian principalities to the Duke of Modena, so leaving Piedmont free to take Modena and possibly Parma. A third suggestion by Lord Palmerston, which Cavour had turned down in December, was to give part of the Papal States to Tuscany in return for some unspecified compensation to Piedmont elsewhere.

The Papal States were by general admission very badly governed. Between the Adriatic Sea, the Apennine mountains and the River Po there were four regions under the authority of Cardinal Legates, assisted where necessary by Austrian garrisons. These Legations, loosely if not quite accurately referred to as the Romagna, were not well integrated into the Pope's kingdom and had witnessed many minor revolts against him and his predecessors. Moreover the presence of Austrian garrisons was a clear breach of the treaty settlement of 1815, and Cavour could therefore appeal to international law against them. He could also appeal to French resentment against any extension of Austrian influence in central Italy; and furthermore took care to send exaggerated stories to the Protestants in England about persecution and tortures by the papal Inquisition.

Once various possibilities for future diplomatic action were raised, the next problem was how to gain admission to the peace congress on a footing of equality with the other powers. Although he told Parliament that this would present no difficulty, he had no authority for saying so, and Piedmont was in practice excluded from preliminary conferences between Austria and the other allies. To win support on this point, secret messages were sent severally to England and France with conflicting assurances that, if the Piedmontese were given what for form's sake could be called equal status, each of these two countries would find in Piedmont a faithful ally against the other. The French were told in addition that Cavour would support them against Austria, while the British were privately informed that he would not only back them against France but could be relied on to crush the revolutionaries in Italy and exorcise the 'spectre of papism'. Both countries were reassured that he would be happy to have a merely nominal status of equality at meetings, and that if this were allowed he would tactfully abstain from intervention on any point that did not concern him directly.

While these matters were being considered, he invited Azeglio to represent the country at the peace congress in Paris, because Azeglio was someone whose voice might count more than his own with the French. Cavour was asked by the other Piedmontese ministers to lead their delegation himself, but refused because he also feared that a subordinate status would mean loss of face, and failure to win substantial concessions might bring his political career to a premature end. Azeglio, despite ill health, let himself be persuaded, and was also allowed to believe that there was no chance of having to take a merely secondary role but that he would find himself on the same footing as the other delegates. Only when Azeglio discovered that this crucial issue had not been settled did he withdraw his consent, protesting that Cavour had been deliberately deceitful.

Azeglio was additionally upset by something else, because he was specially requested to draw up a memorandum to Napoleon asking for the annexation of Lombardy and the central duchies, but Cavour then refused to use it. Azeglio's memorandum included a request for Piedmontese annexation of Parma and Modena, and for the formation of a customs union between the various states in Italy; also a proposal to bring the temporal power of the Pope to an end. However, Cavour on second thoughts realized that this was too much to ask: far better, as Palmerston suggested, not to be so specific and not to arouse too much hostility too quickly.

Cavour therefore decided that it would be expedient not to antagonize Austria by asking for annexations, but instead to demand liberal reforms in Lombardy, Naples and the Papal States. He knew that this programme would not greatly appeal to the *italianissimi*, but it was more realistic and practical than theirs. He now agreed, albeit reluctantly, to attend the congress in person, where he would pose from the outset as a trustworthy moderate whose demands would not be excessive. At a later stage it might or might not be possible to bring some of Azeglio's suggestions forward.

He arrived in Paris to discover that he had not been invited to attend further preliminary meetings; but the chief British representative, Lord Clarendon, hoping to find in him a useful supporter, successfully objected to his absence on the grounds that Piedmont had been a loyal ally and would surely have something to contribute. Cavour at once set himself the task of being as agreeable as possible to the other delegates, including Count Buol the Austrian representative, who he knew would be his chief adversary. For the next two months he and his staff stayed in a luxury hotel with no expense spared, and he did not forget to invite the Parisian journalists to his lavish entertainments. Always free with tips, it was usually his practice to act on the assumption that it was undignified for someone of rank to question even the most excessive bill of a tradesman or hotelier.

Azeglio could never have behaved with such style, but Cavour thought it important and was ready if necessary to pay twice the going price so as to establish the proper dignity of his country. Clarendon was agreeably impressed with someone who was not only convivial and friendly but was the only other liberal delegate in the congress; he found Cavour 'an excellent colleague and one of the few foreigners I know who is like a practical well-educated English gentleman . . . one of the most moderate but at the same time most practical men I have ever had to do with'.

What Clarendon would not have known was that the chief Piedmontese delegate arrived in Paris with a preconceived intention of befriending the representatives of autocratic and defeated Russia, on the assumption that they might be more helpful than others in pushing Italian interests. A few days earlier Cavour had been agitating for an even more extensive war against Russia, but he now spoke of the Russians as his 'most faithful ally'. He brought with him money from the secret service funds for bribing the Russian and possibly also the Turkish delegates, though the documents were later doctored to conceal this intention. He also turned upside down his earlier excuses for fighting against Russia. Instead of her being a dangerous threat to liberty and to the other emergent nationalities, it was suddenly important to prevent the Russians from being too much damaged by the congress. Such an attitude was bound to annoy the strongly anti-Russian British, whose help he would also need, so this was something else that had to be kept as secret as possible.

The chief Austrian delegate was a former acquaintance from the whist table. The French delegation was led by Count Walewski, the illegitimate son of Napoleon I, who at once revealed himself as an enemy of Italian hopes. The Emperor remained in the background, but careful arrangements were made so that the Piedmontese representatives could send private messages to him without Walewski knowing. The main intermediary with the Tuileries was Napoleon's physician, Henri Conneau, whom Azeglio had earlier employed for a similar purpose. Another go-between and informant was the Comtesse di Castiglione, a former mistress of Victor Emanuel's, who was having an affair with the Emperor and whose help Cavour secured by promising a junior diplomatic post to her father. Whether she was ever of any real help is not clear.

He already knew that Napoleon and Palmerston were not unalterably opposed to an extension of Piedmontese territory. Palmerston had hinted at Lombardy; Napoleon preferred Parma, and the English agreed that this might be more practicable. The Bourbon Duchess of Parma and the Austrian Duke of Modena could perhaps be sent to govern the Danubian principalities, thus leaving room for Piedmontese expansion in Italy. Another suggestion was that Victor Emanuel's cousin, the Prince di Carignano, could be married to the widowed Duchess of Parma and sent to Moldavia with the title of King. Cavour was sure that this not very interesting Prince would 'regenerate the Roumanian race' and be a popular appointment among his new subjects. But there was one difficulty, quite apart from the Prince's own inclinations. The recent war had been fought to defend the integrity of the Turkish empire, an objective to which Cavour was committed by a formal treaty, and it would be ironic if Turkey lost her outlying provinces merely to compensate Piedmont. An alternative and even more fanciful suggestion by Palmerston was that the Prince and his enforced bride could be despatched to displace King Otto on the throne of Greece.

There was something oddly unrealistic about the way these various expedients were conceived one after the other, each of them wilder than the last. Equally implausible was Cavour's suggestion to give defeated Russia part of Turkish Moldavia, based on the strange idea that this would make the peace so disliked in England that Palmerston might be forced to allow Piedmont some annexations in order to recover his popularity. Alternatively the British might lend some soldiers to help the Piedmontese conquer Sicily; or else Carignano could be sent to replace King Ferdinando on the throne of Naples. Similarly unrealistic was the idea that the congress might let Piedmont annex the papal Legations. Here the main difficulty, apart from the presence of Austria, was that Napoleon had to reckon with a very large Catholic population in France, and the Empress was hoping that the Pope would stand godfather to the child she was expecting. Any tinkering with the Papal States was thus out of the question.

At the end of March the peace treaty was signed and Cavour alone had gained nothing of what he wanted. He was so crestfallen that he spoke again of leaving politics altogether, and this was one of a dozen occasions in his life when he talked of possibly emigrating to America. As he wrote to the King, only a war against Austria would now solve

Italy's problems, and in desperation he said as much to the Emperor, though he had been clearly told that France could not contemplate another war 'for the moment'. Evidently the Austrians were emerging from the congress as the real victors without having made any of the sacrifices that Piedmont had in sending troops to the Crimea.

Napoleon had agreed that the subject of Italy would be raised in the congress once peace had been signed, but Cavour's belligerence and anticlericalism made the Emperor less than eager and it was left to Clarendon to take the lead when the matter was placed on the agenda. Although no formal decisions were taken at this meeting on 8 April, it was a great achievement that the plight of Italy was discussed at all, especially at what was a major European conference. The represent-atives of France and England on this occasion both criticized the misgovernment of the Bourbon King of Naples. Clarendon, however, did not receive much support when he also asked for reforms in the Papal States, and some of his denunciation of papal misrule had to be tactfully deleted from the record. Clarendon also cited the presence of the Austrian troops in the Legations as being in violation of inter-national law. Cavour took care to be much less outspoken when his turn came to speak, for he was anxious not to offend Napoleon or the Russians and had by no means given up hope of allying with Naples. Even though this short debate on 8 April was his one positive gain from the war, he called it a thoroughly unsatisfactory result.

In private conversation he was anything but moderate, and to the British he again spoke wildly of planning to fight Austria in the near future and depose King Ferdinando of Naples. He hoped that his friends would thereby realize that if someone as moderate as himself could think of war, Italy must be suffering serious wrongs which other countries should help him redress. Clarendon's reply, according to Cavour's uncorroborated account, was that England was delighted with the idea of such a war and eager to join in fighting Austria for the 'aggrandisement of Piedmont'. Cavour accordingly sent a note to Turin to say that he intended to deliver Austria an ultimatum as soon as Piedmontese troops returned from the Crimea. He was sure that France as well as England was prepared to fight, and hence that victory would be certain.

This reference by him to a British and French desire for war is unconvincing because it is directly contrary to everything else that we know, and Clarendon, when Cavour's private documents on the subject were published many years later, categorically denied that he could have possibly said anything so contrary to the basic principles of British foreign policy. Austria was England's chief ally, and on the very same day as this supposed anti-Austrian conversation, Clarendon was in fact negotiating a formal treaty of alliance with Buol. England did not even possess the kind of army that could be used effectively against Austria, and in any case another European war was the very last thing that British interests required. Clarendon looked back later on Cavour in Paris as someone he liked and admired but who 'was demented about his Italian schemes and perfectly unscrupulous as to the means by which he brought them about'.

These illusions about British policy were one of the more serious mistakes of Cavour's career and it is the more unfortunate that they are hard to explain. There is no conceivable reason why the English representatives should have wanted to deceive him into thinking that he could rely on their military help. Just possibly the two men misheard or misinterpreted each other when speaking French; or possibly the Italian spoke so guardedly that the Englishman thought they were talking of a war of aggression by Austria; but these explanations are unconvincing. Cavour tried to persuade his colleagues that his plan for an immediate declaration of war on Austria was no symptom of 'cerebral fever' since he had never felt so calm in his life. Perhaps, however, this was one of those dramatic and stressful moments when, as the King later recalled, he was in such a state of excitement that reason deserted him and he lost any recollection of what he said.

Whatever the explanation, Cavour suddenly decided to change his plans and go to London, though it was a visit that he almost at once regretted. The fact that he did not first consult Clarendon about the advisability of this journey makes it even harder to believe that the latter had encouraged him to think of war. Nor did he mention fighting when he arrived in England. On the contrary he told Queen Victoria in Buckingham Palace that, though he was a little disappointed, the congress had been a success. To Palmerston he apparently spoke only of wanting peaceful reforms in Italy, and the British government, delighted to hear it, promised that they would back him in securing not only liberal changes in Naples but also the withdrawal of Austrian troops from the papal Legations.

At this point Cavour committed another minor *gaffe* when he persuaded the opposition in London to put pressure on the government: by furnishing the Tories with facts for a parliamentary debate he possibly hoped to coerce Palmerston into doing more for Italy. When his somewhat disingenuous intrigues were discovered he confessed that he was at fault, making the implausible excuse that he was ignorant of party divisions and the conventions of parliamentary behaviour. Clarendon was greatly annoyed by what he called this unprincipled and unskilful conduct; the English politician confirmed his regard and friendship for Cavour personally, but said that henceforward he would no longer be able to trust such a person, and that anyone working in this underhand way to start another European war – let alone a war against England's major ally – would now find liberals and Tories forewarned and united against him. Here was a major reverse for Piedmontese foreign policy, because a useful ally had been turned into a potential enemy.

Back home in Italy after an absence of two and a half months, Cavour discovered the administration languishing without his guiding hand. He had tried to keep in touch from a distance, even over minor matters of administrative detail, and more than once had sent from Paris a threat of resignation when he thought his wishes were not being precisely followed. But in Turin the main issue in everyone's mind was the peace settlement. Various politicians had been betting on what annexations he would secure. Returning empty-handed after a war that he knew had been unpopular, naturally he feared for his political future.

Opposition voices in Turin were nevertheless subdued. In Parliament Cavour had to concede that an earlier peace settlement in 1815 had given Liguria to Piedmont without the country being represented at a congress, whereas in 1856 a costly war had ended with no territorial acquisitions, with no relief for the many ills of Italy, and Austria still in a position of almost unchallengeable supremacy. Brofferio complained that Parliament had been pushed into the war on false pretences. Solaro della Margherita, who had opposed the unprovoked declaration of war against Russia, now argued that the army had fought with courage only to be let down by inept diplomacy in Paris; he was angry that the Austrians had humiliated Piedmont by being able to draw public attention to her military occupation of the principality of

Monaco. Evidently the Piedmontese were as much in violation of international law at Monaco as were the Austrians in central Italy.

Cavour in his defence laid certain documents before Parliament but only on the strict condition that they remained absolutely secret. Whatever their tenor, most of the deputies accepted his rejoinder that it was a triumph to have been admitted to a congress on the same terms as the great powers of Europe. He tried hard to play down as of no consequence the fact that on 15 April France and England, without informing him, had signed a secret treaty with Austria to guarantee the status quo in Europe – though that status quo was in fact the very last thing he wanted. He tried to claim as a great success that the integrity of the Turkish empire had been sustained against Russian aggrandise- ment, but was careful to keep secret his own attempt to violate that integrity and his own private discussions with the Russian delegates about a possible joint war in the future. He pointed out that Naples and the Papacy had been publicly branded at Paris for their misgovern- ment. Austria likewise had been reproached for manifest breaches of international law. And he untruthfully tried to convince the deputies that no one, least of all himself, had ever expected that France and England would do more.

CHAPTER 10

Economic Policy
1852 – 8

The reduction of tariffs since 1850 had confounded at least some of the critics by its beneficial effects; customs revenue had admittedly fallen, but the loss was more than made up by an increase in trade and general prosperity. Cavour was not so dogmatic a free trader as some of his associates and did not shy away from centralized intervention in the economy where he thought it necessary. What he called 'the timidity of our capitalists' and their 'lack of any spirit of association' left him with little option. Subsidies and monopolies were therefore given to the railways, to the postal and telegraph service, to banking and ship-building, though he hoped that this kind of activity would be reduced in time. The officially subsidized electric telegraph linked Turin with Genoa in April 1852 and with Paris in January 1853; and despite the prophets of gloom this telegraph service was covering its expenses and paying ten per cent on borrowings within the year.

With respect to the postal services, Cavour was able to profit from the experience of the 'penny post' in England, where, as he carefully observed, an initial loss of revenue was quickly made up as the volume of correspondence increased. He accepted that the post should be a public utility rather than a source of revenue. By almost halving the stamp charges for mail he had to report a loss in 1851–2, but was in profit the following year.

Another less successful venture was to set up the Transatlantica shipping company in 1852–3 with substantial government aid. Genoese long-distance commerce was mainly with ports in the Black Sea, and almost never did any vessel venture round the Cape of Good Hope, but now that England had dropped her exclusive Navigation Acts there was every chance of winning a bigger share of world trade if ocean-going ships were built. Cavour mistakenly argued that such

94

ships could be quickly adapted to military use if necessary. A parliamentary commission recommended using iron and not wood for these vessels, though his own view was that despite all the attractions of new technology and his own interest in more speculative methods of marine propulsion, steam would never replace wooden sailing boats for bulk carriage. Only the experience of the Crimean War convinced him that he was wrong.

The commission was doubtful about the whole idea of launching a service to the two Americas, and Cavour admitted that such a service was bound to begin at a loss, especially on the New York route where trade with Italy was small. He himself thought that New Orleans would be a more profitable terminal than New York. But his chief hope was in a regular service to the River Plate, where a colony of some sixty thousand Ligurians and Piedmontese was well established around Buenos Aires and Montevideo: colonists living in this area were already rich enough to buy a great deal from Italy as well as to send substantial sums to their families at home. He hoped incidentally to capture a large part of the transit trade between Switzerland, Germany and South America. But the venture was badly timed and inexpertly costed. Only five of the seven ships planned were in fact built, and they proved so unsuitable for transatlantic traffic that a few years later they had to be sold for a quarter of their cost. A good deal of money was thus wasted, in part because the project had to be based on official guesswork rather than commercial calculations of profit and loss.

Another grandiose project that he never carried through was rebuilding the port of Genoa. In 1850, Azeglio had made a study of this problem, and had identified the need for new docking facilities and other transport linkages if Genoa were to compete with Trieste and Marseilles in attracting the transit trade from central Europe. Cavour always retained a slight animus against the Genoese, just as they did against him, and hardly anyone from Genoa entered his circle of close acquaintances. The bombardment of 1849 was not easily forgotten by either side. He complained at the anomaly that this 'commercial metropolis' of the kingdom would not put up the money required for modernizing its own harbour; also that its merchant oligarchy was always grumbling at being asked for too much tax; and that such a rich town remained a centre of revolutionary disaffection. He eventually went so far as to obtain a detailed feasibility study from an English firm of consultants; but the port of Genoa was rebuilt only after his death, when a large legacy was received for the purpose from an expatriate banker who died in Paris.

It took Cavour many years to abolish the antiquated and restrictive practices of the dozen guilds of maritime and port workers in Genoa. But one privilege that he was in favour of at least partially preserving was in Nice, a free port with tax exemptions designed to attract wealthy tourists in search of winter sunshine. Nice was another town where he had few close friends, and there was an additional problem that some citizens were hoping for annexation by France. So primitive were communications over the mountains that Nice was more accessible from Paris than from Turin; it was even said that goods could be taken there more cheaply from America. When Parliament abolished the *porto franco* in 1853, he tried to compensate by building roads to integrate this peripheral region more closely into the kingdom, but it proved a very expensive operation and was never completed.

Adjoining Nice, the principality of Monaco was an independent state surrounded by Piedmontese territory, and for many years its independence was an object of envy. A garrison of Piedmontese soldiers had occupied the greater part of Monaco ever since the revolution of 1848, and Cavour, somewhat high-handedly, intended to go still further and integrate the occupied villages of Menton and Roquebrune into the Piedmontese customs system. The ensuing controversy with Prince Florestan of Monaco was a continual nuisance to France and Britain who were called on to mediate, and this minor military occupation helped to weaken Cavour's arguments against the illegal presence of Austrian troops in central Italy. The French envoy to Turin called the Piedmontese blockade of this principality more arbitrary than Austrian behaviour and 'an unparalleled example of tyranny exercised by the strong against the weak'; and the American envoy said much the same. Cavour, perhaps because of these criticisms, would not accept arbitration and always refused to offer what others thought would have been adequate financial compensation to the dispossessed prince. He even tried to win foreign sympathy for his annexation of the whole principality by protesting that Florestan was immorally setting up a centre for gambling in Monaco, without explaining that the Piedmontese government had a strong financial interest in a rival casino at Aix. The problem was still not settled when, in 1861, Menton and Roquebrune were purchased by Napoleon from the Grimaldi family and annexed to France.

* * *

Of major interest was the building of railways linking Turin to Genoa, Milan and the French frontier between Chambéry and Lyons. This was part of a scheme outlined in the time of Charles Albert, but it was Cavour who overcame the practical problems of finance and technology. Not much money could be found locally, and hence the main lines had to be built either at government expense, or preferably with generous guarantees given by the government to foreign investors. The line to Genoa had extra problems because of very steep inclines and tunnels through the Giovi pass in the Apennines. It was a great moment for the country when this line was opened in 1854, and both houses of Parliament suspended their sittings to attend the ceremony. Thomas Bartlett's new boring machine employing compressed air was used for the Giovi tunnels and was later greatly improved by the Savoyard Germano Sommeiller for the far more difficult problem of tunnelling through the Alps.

Equally important was the railway running from Turin to the Alps, beyond which it was intended to link up at Modane with a line through Savoy to Lyons and Paris. Nearly all the money for this line came from France – in particular from the Parisian bankers Laffitte and Rothschild – and a number of English engineers including Thomas Brassey had a large share in the planning and construction. One of Cavour's controversial but brave decisions was when he persuaded Parliament in 1857 to pledge the country's credit for an eight-mile tunnel through the Mont Cenis, an enterprise that he called the most stupendous engineering feat of modern times. This tunnel was not complete until long after his death, and until then travellers to France had to change at Susa to use horse-drawn carriages and sometimes sledges for fifty kilometres of the way. He justified the huge expense by the fact that three-quarters of Piedmontese exports went to France, and mostly by sea. Almost a thousand kilometres of railway – half the total mileage in the peninsula – were operating in Piedmont by the end of the decade, and already could be seen as a fine investment that was changing the whole economy of the country.

The encouragement of industry by government action was not one of Cavour's primary aims, because fuel and raw materials were lacking and so was a socially accepted habit of active engagement in industry and commerce. Nevertheless, he himself was by temperament a gambler and entrepreneur whose personal example in this field was infectious. He was sorry to have to acknowledge that until 1848 there had been hardly a single example of joint stock enterprise in Piedmont, and on becoming a minister said he would like to 'inebriate' the country with the habit of speculative investment. One among many reasons for this was that only by increased economic activity would tax revenue be increased. Several years later he had to admit that the expansion of credit had gone too far and investment was being directed rather into a stock exchange boom without sufficiently helping the economy. By abolishing existing laws against usury in 1857 he was again attempting to make credit more readily and cheaply available, and though the critics called this a moneylenders' charter that would mainly benefit the rich, it was a necessary and overdue reform that helped to put Piedmont ahead of other Italian states.

The metallurgical industries, especially those based on the inefficient iron mines of Aosta, were among the sectors of the economy hit by a reduction in protective duties, but Cavour was on firm ground when he pointed out that protection had operated in the past to keep such industries unprofitable and antiquated. Those that could survive under competitive conditions would be far more healthy. The mechanical industries (of which there were very few before 1850) did better on the other hand; and he was not so extreme a believer in free enterprise that he would not allow some 'inducements' – for instance to assist with the provision of machines and skilled workers for manufacture, or at least for repairs and maintenance. A dozen locomotive engines were built in the late 1850s. He also tried, with not very much success, to shift the general pattern of education so as to provide more technical instruction instead of so much Latin and philosophy. His own schooling was unusual in having been predominantly mathematical and scientific, and though he regretted that it had been too one-sided, he firmly believed that an almost exclusively classical and literary education was one of the major reasons for the country's economic backwardness.

The biggest industrial success effected by lower rates of duty was in textiles. Even the cotton industry, which might have been expected to lose by exposure to competition from well-established English factories, continued to expand. Silk manufacture, which hitherto had been so protected as to constitute a virtual monopoly, was in fact stimulated by competition into buying new machinery for spinning and weaving; and though the treasury lost temporarily by the consequent reduction in customs duties, exports more than doubled in four years. Chinese raw silk was even brought into the country from England to be manufactured and then re-exported back to England.

As the taxable capacity of the country grew, Cavour remained convinced that he could bring revenue and expenditure into balance and so acquire a new credit-rating in the eyes of foreign bankers. Here was another reason why he kept the finance ministry in his own hands. On becoming Prime Minister in 1852 he said he hoped to balance the books during the course of 1854, or at the latest in 1855, and this he called an 'absolute duty'. In December 1853 he confirmed that the finances were on their way to being back on target and that a balance would be reached in 1855. To make this possible he promised to be miserly in every branch of expenditure.

At this point, partly as a result of the war against Russia, most of Europe experienced an economic recession that upset all forecasts of revenue. An additional burden was the actual cost of the war, especially since Cavour was adamant against accepting any grant from his allies that might seem to be payment for mercenary troops. Instead, after failing to get a loan in Paris, he borrowed twenty-five million *lire* at a low rate of three per cent interest in London. This sum, which he privately thought would be more than sufficient, was in fact estimated by the British government to be much more than the war would cost. But in October he requested a second twenty-five million, and on his visit to London in December a third, until the premature ending of the war made further funding unnecessary.

Apart from wartime borrowing from abroad, there was a very considerable influx of French capital into railways, banks, mines and insurance companies: altogether this amounted to over a thousand million *lire* during the decade and is a good index of the confidence that Cavour's management of the economy inspired. As well as Rothschild, against whose attempt to 'Jew' him he protested more than once, he used other bankers: Laffitte, Hambro, and Péreire's Crédit Mobilier. It was important to force Rothschild to offer competitive terms, and equally important that as many northern investors as possible should acquire a material interest in the prosperity and expansion of Piedmont.

Almost immediately after becoming a minister, Cavour had asked

Parliament to increase taxation quite considerably, and more than once threatened resignation if this were not agreed. His governing principle was that taxes should fall with some degree of relative proportionality on every class of citizen; but they should be designed to interfere as little as possible with the accumulation of wealth or economic growth. He continued to aim at reducing the indirect taxes on necessities, which fell most heavily on the poor – though here he was sometimes accused of fine words supported by too little action. Repeatedly he said he would like to abolish the State lottery which was a bad and 'immoral' tax, though in practice he found it was impossible to abrogate such a useful form of revenue. Parliament nearly always granted his requests, but naturally there was a good deal of resentment: the self-employed professions, especially the lawyers, were the most vocal among the deputies and until now had been immune from the burden of direct taxation.

He still sometimes thought of introducing a general income tax, and used to pursue Disraeli and Gladstone with requests for information on the practice in England; but concluded once again that it would not work. If individual declarations of income were dishonest and un-reliable in England, he thought they would be more so in Piedmont, and was unwilling to give government inspectors the right to inspect private account books. As he told Parliament, the new tax introduced in 1851 on traders and the professions was producing less than ten per cent of the sum that would have been payable on the basis of honest declarations.

Among the criticisms made by opposition deputies was that Cavour dealt too lightly in taxing financiers, banks and holders of government stock. Owners of large estates, by his own admission in 1855, also continued to pay less tax than in other European countries and proportionally less than they had done earlier in Piedmont. Occasion-ally debates took place about introducing a new and more accurate land survey to remedy such a palpable inequity, but Cavour had some doubts about its feasibility and never made this a matter for a vote of confidence, so that at the time of his death the *catasto* (land register) was still very defective and the problem of land tax largely unsolved. This allowed the charge to be levelled against him that, despite his genuine wish to help them, in practice poorer people and some of the middle classes continued to pay more in taxation than their fair share.

Notwithstanding every effort and repeated undertakings, not only did imports continue to be greatly in excess of exports, but the budget remained unbalanced and became more so. In January 1856, Cavour apologized for this, saying that the exceptional difficulties of war and bad harvests were responsible for a merely temporary failure, and a year later announced once again that a balance was on the point of being achieved; but he was being disingenuous because, apart from the fact that the figures had been doctored to look good, he was already preparing for another war against Austria that he well knew would mean greatly increased expenditure.

The opposition accused him of becoming so preoccupied with foreign policy that he had less and less time to consider problems of the domestic economy. Revenue went up, exports increased, more people were buying government bonds, the number of small holdings increased: all these were signs of prosperity. But of course not everyone gained. From the newspapers it appears that there were many bankruptcies among those who failed to adjust, and while financiers and some industrialists prospered, others had a difficult time. The national debt was nearly ten times as high in 1860 as in 1847. In compensation, many other changes in the economy were beneficial and they fully justified Cavour's confidence, foresight and sense of enterprise.

As a farmer and *laisser faire* liberal, he at first resisted interference by the government in agriculture, believing that the liberty of individual citizens should be the primary consideration. For the same reason he was angry when the civic administration of Turin tried to restrict the right of property-owners to build as they thought fit. He used to vote against proposals to limit the absolute right of landowners to cut trees and pasture their goats in the mountains, though later he came to recognize that the general interest might in this case override the interest of individuals. The Ministry of Agriculture was abolished in 1852, but he revived it in 1860, and one reason for doing so was that the progressive denudation of the mountainsides was creating serious problems that needed collective attention. He also agreed that government aid could properly contribute towards improving animal breeds and encouraging farmers to use better agricultural implements.

Irrigation was another problem where individuals were relatively powerless and the community had a special interest, above all in the province of Vercelli where his own farm of Leri was situated and rice was a principal crop. In general he criticized landowners who selfishly used irrigation canals to maximize profits at the expense of their neighbours; nevertheless, although he sued someone who tried to restrict his own use of water, he spent thirty years in relentless litigation against another landowner who appealed to the ancient right of aqueduct to take water through the Cavour estate.

As a minister he greatly helped landowners in his own territory of the Vercellese by improving the canal system at government expense, and was accused, with some justice, of sacrificing public welfare on this issue to his own immediate interests. He also encouraged the building of a public road near his own farm and had earlier tried to deviate the main railway in order to help his constituents. But his principal assistance to agriculture in this area was the practical example which he set as a farmer, by proving the value of guano as a fertilizer and experimenting with agricultural machinery of one kind of another. An English hydraulic engineer was brought to Leri to advise about applying the techniques of subsoil drainage, and the information was made available to others.

Cavour as an employer had the reputation of being very exact over the precise fulfilment of contracts by his 'subjects', as he sometimes continued to call them. Normally a surplus of labour in the countryside made it easy to dismiss workers, if for example their wives refused to work when required to, or even if they set a bad example by following his own practice of keeping a mistress. But he was generous, especially in difficult times: always anxious to provide good housing, or food after a bad harvest, or to give fuel and clothing for those too old to work, or dowries so that daughters could find a husband. Whereas many Piedmontese villages had no medical doctor, at Leri he provided one and also a pharmacist whom foreign visitors sometimes met at his dinner table. Occasionally he paid to buy his men off their military service and send the sick to a sanatorium. William de la Rive made the interesting comment that he habitually treated prince and peasant alike, not from calculation but out of human respect and natural inclination.

Cavour often used the phrase *noblesse oblige*, recognizing that his own privileged position carried a corresponding duty to the rest of society. De la Rive described him as 'an aristocrat by birth, taste and nature', who was 'too refined to understand the masses or be understood by them', and he himself confessed that he had begun by assuming that aristocrats were 'by nature superior to the bourgeois classes'; yet he learnt from the experience of England that a proper regard for the underprivileged, by giving them a better share of wealth and capital, would be a useful means towards averting social unrest. The European revolutions of 1848 were attributed by him largely to the egoism and ignorance of the rich, and one of the principal lessons he learnt from 1848 was that the serious problems of the day were increasingly social as well as political. He once hazarded the suggestion that the world was moving inevitably towards what he called socialism, in the sense that more and more people would come in time to exercise political power, and that this was something over which it was futile to repine. Hence, bettering the lot of the poor might offer the last chance of escaping a catastrophe. It might be the only way to prevent social conflict from complicating other political issues and making the national question far harder to solve.

Social reform, however necessary, was not in Cavour's opinion a task for the state so much as for individual employers of labour, and he optimistically expressed confidence that what he referred to as 'the well-known spirit of philanthropy' among the propertied classes would suffice to help the poor during periods of economic difficulty. He conceded that tax exemptions and even direct subsidies could some-times be permitted in order to help charitable foundations, because any civilized society had a duty to ensure that no one suffered the extremes of poverty; but this precept was not easily translatable into legislation. He talked of wanting laws to control the employment of women and children, especially as they were expected to work far longer hours than in England. In practice this good intention went by default because Parliament had more urgent business than social reform, and he noted with some dismay that the number of small children working in the rice fields continued to increase.

Although he was at pains to argue that real wages and standards of living were rising in general, the figures varied so much from place to place and from time to time that they can with difficulty be quoted in support of any general conclusion. When critics pointed to the fact that some eight thousand people were emigrating each year to South America, and others to France, while some villages in Liguria were entirely abandoned, he replied that this was not necessarily an index of extreme poverty. He could argue quite rightly that, though prices were rising, poorer people gained more than others from the reduced taxes on cereals which were their basic food; and there were also lower taxes on salt, of which the average annual consumption was as high as eight kilograms per family. Opposition deputies replied that employers often took this as an excuse to reduce wages proportionally. Reports were received each year of deaths by starvation and in bad years many people were kept alive only by private charity.

Cavour's speeches indicate that he took the problems of pauperism very seriously. But he hoped that the situation was improving. He mentioned that almost all agricultural workers were now in possession of some kind of footwear, at least for use on festive occasions, so that the reduced tax on leather would help to alleviate what was, apart from cereals, the chief item of expenditure for many families. He knew that either maize or chestnuts were almost the only food over large areas, while meat was still eaten no more than once or twice a year by perhaps the great majority. But he was glad that consumption of wine and beer was rising among town populations, and hoped that labourers in the rice fields would one day afford to buy more wine to fortify them for the exceptional fatigue of their work. A further advantage was that another narcotic, tobacco, was being bought by richer peasants, thereby incidentally providing a helpful addition to tax revenue.

The one region of the kingdom that Cavour knew not at all was Sardinia. This island, despite the fact that it provided the King of Sardinia with his royal title, was so neglected that some of the basic details of its topography and population were impossible to discover in Turin. Parliament was told about the abundant oak forests of Sardinia, whereas those easily accessible had been largely cleared. Cavour refused to believe all the complaints about Sardinian poverty, but admitted that there was at least some cause for concern. Malaria and brigandage were permanent problems, and civil disobedience in Sardinia sometimes reached the point of being called an endemic civil war. Roads were so lacking that Alghero – one of the main towns, the inhabitants of which spoke pure Catalan – could be approached only by sea or on horseback. Cagliari, the regional capital, had an entirely inadequate water supply that was becoming more of a problem each year. Since few villages possessed a school, ninety-five per cent of the population in the countryside was illiterate, while many areas continued to use barter instead of money – one result of which was that taxes were hard or impossible to collect. Most Sardinian deputies in

Parliament belonged to the two extremes of right or left with whom Cavour had little in common, and when some of them invited him to visit the island to see what could be done, he had to reply that he was too busy.

Feudalism survived legally in Sardinia until 1836, with private baronial courts and bonded serfdom still in existence, and some feudal practices long survived their legal abolition. To relieve such a collection of problems, Cavour could allocate resources for road-building and send troops in the illusory hope of suppressing brigandage; he also laid an under-sea cable and abolished the customs barrier between this province and the mainland; but basically he had to rely on the doctrinaire belief that a régime of free parliamentary government would eventually – he said, quickly – bring conditions on the island up to the standards prevailing elsewhere. Nor did the Sardinians have any more practicable solution to offer. Their negative criticism was that he treated the island as a conquered colony and sent officials there as a punishment. Any magistrates or policemen arriving from the mainland were bound to find the local language and customs unintelligible. Sometimes the government could make its presence felt only by suspending constitutional guarantees and applying martial law, in exactly the same manner as the much despised and much criticized Neapolitan Bourbons in Sicily. Outside observers commented that the autocratic Bourbons sometimes seemed to be more enlightened than the constitutional government of Turin.

One of the difficulties inherited from feudalism was that millions of acres in Sardinia had no ascertainable landlord but were held in collective ownership: barons, villages, and peasant commoners all shared an ill-defined form of common property that made proper cultivation of the land impossible. Cavour repeatedly promised that this would be changed, but several attempts never got very far. Sometimes parliamentary debates on Sardinian affairs had to be suspended because mainland deputies were too little interested to make up the necessary quorum; sometimes the government itself was responsible for inaction by concealing the worst facts, fearing that they might shock the public and expose dishonourable truths to the outside world.

Cavour did not try very hard to hide his distaste for this intractable subject, and publicly referred to Sardinians as lazy, dirty, unenterprising, over-sensitive and quarrelsome. He blamed them, just as he blamed the Genoese, for being unwilling to help themselves and for always calling upon the government to wave some magic wand. He advised a friend not to take a job in Sardinia until the island became more 'civilized'. After many frustrations, he lost patience and ordered the intendants to ignore local opposition and impose continental standards of order and morality. But this was less a solution than a confession of failure.

CHAPTER 11

Foreign Policy
1856 – 7

In April 1856, as soon as peace was signed with Russia, Cavour abruptly got rid of his Foreign Minister, Cibrario: in fact he provoked the latter's resignation by sending him a deliberately impertinent letter over a trifling incident where Cibrario was in the right, and then gave the public excuse that the resignation was due to ill health. The experience of two months in Paris had taught him about the pleasures and possibilities of diplomacy, and he was eager to preside over what he now saw to be the most important department of all: foreign affairs. From daily contact with the leading statesmen of Europe he had discovered how, by his own special brand of persistence and ingenuity, he could play on their weak points and exploit their national rivalries so as to take the Italian question one stage further.

When he appeared in Parliament to justify the peace settlement he won a large majority. Naturally nothing was said about his mistakes. For example, the deputies were inaccurately informed that he had never been so naïve as to think that England or France could be persuaded to fight on Italy's behalf. Furthermore he warned them that diplomacy by itself would solve nothing – the implication being that blood, iron and financial sacrifices would also be needed before the hegemony of Piedmont in the peninsula would be generally accepted. The Republic of San Marino had sent a memorandum to the peace congress about constituting an Italian federation in which Piedmont would have no special pre-eminence: that kind of suggestion had to be firmly nailed as erroneous and impractical. His own view, speaking in private, was that Piedmont would have to fight Austria at some point during the next three years. To his friend Salmour he talked unrealistically of marching on Vienna as soon as he had recruited a hundred thousand soldiers, though on reconsideration he thought it might be best to wait until there was another European conflagration that could be turned to advantage.

Of course he was careful to conceal such aggressive intentions, especially from the French and British, telling them instead that he was glad to keep a strong Austria as a buffer state against Russia: but he also hoped to convince them that they should nevertheless back Piedmont in Italy as a counter to Mazzini's more revolutionary objectives. He also sent to Vienna an envoy who had friendly – and, for obvious reasons, not much publicised – talks with Buol. The Austrians explained to this envoy that their troops would soon be withdrawn from the Romagna; they were waiting only until there was a chance to discuss mutual grievances and receive reassurance that the Piedmontese were not intending to make further trouble.

Cavour had far more bellicose ambitions than to be attracted by such pacific talk. In April he had mistakenly convinced himself that English politicians would agree to fight for the aggrandisement of Piedmont, and in June was still half-hoping that England might be persuaded to join him in a joint war against Austria in the not-so-distant future: and of course to obtain their help it would have to seem a defensive and not an aggressive war. Somehow he convinced himself that it would be an easy war for the English to fight and one demanded by their own public opinion. What he told Clarendon was that England's national interests ought to make her intervene in Italy, if only to prevent France from obtaining a predominant position in the peninsula. He thought that a Pitt or a Canning would already have seized on such an obvious point.

But he was wrong in his assessment of British interests, and wrong also in failing to understand that public opinion in London was firmly against intervention on such an issue. Palmerston offered him military help but only against Austrian aggression, which was most unlikely to take place. Cavour's warlike talk in Paris to Lord Clarendon had given the game away, because he had explained his intention to provoke the Austrians into fighting; hence he could count on no help but only fierce opposition from London.

One Piedmontese interest where Protestant England might nevertheless be counted on to give assistance was in encouraging the Austrians in their intention to withdraw from the papal Romagna. About eight thousand Austrian soldiers were there on the plea that the Pope needed them to keep law and order, but some English politicians were afraid that, on the contrary, their continued presence could produce the spark to ignite the revolutionary war that most Europeans wanted to prevent. Cavour stood to win either way: if the troops left, that would be an indication of Austrian weakness which he could exploit; if they stayed, the Romagna would remain a useful flash-point for a revolution that, even while pretending to oppose, he might secretly encourage and utilize.

While negotiations were continuing over this possibility, Cavour made another attempt in the summer of 1856 to secure an agreement with the Vatican which would have added substance to his reputation as the leading statesman in Italy. Pius IX had informed the British government that, though he accepted the imperative need for reform, he could go no further in secularization without destroying the whole system of papal administration, and if force was used against him 'he was ready to retire to the catacombs'. Cavour knew that emissaries from the royal court in Turin were again in touch with Rome and secretly promising a veto on any further anticlerical legislation; once again, therefore, he put up his own counter-proposal indicating that he would permit greater freedom to the Church if the Pope would consent to some major concession, for example over civil marriage. This initiative was firmly rebuffed in Rome. At the same time the ministers tried to persuade the King not to continue a parallel and secret policy with his own private agents and ciphers about which the government was supposed to know nothing. Victor Emanuel told a Swiss visitor about another altercation with Cavour, who had angrily started kicking the royal furniture and broken a clock.

But on the main issue – that of fighting Austria – monarch and minister were at one, and though neither man came round to liking the other, this common aim bound them together in practice. As a preliminary step they agreed on building new fortifications at Alessandria that could be aimed only against Austria. With scant respect for constitutional propriety, the necessary expenditure was authorized by royal decree, and this was done deliberately a few days after Parliament went into recess: mindful of the narrow vote of approval four years previously after the equally unconstitutional decision to fortify Casale, it seemed expedient to delay any public debate on rearmament until most of the basic construction at Alessandria was complete.

Tuscany was another region where, since Victor Emanuel's cousin the

Grand Duke Leopold was a subordinate ally of Austria, a little minor provocation might be both possible and profitable. The Piedmontese diplomatic representative in Florence already had orders to organize a network of secret sympathizers. In May the ambassador received a further request from Turin that these sympathizers should be instructed to start some moderate agitation and, if possible, make an undercover attempt to suborn elements in the Tuscany army. They were informed that Piedmont needed some evidence of unrest so as to persuade England and France that the whole of Italy was eager for liberation from Austrian influence; but they were also told that the agitation had to appear completely spontaneous or else it would not be convincing; moreover, in order to appeal to Napoleon, the agitation would have to be 'more national than liberal in character'.

A third area for exerting pressure was the Duchy of Modena, especially the region of Massa and Carrara which immediately adjoined Piedmont and where some people strongly resented the ducal government. Here the workers in the marble quarries had over the centuries developed a tradition of forming associations for industrial or political action, and it was known to be one place where Mazzini possessed devoted adherents who were prepared for violent agitation in the cause of patriotism. In July a group of activists were allowed to cross from Piedmont into Massa hoping to launch a general insurrection, but found almost no local support, and Cavour shrewdly back-tracked in order to help the ducal government arrest those responsible: the ten ringleaders were then tried and condemned by the courts in Genoa and Turin. His own commitment against uncontrolled revolutionary action was such that, much as he needed obvious symptoms of unrest, he recognized that more could sometimes be gained by warning the Duke of Modena and the Grand Duke of Tuscany when he had information that insurrections might break out.

His behaviour was certainly ambiguous. So sure was he that Mazzini's brand of agitation would fail, and so much did he want the reputation of being the great enemy of this republican revolutionary, that he had perfectly understandable reasons for warning the other rulers of Italy about possible uprisings. Where his sincerity became questionable was in the covert encouragement he simultaneously gave to the extremists in the hope that some kind of quasi-revolution would take place and provide him with an excuse to intervene.

For example, he had sent to London for a daguerreotype portrait by which the police could recognize Mazzini if an attempt was made by the latter to return to his native Genoa, and he offered considerable sums of money to bribe some of Mazzini's associates into betraying the latter's plans and whereabouts. Nevertheless, whether or not his actual address was known, this condemned criminal lived for several months of 1856 in Genoa unmolested by the police, and evidently was allowed to go ahead with organizing an insurrection in Modena after he had given some kind of private undertaking that the rising would not be ostensibly republican. This mysterious episode indicates Cavour's readiness to play both sides at once. He needed revolutions, but also needed to be thought a strong anti-revolutionary; he wanted evidence of rebelliousness, but without any risk that a revolution could actually succeed, and preferably with merely enough turbulence to permit him to intervene and 'restore law and order'.

Many of his closest collaborators had begun their careers as disciples of Mazzini, only to desert this hardened revolutionary as they observed that repeated attempts at popular insurrection met with little support among ordinary people. There were still some republicans living in Turin, but the more extreme among the refugees had by now been shipped under armed guard to North and South America. By the end of 1855, some of the Italians from other parts of Italy who were refugees in Piedmont grouped together into what later acquired the name of the National Society. Their acknowledged leader was the Venetian, Manin, who had not been able to find a job in Piedmont and was living in Paris; Manin's chief assistant, Pallavicino, was a Lombard; and these two were joined in 1856 by the Sicilian, Giuseppe La Farina, who became the Society's executive secretary. Their paramount aim was the unification of all Italy, and though most members of this association would, like Manin himself, ideally have preferred an Italian republic or confederation of Italian republics, they increasingly realized that monarchist Piedmont, as the most likely instrument of unification, deserved qualified support if only the Piedmontese ruling classes could be made more Italian and less municipalist in sentiment.

Cavour was quick to seize on the possibilities offered by this group of patriots. He saw Manin twice during his first few days at Paris in February 1856, and had a third long conversation before leaving in April. The two men established that they shared some common ground. Cavour told others that he found Manin to be honest and potentially useful, though too utopian, too eager for popular revolution and too much preoccupied with 'the idea of Italian unity and other such nonsense' – this phrase was later tactfully deleted from the published edition of his documents. Manin, for his part, learnt that the Piedmontese representative at the Paris congress was in his own way a patriot even if not a believer in national unification. While the pro-government newspapers in Turin continued to speak with contempt and even disgust of Manin and his friends – Manin sadly confessed that he had to rely on English newspapers to publish his views – nevertheless the few hundred members of the National Society assumed that Cavour would be 'too intelligent and much too ambitious' not to support them should they become sufficiently strong, if for no other reason than because they would constitute a further means of dividing the republican opposition. Rattazzi and Castelli worked covertly to encourage what could be recognized as a very useful potential alliance.

In July 1856 the National Society gained a valuable recruit in Garibaldi, and soon afterwards this revolutionary soldier was summoned by Cavour to a meeting at which the idea of a future war was almost certainly discussed. In September, La Farina saw the Prime Minister and, according to La Farina's recollection some years later, Cavour said that he would accept the idea of national unification as a long-term objective; but since he had little information about other regions of the peninsula, and since he might well need a body of brave men who could agitate when told to do so without expecting any overt support from Turin, he would like the advice and practical help of the Society. La Farina wrote at the time that Cavour, though still not completely trustworthy, could be a useful ally and might be pushed into braver action in course of time.

La Farina was a southerner and may well have suggested that, as the Papal States and Modena had powerful protectors elsewhere in Europe, the most vulnerable area for action might be not central but southern Italy. One reason for this vulnerability was that France and England had agreed in Paris to denounce the misgovernment of Naples and Sicily, which they feared as a possible cause of revolution that might embroil the rest of Europe. More than once Cavour thought vaguely of obtaining English help for landing troops to annex Sicily and perhaps placing a relative of Victor Emanuel on the throne of Naples, only to dismiss the idea as unrealistic.

Napoleon III's cousin, Lucien Murat, had a claim to the Neapolitan throne through his father Joachim Murat, who had been King of Naples under the great Napoleon. In Paris, Cavour met Lucien as well as Manin, and decided that though a 'Muratist' solution in Naples was far from an optimum solution, it might possibly be acceptable as a useful means of involving France in a more general move to extend the frontiers of Piedmont. Cavour knew almost nothing about the south, but some Neapolitan exiles in Turin were ready to back Murat, so he saw this candidature as a possible step towards 'the independence of Italy and Piedmontese aggrandisement'. Ready as always to play both sides simultaneously, he took the precaution of warning London in the hope that the prospect of a French dynasty in Naples might alarm the English and persuade them to help Piedmont more actively.

In October 1856, England and France jointly broke off diplomatic relations with King Ferdinando of Naples after he ignored their urgent and repeated request to modify his absolutist régime. Cavour saw this as a promising development and wanted to follow their example, but they advised him not to. He was further frustrated when they stopped short at severing relations whereas he had hoped that they would go further and use force to make the King abdicate. On second thoughts he therefore decided to go to the other extreme and dissociate himself from their diplomatic offensive against Naples. Indeed, he conceived the quite different idea of inviting Ferdinando to join him in defying any improper intervention by outsiders from northern Europe, and secretly suggested that an alliance between Naples and Piedmont could decide the future of Italy. But the Neapolitan government was not interested.

One good reason for greater friendliness towards the Bourbon dynasty of Naples was that this part of southern Italy was under Russian protection, and Cavour now needed to renew what he described as 'the links of friendship that for centuries have bound together the royal houses of Romanoff and Savoy'. He still sometimes agreed that the Slavs were a potential threat to western society and culture; on the other hand, Russia might one day be induced to fight the Austrians for supremacy in eastern Europe, and he therefore sent a message to tell the Tsar that Russia was 'incontestably' the one ally in Europe that he could trust. When the British reproached him with his growing cordiality to their recent enemy, he denied what he denounced as a malicious rumour spread by the Austrians. As a counter-charge he accused the politicians in London of repeatedly changing their minds in politics; by contrast, he insisted that his own entire loyalty and good faith made him a thoroughly dependable friend; nor would he, unlike England, ever ally with an absolutist power. When a colleague remarked on this piece of minor untruthfulness, he replied that in politics one must be flexible and never doctrinaire.

Towards the end of 1856 French and English interests in eastern Europe began to deviate rapidly when Napoleon saw the Russians as a potential ally in a future European war. This presented Cavour with a difficult choice. He needed the help of all these countries if possible, but though he told the English that they were his real ally and that he feared that France wanted only to dominate in Italy, he knew that France was much more likely to assist him in fighting Austria. So, albeit with occasional reluctance, he decided that he would have to support Napoleon on every issue of foreign policy. He thus favoured the fusion of Moldavia and Wallachia into a single country. Apart from French wishes on this matter he argued that a united Roumania would be another Latin state and hence another potential ally. In the future this country might constitute an exploitable threat against Austria; or alternatively Roumania might one day be sacrificed to the Austrians in return for their surrender of Lombardy. Either way, it could be useful.

Another controversy arose over Russian claims to the town of Bolgrad. At the Paris congress a decision had been taken to keep Russia away from direct access to the Danube, but she was allowed to keep a Bolgrad that was clearly marked on the map well north of the river. Some months later the Russians produced another much smaller Bolgrad further south, and their claim to it was approved by Napoleon as part of a plan to secure a Franco-Russian alliance. When the British opposed this as a manifest breach of the treaty settlement, Cavour at first tried to avoid committing himself. Under pressure he agreed that the French and Russians were strictly in the wrong; yet on what were said to be grounds of principle he preferred to be conciliatory and support their case, only to change back again when Napoleon altered direction and asked Piedmont to vote with England. Cavour was embarrassed but agreed to play out this 'comedy', though some people thought that such vacillation reflected on his judgement and perhaps his courage.

The difficulties of his position were exposed by the dispute over Bolgrad. Of his two principal allies, he had to accept that the British were learning to look on him as someone who could not be trusted and indeed who was trying to precipitate Europe into war; whereas the imperial government in Paris was so secretive that French policy was sometimes impossible to understand. He therefore thought it expedient to resume a more passive role in foreign affairs, as he waited for some 'accident' to happen that would enable a watchful and clever diplomat to 'seize fortune by the forelock'.

Whether or how far he believed by now in the practicability of Italian unification is uncertain. Despite what La Farina wrote subsequently, his remarks about Manin's utopianism suggest that he regarded such an idea as altogether too doctrinaire and 'Mazzinian'. He strongly believed that Italy should free itself from Austrian control, but was too much of a realist to make national unity a directing objective for practical policy over the foreseeable future. A thorough believer in national identity would hardly have favoured, as he did, allowing an Austrian Duke to rule Moldavia, or a Hohenzollern prince to govern Tuscany, or the Frenchman Murat taking the throne of Naples, or the Piedmontese Prince di Carignano that of Greece; nor would he have suggested Russian annexation of Galicia or Austrian annexation of both Roumania and part of Greece. His friend Salmour recalled that he always spoke of the 'emancipation' rather than the 'unification' of Italy. He subsequently admitted to the Comte de Rémusat that it was Manin who first put the idea of unity into his head as a possible aim; some people were convinced, however, that he never believed seriously in Italian unification until Garibaldi's victories in 1860 showed him that it was politically practicable.

The Kingdom of Sardinia was still to a considerable extent French by language, and by straddling the Alps still included a large area of present-day France. But by 1857 the general orientation of public opinion at Turin was becoming directed much more towards the rest of Italy – to the east and south-east – and less towards Savoy in the north-west. The Italian language was normally used in Parliament, and Italian was replacing Latin in the school curriculum. In February 1857, under pressure from the newspapers, the civic administration of Turin changed the name of the town's 'Gate of Italy' to the 'Gate of Milan' as confirmation of the fact that Italy was no longer alien territory as it had been in previous centuries. Cavour now spoke less of

Piedmont and more of Italy. To mark his championship of Italy at the Paris congress, subscriptions arrived from Naples and Milan for commemorative medals to be coined in his honour, because in every other region of Italy there were some people who looked to Piedmont as their main hope in the struggle against Austrian dominance.

The exiles who had come from other Italian provinces to live in Piedmont had diminished in number: some put the figure at only fifteen thousand, which must be much nearer the truth than the hundred thousand given by others. Some of these exiles, including the Marquis Pallavicino from Lombardy and Dr Farini from the Papal States, had been given citizenship. Many had become important in politics and intellectual life: the engineer Paleocapa from Venice, the economist Ferrara and the journalist La Farina from Sicily, the writers De Sanctis and Massari from Naples: these and many others were helping to make the inhabitants of Piedmont more conscious of their common bond with other Italian regions.

Not all of the exiles were well integrated into the community. Some continued to grumble about a virtual boycott by Turin society, and even of discriminatory harassment by the police. De Sanctis complained that, compared to what he had experienced in Switzerland or Naples, Piedmont was culturally a barren and almost barbarian desert. Some, for example the writer Niccolò Tommaseo, disliked Cavour as a great deceiver and corrupter. Pallavicino, who had spent years in an Austrian prison for his political beliefs, remained doubtful and complained that not a single member of Parliament in Turin supported the National Society – nor did any prominent journalist except La Farina. Pallavicino believed that few Piedmontese were interested in or understood the rest of Italy. Repeatedly it crossed his mind that Cavour might be merely pretending and in reality was aiming at Piedmontese expansion across northern Italy, with little serious thought for the rest of the peninsula. Manin, too, although by now he regarded Piedmont as the best hope for Italy, was still not sure how far her ministers could be trusted.

At the beginning of 1857, Cavour was anxious to demonstrate that he was uncommitted. There were distinct advantages in being vague about where he stood between France and England, between whole-hearted patriots and gradualists, even between peace and war. Though his aim to displace Austria was in fact revolutionary, he wanted conservatives in Europe to believe that, far from accepting the method of revolution, he opposed it strongly, and indeed that for them to support Piedmont would be the best prophylactic against revolutionary agitation. This was the gist of another message that he sent privately to Vienna. In private and public he repeatedly asserted that his reputation for guile and artfulness was quite undeserved, because he invariably followed 'a frank and loyal policy without deception or subterfuge'. Parliament was also told that he had no intention of trying to change the existing frontiers that divided the component states of Italy. To Carlo Boncompagni, the Piedmontese ambassador in Tuscany and Modena, he gave orders to allay any suspicions to the contrary. Boncompagni was told to oppose any increase of Austrian influence in Tuscany and to encourage any move towards liberal constitutional reforms; but also to give positive assurances that Piedmont, having no ambitions in central or southern Italy, wanted to work in complete good faith with the Grand Duke and other Italian rulers.

Meanwhile the Emperor Franz Joseph of Austria was trying to win back public opinion in Lombardy by granting an amnesty for political offences and sending his brother, the Archduke Maximilian, to replace the military administration of Marshal Radetzky. Some of the Lombard exiles were glad to return to Milan in the expectation of enjoying a more liberal régime there, and this lowering of tension and animosity was a setback to Cavour's long-term strategy. But once again Count Buol made the mistake of over-confidently resorting to a further piece of intimidation: on a flimsy pretext about Piedmontese hostility, the Austrian ambassador was withdrawn from Turin, so giving Cavour a chance to issue a dignified rejoinder regretting such a breach in relations but refusing to make any concession.

The British were alarmed at what Clarendon called this 'unpardonably stupid' action by Vienna. They were glad to see Austria's more liberal policy in Lombardy, especially as Cavour had told them that this was precisely what he wanted; but they now were confirmed in their suspicion that his underlying aim was not to lessen discord but rather to increase it. When Clarendon advised a more conciliatory policy by both sides, Cavour replied in an almost threatening note that he would break with England if there was any serious attempt at conciliation. From statements made by Cavour's close associates and friends, including Massari, Artom and de la Rive, it seems that Cavour's private feelings towards the English remained as friendly and admiring as ever, but he had to accept that their desire for peace and European stability forced them to set as much value on an Austrian as a Piedmontese alliance. He also knew that they increasingly distrusted him as unreliable and politically over-dependent on France.

In March 1857, Parliament discussed the fortifications at Alessandria that had been begun – illegally, as Cavour now frankly confessed – a year earlier. Though he won a vote of approval, he was criticized from right and left for relying on a subservient majority in the *camera* to give retrospective sanction to one illegality after another. The conservative Revel repeated the warning that the only way in which parliamentary practice would take deep root in the country was if the legislature were treated with more respect, otherwise liberal institutions would wither. Some critics thought that the government was moving towards what was described as a 'parliamentary dictatorship'. Others complained that Piedmont was being made into a subservient ally of an illiberal government in Paris.

Cavour replied to such criticisms that, where national interests were involved, he must be allowed some latitude. He could not of course admit that he was aiming at war, but some deputies either hoped or feared that another major European war was in his mind. General Lamarmora, the Minister of War, asked Parliament to accept the government's confession of having acted improperly over Alessandria, but also stated his own view that matters of national defence were no concern of Parliament. The same point was made more forcibly by another naturalized exile, Count Mamiani, who called for an end to what he called useless discussion, since 'the dignity of Parliament, as well as the grandeur or rather the sanctity of our national objective, should persuade us to avoid further debate and give the government our unanimous approval'.

In June a warning was received from the French police that an insurrection was about to break out in Genoa, to which Cavour replied that the rumour was without foundation for no revolution could possibly break out in Piedmont. Secretly he was aware that Mazzini's friends in Genoa were planning another expedition, this time to Naples. The fact that Mazzini had again arrived in his home town was known to the government, and their failure to arrest him suggests that they were hoping for him to take some action – action that, if successful, they might be able to exploit or, if unsuccessful, could be used to discredit the republicans. Cavour used to tell people that Mazzini ought to be arrested and executed 'without pity', but when someone objected to this on the grounds that occasional insurrections by Mazzini's party might help government policy, the Prime Minister laughingly agreed that the objection might well be true.

What he had not bargained for was the armed rising that took place at the end of June against his own administration in Genoa. Fortunately for him it misfired and was easily put down. But the Neapolitan exile Carlo Pisacane, after hijacking a Piedmontese vessel, the *Cagliari*, then set out from Genoa for the island of Ponza off the coast near Naples where he liberated a number of political prisoners and landed on the mainland south of Salerno. The local population, to Pisacane's dismay, turned out to be indifferent if not hostile, so the Neapolitan government had little trouble in crushing this ill-timed and ill-prepared attempt, especially since Cavour took the precaution of warning them what might be about to happen; and the brave Pisacane paid with his life.

The angry reaction in Turin was entirely genuine. Cavour did his best to lay the blame on others: for instance on inefficient policemen in Genoa, and on the Austrians whom he now pretended must be subsidizing Mazzini. Bitterly he called Mazzini 'Austria's strongest ally' and 'Italy's greatest enemy'. He blamed the British for having allowed Mazzini to live so long in London and sent a demand for them to expel this 'assassin' to face public execution in Italy. He was especially annoyed that the episode might have exposed to French eyes the inefficiency of his government and its not very skilful collusion with the Party of Action. He took the opportunity to punish any captured rebels, and used their failure as a further argument to persuade good patriots to acknowledge the leadership of Piedmont as the best hope for the future.

His chief concern was that the French would withdraw their support and assume that he must have been conniving with Pisacane. Their alliance was vital – so much so that he again sent word to them that he would back France on every international issue as long as they told him what he was expected to say or do. When they insisted that he must arrest Mazzini, he begged Napoleon to send French detectives to help the local police find this elusive rebel, and did not refrain from some gentle blackmail, hinting that if France turned against him he would resign in favour of a more pro-English administration.

But the French needed his help quite as much as he needed theirs. In July, Cavour's boyhood companion Count de Salmour was at the French resort of Plombières where Napoleon was taking the waters for his health, and the Emperor explained in the greatest confidence that he needed a popular war to establish his dynasty more firmly and strengthen the international position of France. In half a dozen meetings with Salmour, the possibility was discussed that at some time their two countries should conclude a formal alliance to fight Austria; but it was made clear that Napoleon must be left to decide when. Cavour, overjoyed, wrote to congratulate Salmour: 'the Emperor is our best friend, the one person in France who backs Italy, the one sovereign in the whole of Europe who has a genuine interest in the aggrandisement of Piedmont; fighting alongside him we shall reach our goal'.

This was a critical moment for Cavour's policy, and he busily set himself the task of shifting public opinion more in favour of France. He even took the trouble to persuade a young dramatist, Paolo Ferrari, to create French characters who were more attractive than the stock figures of mockery expected by current theatrical fashion in Turin. The Crimean War had not been nearly big enough, but with Napoleon's help something bigger and more destructive might now be possible. What the *Italianissimi* could not win by insurrections, the Piedmontese monarchy might win by French help on the field of battle.

CHAPTER 12

Coalition Politics
1857 – 8

The French alliance was fundamental, but there was a price to pay because Napoleon in return required Piedmont to be less liberal in internal policy. He wanted the *connubio* to be ended, which meant that Rattazzi should be dismissed from his post as Minister of the Interior. In particular he demanded more restriction of press freedom, a further reduction in the powers of popular juries and closer control over the émigrés resident in Piedmont. Cavour succeeded for some months in fending off these demands, especially as he sensed that they presented him with a useful bargaining counter for which he might be able to ask a good deal in recompense; meanwhile he begged that there should be no public request from Paris in case he could be accused of submitting to direction from a foreign power.

Cavour was a genuine liberal in the sense that he sincerely believed that freedom was desirable for its own sake and was normally more effective than repression. In youth he had denounced any form of censorship, on the grounds that repression merely drove opposition underground where it was more difficult to deal with. But the experience of being in government, as he told Napoleon, had pushed him towards a certain degree of interference with the press. He accepted the need to censor immoral or politically suspect books; also any newspaper that professed atheism or questioned papal infallibility. He also sometimes intercepted private letters, despite his claims to the contrary, and he defended the existence of a small-scale secret police force which he said he intended to reduce 'when things return to normal'. Occasionally he adopted what he called the corrupt practice of subsidizing journalists, and secret service money was sometimes used in paying newspapers, as well as in the more regular practice of instructing them what attitude to take over foreign policy.

But there was a strict limit to what could be done, and when the French asked for further curbs on freedom he said he needed time to gauge how public opinion might react. Fortunately, despite disapproval from individual deputies, there was not much to fear from any systematic opposition in Parliament. Brofferio was possibly exaggerating when he said that since between a third and a half of the deputies had either jobs, pensions or at least hopes of preferment in central and local government, there existed a silent, subservient phalanx of supporters on whom the government could automatically rely. But Cavour admitted that after the *connubio* of 1852 any semblance of organized parties had virtually disappeared, leaving only isolated critics to contend with, and he partially explained this by the patriotic enthusiasm generated at the thought of a possible 'third war', or *terza riscossa*, against Austria. The deputies of the left, having mostly lost their separate cohesion when they sensed the prospect of war, had given up the caucus meetings where once they used to discuss policy, and Cavour knew that most of them, even if with reluctance, preferred him to any likely alternative. Others on the moderate right had good reason to hope that the Prime Minister's formal link with Rattazzi's friends was growing weaker, and believed that his doctrine of the *juste milieu* would eventually persuade him to move back towards the right and terminate the *connubio* which in their estimation had dangerously divided the old ruling class of the country.

Though party opposition had diminished, there was of course opposition by individuals to what Cavour had so far achieved or failed to achieve. From both extremes came criticism of his economic policy: for instance, criticism of repeatedly broken promises to balance the national budget, and of a huge debt piling up to be a burden on the future. The Marquis Costa de Beauregard, an entrepreneur who had once been Cavour's close associate in railway construction, could not understand the repeated refusal to introduce an income tax, nor could he excuse the apparently deliberate concentration of power in one man's hands: overcentralization of power, he said, was permitting a self-important and not very efficient bureaucracy to misgovern unchecked. Costa blamed a 'parasitic administration' for acting as a brake on the development of commerce and industry. From a different point of view, a former journalist on the *Risorgimento*, Francesco Ferrara, argued that Piedmont could not expect other Italian states to accept her primacy so long as her penal laws were sometimes harsher than theirs, her universities less distinguished and her system of local government less free.

Another former colleague, Giorgio Briano, acknowledged that free trade had helped some individuals – more of them foreigners than nationals – to become rich, but maintained that it had not done nearly as much as Cavour claimed in creating new jobs or raising the basic standard of living. In one of his increasingly rare speeches Revel agreed with this verdict. Solaro della Margherita followed Briano in arguing that the government was in practice if not by intent encouraging the spread of indifference and scepticism in matters of religion, while anticlericalism inside the administration, typified by the freemason Rattazzi who was Cavour's chief colleague, was creating a divisive crisis of conscience for many Catholics. An almost opposite complaint was voiced by Brofferio: that ministers had broken their promise to legalize civil marriage and, despite the law of 1855, were leaving many monasteries with their riches intact.

The newspapers, including some that backed the government, continued to remark each January in their annual summary of events that the previous year had brought few if any of the basic reforms promised regularly ever since 1848. At the start of each parliamentary session there was usually an undertaking to make changes in the administrative system and in the organization of education and justice. But some people on both right and left complained that insufficient time was allowed for Parliament to discuss urgent internal matters. Some blamed the *connubio* in the sense that Rattazzi's progressive centre-left, by entering the ministerial coalition in 1852, had deprived the country of the organized opposition and criticism that any healthy Parliament required; or in other words that, once the centre-left was inside the gilded cage of government, any efforts at reform were being frustrated by the need to avoid controversial issues and so prolong the alliance between component elements of the coalition. Rattazzi himself made this point and complained that the government was not allowing individual ministers to carry out their agreed programme of liberal reforms. Without clear choices being presented to the public, without firm and positive direction by a united Cabinet, without a proper allocation and delegation of responsibility, the inertia of bureaucracy resulted in delaying or preventing change.

One example was prison reform, which had been one of Cavour's earliest interests. He had to admit that Piedmontese prisons were in a deplorable state, and was embarrassed at having to explain why conditions were little better than those in Naples that had aroused Gladstone's indignation six years earlier. Gladstone's denunciation of the Neapolitan prisons had been given enormous publicity, some of it organized from Turin, and had done more than anything else to turn European public opinion against the Bourbon régime in Naples. Fortunately Lord Vernon's indictment of the Sardinian prisons in the same year passed almost unnoticed in the rest of Europe.

Cavour knew there was a problem, but had little time or money to put into effect a plan of reform prepared in 1851. Horrifying figures were produced in 1854 about the mortality rate in the prison at Alessandria, yet priority was given to spending money on the prison chapel rather than to making conditions more hygienic and less inhumane. Four years later it could still be said that a prison sentence at Alessandria, because of the number of fatalities, was almost equivalent to imposing the death penalty; while the Genoa prison, where inmates could not stand upright in crowded and stinking cells, was as bad as those in Naples. Cavour could not deny some of the worst facts, but reluctantly insisted that military expenditure was more important than changes in the prison service; the Turin newspaper, *Il Diritto*, confirmed in June 1858 that the requirements of foreign policy left nothing over for such 'prosaic matters of domestic reform'.

In November 1857, general elections were held. Local elections had recently indicated a distinct move towards the right, and Cavour must have assumed that there was a good chance of removing from Parliament some of the irreconcilables on the far left. His position also might be strengthened if Rattazzi's centre-left, despite forming part of his governmental coalition, were to be reduced in numbers. He was convinced that the country was behind him and he would score a notable victory. But, just as he had misjudged over the Genoa rising in June, so he much more seriously misjudged the extent of resentment against his policy of higher taxes and secularization. Solaro della Margherita and the clericals worked unobtrusively to set up an electoral organization and put up a single agreed candidate in each constituency, whereas the disorganized liberals sometimes put up four or more who took votes from each other. This novel but efficient form of electioneering caught the government completely by surprise. There was general astonishment when one bishop was seen marching to the polls with two hundred of his clergy in procession behind him.

Cavour's personal religious beliefs were still no easier to define than they had been in his youth. He called himself a Catholic; but he does not seem to have attended mass or confession, and though a friendly priest promised to disregard papal excommunication and provide him with the comforts of religion on his death-bed, some of those close to him thought that he had an easy conscience in matters of faith and was mainly anxious not to give offence by publicly defying the established religion of the country. The testamentary dispositions he drew up in 1857 contain none of the religious sentiment and none of the references to the deity mentioned in his earlier will of 1849. Such facts are very far from being conclusive, but it is hard to deny that he remained fundamentally if moderately anticlerical. He used to refer to his own 'antipapism', and wrote just before the elections that he envisaged no chance of conciliation between Church and State: he was in fact resigned to this *dissidio* continuing. Indeed it offered positive advantages, since 'coming to terms with the Pope would mean Piedmont forfeiting any influence in the rest of Italy'.

Despite Pius ix's warning that only in catholicism was there any possibility of salvation, Cavour believed in toleration of other creeds and still had little patience with dogma. He had found a genuine sense of religion to be more developed in England and Scotland where liberty and an indulgent forbearance prevailed, while Catholic Italy was the one country above all where religious sentiment was flagging. He disliked the fact that although the constitution of 1848 stipulated freedom of worship, the antiquated penal code denied it, and traditionalist magistrates preferred to obey the code rather than the constitution. He had to explain to Protestants that much as he would like to change the law, and indeed would change it when public opinion was ready, he could not allow their ministers of religion to provoke disturbances by distributing bibles or indulging in overt evangelism. To the great scandal of the bishops, some Waldensian churches were permitted in the bigger towns because the sect was well established in some areas of the country, but this was a controversial field of policy where Cavour moved slowly and with caution.

The British ambassador reported that despite the resurgence of clerical activity, the elections took place in November 'with good order and good temper on both sides'. The liberal candidates were so sure of being elected that many and perhaps most of them did not address meetings or even visit their constituencies. It therefore came as a shock when Cavour himself obtained only a small majority in Turin and was the sole member of the Cabinet to win outright, while the two centre-left ministers, Rattazzi and Giovanni Lanza, failed to get a clear verdict and had to fight a second election *en ballottage* later. General Lamarmora failed completely and was obliged to find another constituency. In the new *camera*, those deputies on the left who were outside the governmental coalition won only about ten per cent of the seats; the centre-left was also reduced, in part because Rattazzi's candidates were sometimes competing with Cavour's and only agreed to join forces in the *ballottage*. These two centre groups of the coalition were together down by a third, and could no longer be sure of holding an absolute majority.

The moral victors were the right, who gained fifty seats to take almost forty per cent of the places in the *camera*, and within this number the extremist followers of Solaro greatly outnumbered the more moderate group round Revel. In Savoy, only two out of twenty-two deputies were liberals, and nearly as great a collapse was registered in Sardinia and Liguria. Solaro was himself elected outright in four places, and survived to the second election in three others. This was an astonishing turn of fortune.

Cavour sought what comfort he could for such manifest opposition to his government among the electorate. He admitted that in normal times he would have had to resign, but 'exceptional circumstances' forced him to stay in office. One compensating factor was that the monarchy was obliged to support him, since only with his liberals in government was there much chance of a *terza riscossa* against Austria. Another advantage was that there would now be something like a two-party system between Cavour's own moderate liberals and the clericals; and happily most of the latter were not only inexperienced and quite new to Parliament, but so extremist that he would hold many of the trump cards. Yet another incidental compensation was that a quarter of the deputies were titled aristocrats, a class that hitherto had tended to stay outside the lower house of Parliament but who would be less dangerous inside the *camera* than out. One day, he thought, such people might form an alternative and more conservative government;

and he added enigmatically that this 'would perhaps be a gain for the country'.

Here was a pious hope or fear for the distant future. He saw his immediate task as being to remain in office and resist any attempt to put the clock back, resolutely reasserting his control over Parliament, if necessary with intransigence. In December when one of the new clerical deputies challenged him to another duel, he accepted, but fortunately the affair was settled peaceably. To avoid being caught unawares in future, a Liberal Association was created in time to plan for the supplementary elections, and this was a welcome sign of greater political sophistication. Less acceptable was Cavour's arbitrary decision to exclude some of the opposition deputies before they could take their seats.

A quarter of the deputies, whether for trivial or serious reasons, had the validity of their election challenged when Parliament assembled, and months of debate were then devoted to a close scrutiny of carefully selected cases. One issue raised was the category of ecclesiastics with 'cure of souls' who were technically ineligible under the electoral law of 1848. Until now, the regulation had been interpreted as allowing non-resident canons to become deputies since they had no such cure, but now that the elections of 1857 sent nine ecclesiastics to Parliament, this interpretation was revised so as to exclude them by a transparent piece of retrospective gerrymandering.

By another restrospective regulation it was decided to annul any elections where the clergy could be shown to have used 'spiritual pressure' on behalf of their candidates. Priests in their capacity as citizens could not be prevented from voting and putting up candidates, but the argument was advanced that if they employed spiritual authority to influence their parishioners they would have an unfair advantage. Such pressure was of course hard if not impossible to prove except in the most blatant cases, and it was pointed out that equally unfair was the pressure put on civil servants to secure the victory of ministerial candidates. No doubt it had similarly been improper of Brofferio to delude voters into thinking that clerical candidates would reintroduce the burning of heretics and the tortures of the Inquisition. Others called it unfair when government supporters used bribery, or when civil servants were threatened with dismissal if they backed the opposition. But Cavour singled out 'spiritual pressure' as the main problem and went so far as to mention the distant risk of civil war if intervention by ecclesiastics in elections were not strictly circum-scribed.

About ten per cent of the elected deputies were thus excluded for one reason or another, despite the objection that the centre and the left were for the most part unseating their opponents on the right. Against the argument that magistrates would be the best judges of electoral malpractice, Cavour put forward the dangerous doctrine that Parlia-ment would show more impartiality than courts of law. The extreme conservatives in the *camera* were sometimes shouted down when they argued that this sort of behaviour made a mockery of constitutional government, though some of the government's supporters privately admitted that such criticism was not far from the truth. Opposition members were censured by the chair when they tried to make this a public issue.

One result of the reverses sustained in the election was to make the government more vulnerable to pressure from France. When Napoleon was asked by Cavour what should now be done, the advice once more came back to get rid of Rattazzi. Cavour knew that his Minister of the Interior had become increasingly unpopular among moderate as well as extreme conservatives, and since the centre-left had now lost a number of seats, their support had become as much a source of weakness as strength in the overall balance of Parliament. Indeed Cavour was afraid that if he did not shift slightly towards the right, the government might fall. He acknowledged his past debt to Rattazzi, who was the most intelligent, judicious and efficient of his Cabinet colleagues and was very far indeed from being the dangerous radical that some people imagined. Yet in his opinion Rattazzi had been at fault by 'exaggerating the parliamentary system' and allowing the deputies too much influence – quite apart from the fact that the Ministry of the Interior ought to have been more active in using its considerable powers of official patronage to support ministerial candidates at the polls.

Cavour therefore persuaded the other ministers that Rattazzi must be made to resign. Some of the Prime Minister's friends – for instance Castelli, Farini and Lanza – were not happy about this breach with the centre-left, especially as the way it was carried out required some subterfuge and left painful scars behind; but Rattazzi was sufficiently public-spirited to realize that the French alliance as well as the government itself would be stronger if he surrendered his post. Cavour then decided, though with some reluctance, that he himself should take over the interior ministry in addition to that of foreign affairs: he could think of no other capable replacement, and any new appointment might weaken his coalition by shifting the government too obviously in one direction or the other.

The final impetus to a major change of policy was the shock generated when, on 14 January 1858, Felice Orsini attempted to assassinate Napoleon in Paris, missing his target but causing terrible casualties when bombs exploded among bystanders. Cavour's instinctive reaction on hearing the news was to pray that the assassin was not an Italian. His embarrassment on hearing the name of Orsini may have been compounded by the knowledge that the government had recently been in touch with this firebrand and his accomplices, who indeed had been given a small amount of money from the secret service funds as non-Mazzinian activists whose help might one day be useful. To pacify the Emperor, the government reacted by sending more suspected agitators to America and others to internal exile under police surveillance. The French expressed their thanks; but, since this was not the first time an Italian had made an attempt on the Emperor's life, they felt entitled to demand more forceful action. Cavour did his best to modify their anger, explaining to them that after the elections his majority was in danger and he did not want the additional risk of taking repressive action that might undermine a perilously poised parliamentary alliance. But the reply came that no half measures would be acceptable: Cavour had incurred 'obligations' to Paris, and he must make a choice between allegiance to France or to England, between repression or tolerance. Napoleon increased the pressure and warned that if the Piedmontese wanted his friendship they must do precisely what he asked. Otherwise he was prepared to ally with Austria and if necessary occupy Piedmont by force of arms.

In the face of such a threat there was no room to manoeuvre and little alternative but to submit. At the end of January a radical newspaper, *La Ragione*, was brought before the courts in Turin for what seemed a defence of Orsini, and was acquitted by a jury composed of sound professional men. This finally persuaded Cavour to propose a law that would further reduce the independence of juries and introduce greater control over the press. He informed the French that he could expect only moral support from England and no soldiers from that quarter for the *terza riscossa*; he would therefore do what Napoleon required and compel Parliament to agree, if need be by another threat of resignation.

When he submitted his proposals to the *camera*, a parliamentary commission alarmed him by recommending that his suggested law should be rejected for being too obvious a sign of foreign pressure. This brought out his exceptional resources of eloquence and cajolery. He at once set himself to persuade individual deputies that the future of the country was at stake. He spoke privately with many of them, even with Brofferio who absolutely refused to give way. In a major speech he continued to deny that he was under any pressure from France; indeed he guaranteed that he would never so much as contemplate a measure backed by foreign pressure of any kind. He hinted instead that the life of Victor Emanuel might be in danger if the police and the courts were not given greater powers. He hoped that one day it might be possible to go into reverse and extend the jury system instead of restricting it, but for the moment there were considerations of larger national policy that made some degree of repression essential. The dismissed Rattazzi generously came to his help, and so did other individuals on both left and right who usually voted with the opposition, with the final result that both houses of Parliament agreed to grant him the special powers he required.

In the supplementary elections to fill the vacancies that he had created, all Cavour's considerable powers as Minister of the Interior were employed to have moderate liberals elected, with almost complete success. Local government officials, whether provincial intendants, mayors or minor civil servants, were instructed to bring pressure to bear in favour of government candidates: failure might mean, and sometimes did mean, loss of their jobs. The opposition called this another dangerous breach of constitutional convention, but Cavour in reply said that though he would never know and consequently could not object if civil servants voted against the government, they must in such cases keep their views strictly to themselves. He agreed that 'moral pressure' by a government servant might sometimes be as wrong as spiritual pressure by the clergy, and admitted that excessive influence and covert bribery or threats might occasionally have been used. Promises were certainly made in some areas that a favourable vote would bring material and financial advantages.

Such procedures could always be justified on the pretext of a national emergency, and the same argument was used for suppressing the Genoese republican journal, *L'Italia del Popolo*. This paper had a circulation of no more than four hundred copies, half of which were distributed free, and Cavour agreed that it did no harm at all; but French wishes had to be obeyed. He informed the local authorities at Genoa that at the specific request of France the paper must be silenced 'without bothering if the methods employed are legal or not'. As it was not possible simply to suppress it – not at least without contravening the constitutional guarantee of press freedom – he wanted it harassed by every possible means, its writers put under preventive arrest and its printers bribed. Judges were privately informed that harsh sentences were required in the national interest; and he prescribed close supervision of the workers' benevolent societies in Genoa, as they were equally suspect for fomenting opposition against the government.

Apologies had to be sent to Napoleon to excuse the fact that *L'Italia del Popolo* nevertheless took so long to die. Four editors were imprisoned in quick succession, but released for lack of evidence; fifty issues were confiscated over the next few months; and finally, when the paper's finances were so ruined that it was forced into liquidation, the government was surprised and annoyed that most other newspapers greeted its demise with regret. One specific criticism was that its disappearance was clear evidence of obedience to a foreign power and so would reflect discredit on the country. Another criticism was that such a blow against press freedom would be a precedent that a future conservative government might use for a more dangerous and less worthy purpose. Cavour claimed to be a dogmatic believer in freedom of the press, yet when Lord John Russell pointed out to him that only newspapers of the opposition were being suppressed, he agreed that this accusation was true and promised that he would try to behave differently in future.

The first few months of the sixth legislature were not easy. It was fortunate that Rattazzi, who did not like the new policy to restrict juries and the press, advised his political friends to support the government so long as the alternative was an administration led by Revel or someone even more conservative. But by now a dangerous breach was opening between the two leading liberals in Parliament. This was less over policy than because Rattazzi thought Cavour had been authoritarian and deceitful in an attempt to concentrate yet more power in his own hands. Rattazzi said, rightly, that he himself had treated the Prime Minister with loyalty and friendship, without ever trying to assert an independent position inside their coalition; Cavour, on the other hand, had been less than frank in intriguing with other ministers to undermine the *connubio*, and for reasons that had never been clearly explained.

Partly because of this breach, the parliamentary session of 1858 produced little in the way of political reforms, as Cavour himself admitted. Others called it the least productive session since 1848. Far too much time was wasted in a prolonged 'verification' of the election results, which indeed continued for six months until June, although Cavour had once said that two days ought to be more than sufficient. Initially many reforms were again promised, in local government and the central administrative system as well as in revising the penal code and further reducing ecclesiastical privileges. But the government then had to excuse its inaction by arguing that the elections had produced a Parliament in which such reforms had to take a low priority or be discarded altogether.

Education was another field where improvements were slow in being introduced. Half the population of Piedmont was illiterate, and in Liguria over two thirds, while in Sardinia the figure was as high as ninety per cent; yet most teachers in elementary schools continued to earn less than three hundred *lire*, and the Minister of Education admitted that this salary would have to be more than doubled to constitute a living wage without the need for an additional part-time job. Part of the trouble was that there were seventeen successive Ministers of Education in the thirteen years after 1848. Occasionally they talked of wanting to improve the status of the teaching profession and give greater freedom to schools and universities, but with little result. One of the foremost economists in Europe, Francesco Ferrara, was dismissed from his chair in 1858 on the grounds that he had insulted the government in his lectures, though Cavour in 1849 had protested strongly at what he called the arbitrary and dishonourable dismissal of this same professor on a similar charge by Charles Albert.

Another handicap on the working of parliamentary government was that the deputies who had been elected to Parliament as liberals were divided over many issues, and indeed the party system was so confused that many did not know where their permanent allegiance belonged. Cavour's chief preoccupation until he felt more secure was to abstain from any pronounced move towards the right, attempting meanwhile to modify his majority by persuading some of the less extreme conservatives to join his centre coalition. When asked if it was his intention to make a new *connubio* with deputies of the moderate right, he replied that his was not a party government and that he was trying to 'win the support of the whole *camera* without distinction of party'.

The fact that tactical considerations habitually overrode questions of principle was one reason why some people thought that Cavour's reputation as a model parliamentarian was not entirely deserved. He could still be regarded, though quite unfairly, as an aristocrat who merely posed as a liberal in order to win power. A more plausible argument was that he deliberately confused issues and cut across party allegiance with the aim of ensuring that no concerted opposition should appear. This was good practical politics, but in the formative period of a new parliamentary system there were incidental disadvantages attendant on avoiding points of disagreement around which a clearer party alignment could emerge. He himself, writing to his agent Corio, explained his aim of securing a parliamentary equilibirum in which conservatives would support him in the hope of preventing his moving to the left, while the left would think twice before unseating him for fear that the extreme right might take power instead. Menabrea on the right, who was a future Prime Minister of Italy, criticized 'his essentially eclectic policy as he tries to include many different opinions inside his coalition'. Giuseppe Saracco, another future Prime Minister who was now speaking from somewhere in the amorphous centre, was perplexed by Cavour's 'game of see-saw politics' as he 'flits restlessly between right and left without anyone knowing where he will end up'.

Whatever the objections, it was in practice a skilful policy and was subsequently copied, albeit less effectively, by all his successors in office. So long as some politicians at both extremes seemed to have an imperfect loyalty to the constitution, a mobile centre coalition had the great advantage of providing continuity, avoiding excessive contro-versy, and keeping politics well stabilized. The penalty was that political groups were left with little clarity or cohesion, and the absence of organized opposition meant that there was insufficient criticism and insufficient check on the executive. The lack of any alternative policy or of an alternative government could have minimal disadvantages with a strong Prime Minister who was as moderate and as convinced a liberal as Cavour, but at critical moments and with lesser men could be dangerously corrupting and lead to a thoroughly inefficient style of politics.

CHAPTER 13

The French Alliance
1858

In his conduct of foreign affairs, Cavour was meanwhile aiming to consolidate the reputation he had acquired at the Paris congress. While not thrusting himself forward on major issues, he tried to intervene in as many as possible of the more peripheral international problems to show that he was a trusty ally and a reliable anti-revolutionary. He asked to be allowed to lend a frigate to help subdue the Tai-ping rebels in China; and for India, which had fascinated him since his youth, he offered the same frigate to help the 'heroic British soldiers' put down the 'Indian mutiny'. He set up Piedmontese consulates in Melbourne, Sydney and Shanghai, and hoped there would be enough money for others in India and at San Francisco. He had no thought of founding a colonial empire – not at least for the moment – but the possibility was discussed of creating a penal settlement somewhere overseas, and informal enquiries were made in 1857 about whether Piedmontese influence might be extended anywhere on the coast of the Red Sea or in Abyssinia. His consul in Alexandria had orders to favour the construction of the Suez Canal, without annoying the British by intervening too openly.

In Europe the main task was to strengthen links with France and Russia, two countries which, surprisingly, he said he regarded as champions of national liberation throughout Europe. Further hints were received from the Russians in 1857 suggesting that they were ready to fight against Austria for the aggrandisement of Piedmont – provided that there was no collusion with revolutionaries. Cavour was delighted, and as a sign of friendship allowed them to set up a small naval base near Nice. This brought a protest from London with a reminder that Cavour had justified participation in the Crimean War by the imperative need to keep the Tsarist fleet out of the Mediterranean; but times had changed and, temporarily at least, he ridiculed as ungenerous and myopic this obsessive fear of Russia.

One matter over which he hoped to get English assistance early in
1858 was the seizure by the Neapolitans of the *Cagliari*, the Piedmontese ship that Pisacane had used for his unsuccessful piratical
venture. Its two engineers, like most engineers in the Piedmontese navy
and mercantile marine, were British and had been interned in Naples
with the rest of the Piedmontese crew. Cavour was hoping that pressure
from London would help to get restitution and compensation for this
arbitrary and humiliating act; in which case the Neapolitans would
suffer a useful loss of face and Turin would gain correspondingly in
prestige.

Clarendon offered moral support over the *Cagliari* but no more,
because he was sure that Cavour merely sought another excuse for war.
In any case Lord Malmesbury, who was Foreign Minister in the Tory
government which came to power at the end of February, received legal
advice that there might be no valid claim to compensation for an act of
piracy. Cavour quickly used the columns of *The Times* to publish a legal
opinion giving the opposite view, but then repeated an earlier mistake
and upset Malmesbury by encouraging the liberal opposition in
London to raise the matter in Parliament. In April he bravely
threatened to declare war on the Neapolitans to make them give way,
and asked an unwilling France to help.

For some reason, Cavour expected a Tory government in England to
be more friendly than Palmerston's followers, but he forfeited any
goodwill after this further proof that he was hoping to involve other
countries in what he grimly called 'setting fire to the whole of Italy'.
Malmesbury reminded him that on 14 April 1856 he had agreed with
the other delegates in Paris that he would always resort to the good
offices of a neutral power before contemplating war. Cavour could not
deny this, but in fact he had signed the agreement with no intention of
applying it in practice, and now replied that he could not risk the
humiliation of allowing arbitration over a question of national honour
where he was obviously in the right. The matter ended when the French
asked him to be more conciliatory, and the Neapolitans, under pressure
from Austria as well as England, released the ship and its crew. His
persistence had won a substantial point, even if in the process he had
further upset some potential friends.

* * *

It is impossible to estimate how far the idea of a common Italian nationality had yet sunk into the consciousness of the small percentage of Piedmontese who voted in elections and constituted the ruling class. The diffusion of this idea was still in great part due to the much-maligned exile Mazzini, whose enforced exile in England left him increasingly powerless and out of touch. Cavour himself, although he had no sympathy with popular revolutions and hated Mazzini's fanaticism, was able to confess in private that he at least admired the latter's single-minded devotion to an ideal. In public, however, he had to show himself to be quite uncompromising. The national enterprise had at all costs to be dissociated from democratic or social movements that would have antagonized his friends in Napoleonic France and Tsarist Russia. Too radical a policy would also certainly have alienated the conservative and propertied classes in Italy whose active or at least passive connivance would be needed in the process of national regeneration.

On a number of occasions Mazzini offered to lay aside his republican views and collaborate with the Piedmontese monarchy, but only if Cavour would publicly proclaim the objective of national unity. Members of Mazzini's Party of Action realized that Piedmont gained greatly from their continual agitation, which not only kept the Italian idea alive and in the public eye, but put the monarchy in a better light by comparison, and furthermore gave the moderates a plausible excuse for parallel moves or counteraction – an excuse that otherwise they would have lacked. Cavour used to say that these radicals loved revolution and republicanism more than they loved Italy, but this was unfair and quite untrue. Their opposite criticism was that he feared revolution more than he loved Italy, and for a time this was certainly correct. He himself continued to insist that a wider gap separated him from Mazzini than from the reactionaries.

Quite distinct from the Party of Action was the other more pragmatic group of believers in Italian unification who had broken away to form the National Society. After Manin's death, this society had the wealthy Pallavicino as president and chief financier, with Garibaldi as vice-president. By the end of 1857 its secretary, La Farina, was able to announce that a number of local committees were being formed in other regions of Italy. Then in February 1858 the central committee published a statement of its general programme: members could hold any political opinions so long as they believed in national independence and unification. The programme explained that only national unity would enable Italians to take their rightful place as one of the great powers; nothing less would reconcile the conflicting interests of the different Italian regions, or could arrange to link up a common railway system across frontiers through the peninsula, or could provide a big enough market to make large-scale industry possible.

Until the government could be persuaded to proclaim unification as official policy, members of the National Society saw their role as that of a popular, grass-roots movement aiming to educate public opinion. They had to propagate the idea of national independence and also the belief that, within Italy, Piedmont alone had the resources and the military force needed to defeat Austria. Only Piedmont had free institutions; only Piedmont possessed a statesman of international repute; and therefore the government in Turin deserved at least conditional if not unconditional support.

Yet some members of the Society differed from La Farina in supporting the parliamentary opposition in Piedmont, and probably most of them were more at home with the methods of popular insurrection than with the diplomatic negotiations preferred by Cavour. Almost all of them were former followers of Mazzini who had left him in disillusionment at the unwillingness of all but a handful of idealists to rise in revolution. Not one of Cavour's close friends was a member except La Farina himself, and the few among the Prime Minister's associates who knew much about it seem to have been strongly hostile because they saw it to be largely composed of potential trouble-makers and exiles from other regions. The melodramatic and not always truthful La Farina boasted that for four years without anyone suspecting he met Cavour almost every day before dawn, sometimes using a concealed staircase that led to the latter's room. But this story does not ring true. There would have been little to talk about at even a weekly meeting, and Cavour was a busy person who regularly made appointments before dawn, so that such frequent visits would have been observed and corroborated by other more trustworthy witnesses.

At the end of March 1858 the official gazette in Turin published a private letter to Napoleon, written by Orsini just before he was guillotined for his murderous attempt on the Emperor's life. In this letter Orsini expressed repentance and hoped that Italians would one day compensate the many innocent victims of his crime, but also begged the Emperor to do something constructive for Italy. Most surprising of all was that the letter was forwarded to Italy by Napoleon himself, with a request for Cavour to make it public. Soon the rumour circulated that it must have been written at the Emperor's request, perhaps to discourage any similar outrage in the future. The effect on the public was dramatic. The executed assassin became a hero and a martyr. Cavour pretended to be appalled, but in fact welcomed the request for publication as a paradoxical indication that the French government, far from being antagonized, was encouraged by Orsini's bombs to neutralize or placate the revolutionaries and give practical help for a war of Italian liberation.

The same week, to confirm this impression, another message was sent from Paris by Alessandro Bixio, an Italian banker and close friend of Napoleon, to tell Cavour that he was in a far stronger bargaining position than might have been suspected. Napoleon had many reasons for needing Piedmontese help, one of them being that he feared assassination and had an extraordinary dread of that mysterious and insatiable conspirator Mazzini; he therefore needed a government in Turin that would impose curbs on the press and destroy the prestige and influence of any potential insurgents. But he also wanted practical assistance in support of more positive ambitions. For some years he had been hinting that he was ready to help Piedmont conquer Lombardy in return for aid in winning for France her natural frontiers on the Alps and the Rhine. Moreover, although he disliked the existence of Piedmont's parliamentary system, he knew that only Cavour's liberals would support this grandiose adventure. Several people heard the Emperor refer to Cavour as a 'Piedmontese Machiavelli', as someone who was 'a most unprincipled politician', but who was sufficiently ambitious and unscrupulous to be an ideal accomplice in precipitating the European war that they both for different reasons had in mind. Cavour had almost precisely the same view of Napoleon himself.

One minor attempt to expand the frontiers of Piedmont had already been blocked when first Florestan and then the young Prince Charles of Monaco refused to sacrifice the independence of their small independent principality. With French help, however, there would almost certainly be better possibilities elsewhere in Italy. In April, Cavour at last made an explicit statement about 'our aspirations beyond the

Apennine mountains', and a hint was dropped that foreign assistance might at long last be forthcoming for territorial expansion to fulfil the 'glorious traditions of the House of Savoy'. In private he tried to convince the French that, when the time came, the whole of Italy could be relied on to rise and fight against Austria.

Parliament was simultaneously asked to approve another loan of forty million *lire*. Cavour had been trying secretly – and, he admitted, without authority – to borrow again from Rothschild. He knew that a great deal of money would be needed to finance the *terza riscossa*, though in order not to alarm the banks the proceeds of this loan were said to be required for building railways and docks. The Rothschild family were still bankers to the Austrian empire and, perhaps in part for this reason, were not particularly keen. But half the deputies on the left now voted in favour of floating a large loan after Brofferio and Valerio were secretly told that the aim was a war of national liberation.

A special emissary was at the same time sent to Paris to discover at first hand what precise plans Napoleon had in mind. This envoy was Costantino Nigra, a young man who had entered politics as Azeglio's private secretary and who, as Cavour's favourite assistant, was to have a very important function over the next three years as a personal intermediary with the Emperor. What Nigra discovered in Paris was too secret to mention in unciphered despatches or through normal diplomatic channels; indeed both the French Foreign Minister, Walewski, and the Piedmontese ambassador in Paris, the Marquis di Villamarina, were kept almost entirely in the dark. Napoleon in the deepest secrecy confirmed that he was ready for war if Cavour could manufacture a credible pretext. One condition was likely to be the marriage of Prince Napoleon, the Emperor's cousin, to Victor Emanuel's daughter Clotilde.

The Emperor calculated that the British were so heavily committed to fighting in India that they would be unable in the next year to stop him extending the frontiers of France. His private doctor was sent to Turin to explain in greater detail that French ambitions were very extensive, because in Paris they were thinking of a major war by the 'Latin races' against the Germans, a war that would make France the dominant power not only in Europe but throughout the Mediterranean and the Middle East. Cavour was overjoyed to hear this and eagerly accepted an invitation to visit France for discussions on how the Italians could contribute. The meeting would take place at the same health spa near the Swiss frontier where, a year earlier, Salmour had been given a fairly clear hint of what was proposed.

On 20 July, Cavour arrived at Plombières with a false passport so as not to attract attention – though the news was already the subject of gossip in the newspapers of Turin. As the hotels were full he had to pass the night in a humble lodging-house. The next morning he spent alone with the Emperor, his own report being the only record of what both parties said. No time was wasted before agreeing that the aim was a war that would end only in Vienna after Austria had been driven out of Lombardy and Venice. The more difficult matters were first, the timing of the war; secondly, what public excuse should be given for it; and thirdly, what territorial acquisitions each of the two allies could expect.

Evidently Napoleon had already studied these matters with some care. His opinion was that Italy ought to become a loose confederation of states under the headship of the Pope; after the expulsion of Austria this confederation would of course be a satellite of France. Naples would preferably be ruled by his own relative, Lucien Murat, replacing the deposed Ferdinando. In the north, Victor Emanuel would more than double the size of the existing Kingdom of Sardinia, and would win sovereignty over a total population of about eleven million; this would be much the same size as the Kingdom of Italy created by the first Napoleon in 1805, and in addition to its existing regions could comprise Lombardy, Venetia, Parma and Modena.

When Cavour raised the further question of annexing part of the Papal States he encountered no great enthusiasm, but it was understood that if the war went well he might incorporate the papal Legations of the Romagna. One correspondent was informed by Cavour that there had also been mention of taking the southern papal province of the Marche down as far as Ancona, though this would have meant a greater population than eleven million and was left very much in the air. Another region of the Pope's domain, Umbria, would possibly be given to Tuscany. This would leave Pius ix ruler only of the Agro Romano, in other words some two thousand square kilometres around the town of Rome; but in compensation the Pope would become president of the Italian confederation. Cavour was glad to accept this idea of a federal state, because he felt sure that it would permit Piedmont to dominate the rest of the peninsula.

France was intending to take Savoy and Nice for herself, and Cavour admitted that, by any strict criterion of nationality, Savoy should be French, though he succeeded in putting off the more doubtful matter of Nice for discussion at another time. A further unwelcome French demand was brought up in the afternoon when Napoleon, personally taking the reins of a phaeton, drove his guest through the forests of the Vosges. This was the proposed marriage of Prince Napoleon to Clotilde. Cavour had already been authorized by the King to agree if it was absolutely necessary, but tactfully managed to avoid giving a clear answer and said he would consult her family on his return.

The most difficult question of all was that of finding a pretext for fighting since it would have to be one that would look plausible to the outside world and French public opinion. There was no obvious answer, because their true objective of territorial conquest had to remain secret. They agreed that one possibility was Mazzini's favourite project: to stir up a rebellion in Massa and Carrara. The rebels would be instructed to appeal for help from Piedmont, who would decline in a note containing carefully phrased and provocative criticisms of the misgovernment in Austrian-controlled Italy. Austria might thus be coerced into the sort of irritated rejoinder that could be made into a pretext for war. Napoleon was anxious that there should be numerous signatures on the appeal from Massa, 'or at least they should appear to be numerous'.

Cavour departed from Plombières in a state of great excitement. He first visited Baden, another health resort when he knew that a number of Russian and German politicians were on holiday. Here he chose to be moderately indiscreet about his plans in the hope of gauging how the rest of Europe would react, and from one or two casual remarks he convinced himself that he could count on a benevolent attitude from Prussia and perhaps on Russian military help. This was a false impression, indeed dangerously so, but after the heady speculations of Plombières he was perhaps more gullible than usual and read too much into the polite small-talk of diplomatic exchange. Napoleon, who himself was always extremely reticent, had begged him to be circum-spect lest people should think that they were deliberately planning an aggressive war. But the prospect was too thrilling for complete discretion, and in a matter of days the news had begun to circulate.

The question of Clotilde's marriage was the main issue for decision after returning to Turin. The King at first confirmed his willingness to sacrifice his daughter in such a good cause, but gave way when she had sufficient self-esteem to put up some resistance. Cavour was furious at such feebleness, 'but if the King is weak, I am hard as granite, and to achieve our holy objective I would confront greater dangers than the hatred of a little girl and the anger of the court'. He knew that Napoleon set very great store on linking his dynasty with the oldest ruling house in Europe; indeed Cavour told Layard that dynastic considerations were, together with national vanity, the Emperor's 'only principle'. He also knew that Clotilde was an extravagantly pious girl of fifteen who had nothing in common with a middle-aged freethinker and phil-anderer. In addressing Victor Emanuel, the minister used the in-sensitive and perhaps deliberately offensive argument that Prince Napoleon must possess a kind heart since he had always treated his many mistresses with consideration and generosity. Finally, after some angry altercations, the King gave his consent. Clotilde, with some difficulty, was also persuaded to obey her father's wishes.

Another worrying problem was that the more lenient policy of the Archduke Maximilian in Milan was continuing to gain ground among the Lombard population and winning back support for Austrian rule. Russian and English diplomats reported a noticeable change in public opinion in Lombardy, which greatly alarmed Cavour. He sent a request to Milan for Italian patriots to keep up the tension as much as they could, but some of the replies suggested that this might be difficult, and he concluded that hostilities ought to start as soon as possible before one of his best excuses for a war of liberation began to look too thin.

Meanwhile La Farina was put to work devising a plan of insurrection in Massa to trigger off the war. Cavour approved this plan in October and fixed 1 May 1859 as a provisional date for the rising: he reported with excessive optimism that there would be no difficulty and again gave Napoleon an assurance that the revolution would meet with unani-mous support. As an excited Cavour told his niece, 'this time we shall make war in the Spanish guerrilla fashion where even the women will fight'. Some people suggested that the revolt should take place not in Massa but Tuscany, but he was already disturbed to discover that Florentine liberals were attracted by Napoleon's plan for an enlarged independent Tuscany, and in any case his own slightly contemptuous view of the decadent 'Etruscan race' was that it lacked the energy for a successful revolution. Garibaldi was summoned and agreed to lead an insurgent body which, when the order arrived, would cross the frontier into Massa and march on Modena; after organizing a provisional government, an appeal with perhaps four hundred signatures would be sent to invite Piedmontese intervention, and the regular army would be in readiness to invade.

The next task was to persuade Russia to make a formal military alliance with France and Piedmont. Cavour pinned great hopes on this and agreed that the Russians should be allowed to annex Polish Galicia as an extra inducement. In his impatience he did not sufficiently take into account that they might have a different concept of their national interest and might be merely dissembling without any intention of making war. In November a small Russian battle fleet took up its station at the base leased to them by Piedmont near Nice, and to provide more facilities the convicts at the Villefranche prison were removed to Genoa. No alliance was signed, but a friendly relationship was established and Cavour told people that he was confident that the Tsar would not remain neutral when war broke out.

Prussia posed a more difficult problem. Cavour had already persuaded himself to welcome the possibility of Prussia taking the leadership in Germany as Piedmont expected to do in Italy, and he hoped that the same glorious destiny would provide for the 'aggrandisement of Prussia', also at Austria's expense. In October 1858 his hopes were dashed when a new government came to power in Berlin and informed him that they would possibly be on the same side as Austria. Nevertheless he refused to give up his conviction that 'an alliance between an enlarged Piedmont and Prussia is inscribed in the book of history'; there was still a chance that Bismarck's more far-sighted views would ultimately prevail, and the appearance of a united and powerful German empire could only be welcomed in Turin as another means of upsetting the European equilibrium that had lasted since 1815.

Among Cavour's minor activities was an attempt to influence foreign newspapers and win the support of public opinion elsewhere. He denied doing this, but there are documented examples of money and decorations being employed to suborn French journalists. Scores of articles were in fact planted on various foreign papers during the years 1857–9, most of them written by Farini and Artom, and the drafts indicate that Cavour personally supervised their composition. They appeared mainly in France and England, but also in Spain, Germany and Switzerland. Some were designed to persuade; some were frankly minatory, to compel other governments to be more helpful and sympathetic; possibly, however, they may have had the opposite effect in practice by alerting foreigners to Piedmontese intentions.

Cavour also set himself to stir up insurrection in the Balkans. In the previous year he had made preliminary preparations to 'sow revolution' in the Danubian principalities, where by October 1858 he was looking forward to a major upheaval taking place when he gave the word. Further south he was in touch with an agent from Zagreb who had a plan for creating dissension among Croat units in the Austrian army. Another young official from Cavour's private office, Francesco Astengo, was sent to open a new consulate in Belgrade; Astengo's main task was to work with the Piedmontese embassy in Constantinople, smuggling arms into the Balkans under diplomatic cover, and stirring up trouble in Serbia. The best potential trouble spot was Hungary, and in December the Hungarian revolutionary general, György Klapka, came to Turin with promises about a 'vast movement' gathering strength in that country. Cavour was happy to believe him and told Nigra that this revolution was now certain.

The same utopianism that he complained about in the Mazzinians was revealed in Cavour's confidence that such revolutions could be easily started and controlled. He once told the Prussian ambassador that he was ready to make trouble everywhere, not just in the Balkans, but even in Africa and China: the wider the area of conflict, the better the chances of success. There was something cold-blooded in the way he developed this theme. He talked for instance of starting a German civil war by setting friendly Protestants in the north against hostile and pro-Austrian Catholics in the south, and simultaneously a Swiss civil war in which it would be more expedient to support the Catholics of the southern cantons against the Protestants. A Swiss friend told him that this idea was unpromising, but the Piedmontese envoy in Berne was nevertheless instructed to take soundings. This same envoy was asked to encourage the Swiss to act by making them believe the improbable story that England stood together with France in hoping for a major European conflagration.

The government in Turin thought it had everything to gain from such a conflagration and not much to lose. As Mazzini pointed out, Piedmont was in one sense invulnerable since, even if she were defeated in war, none of the surrounding countries could afford to see her either overrun or deprived of territory. Cavour, too, firmly believed that the British navy, despite political differences, could always be relied on to protect the Piedmontese coast from any invasion. Hence there was good cause for taking risks. In November the French ambassador reported that the gossips in Turin spoke of war as inevitable and were already giving the date as next spring. Some people were even afraid that if the war failed to take place, the existing ministers might be forced to give way to a reactionary and pro-Austrian government, in which case Naples might assume the hegemony in Italy to which Piedmont aspired.

Cavour, however, was so confident of success that he no longer saw much need for discretion. To a visitor from Bologna, Marco Minghetti, he explained how he meant to trick Austria into declaring war so that she and not Piedmont would attract the obloquy of aggression. In December he told a complete stranger, Odo Russell, that he intended hostilities to start during the first week of May. The devoted Massari heard him say that the Austrians would be expelled from Italy 'even if it means desolation everywhere and our cities burnt to the ground'.

Anyone listening to such remarks could no doubt admire the courage behind them, but they were premonitory signs of an over-excitability that became more pronounced during the early months of 1859. In his more level-headed moments he might not have been so easily beguiled by expectations of Prussian help against Austria. Nor would he have tried to threaten Prussia, as he did on 13 January, by saying that if she failed to help him, 'it would be the easiest thing in the world to bring in the Russians' by igniting an explosion in eastern Europe and 'setting fire to the whole continent'. Equally incomprehensible were other remarks about the 'ingratitude and stupidity' that stopped England from fighting against Austria; or about the British army being so pro-Italian that it might use political pressure and compel Malmesbury to fight; or about the possibility that the United States would for some reason threaten war to force England into active military intervention on the Continent. This was lack of realism on a colossal scale.

One vitally important department in which this heavily overworked statesman exercised insufficient control was that of military provision, despite the fact that Napoleon had asked him to make it a top priority. Somewhat light-headedly he had promised at Plombières that he would match a French army of two hundred thousand soldiers with a hundred thousand of his own, which indeed he undertook to mobilize 'quickly'; and he was confident that this would leave another fifty thousand Piedmontese troops in reserve. But the figure was mere guesswork, and under the existing system of recruitment only some sixty thousand effectives could be put into the field. After such explicit promises the French would eventually have good reason to think themselves short-measured.

Garibaldi and the National Society had been confident of recruiting five or six times as many soldiers by adopting a broader-based system of recruitment. Cavour on the other hand, as an ex-officer nurtured in the traditions of an élite professional force, had grave doubts about arming the mass of the people and was obsessed by memories of popular revolutions in 1848. Nor did he stop to think that the French might be making their plans on the basis of the number of men he had promised to provide. He simply assumed that with French and Russian military help, there was no great urgency to keep his promise and recruit a large army. Indeed he was proud of the economies he made in the provision of munitions. In any case unwilling to provoke another clash with the King, he had left the army as very much a preserve of the monarchy, outside direct parliamentary or ministerial control.

The lack of public accountability in this particular field was, according to some deputies, one glaring example where the parliamentary system was proving inadequate. The three principal items of military expenditure – at Casale, Alessandria and La Spezia – had all been entered into without prior notification to the deputies in Parliament. In each case the government had to ask subsequently to be indemnified for what was a deliberate breach of constitutional practice. But no apology could make up for the fact that expensive and perhaps dubious decisions were being taken by a far from infallible executive without any outside check.

It was the same with other preparations for war. Already by January 1859, people in the know were beginning to guess that the whole process of rearmament was too slow and haphazardly planned. Some thought that in order to have an equal voice in the campaign and prevent French dominance in Italy there should be not half as many but twice as many Italian soldiers as French, and Garibaldi was not alone in asserting that this would have been far from impossible. Cavour, however, strongly defended the existing practice of recruitment whereby rich people automatically and easily bought their children and servants out of military service – and this piece of social injustice, which he called 'completely fair', partly explained the disastrous lack of morale among the troops in the wars of 1848–9. There were also too few officers and non-commissioned ranks to deal with the sudden expansion needed in wartime. There were even insufficient uniforms for the troops he intended to mobilize. And the reserves of which he spoke turned out in the event to be virtually non-existent. These were all absolutely vital matters, and it is surprising that so important a part of his master plan was allowed to go by default.

CHAPTER 14

Preparations for War
January–April 1859

At the beginning of January 'our mysterious neighbour', as Cavour called Napoleon, made a public and perhaps provocative remark about a deterioration in French relations with Austria, and this caused a momentary panic on the stock exchanges as a rumour spread that war might be imminent. Ten days later, Victor Emanuel created further anxiety by an unexpectedly bellicose speech at the opening of Parliament in Turin. One phrase, included at the special request of Napoleon himself, spoke of the 'cries of grief' from all over Italy. It was a phrase that Cavour at first thought much too strong, but its effect was spectacular. At the theatre of La Scala in Milan, when the Druids in Bellini's *Norma* started their chorus invoking war, many in the audience rose to their feet and took up the cry, to the chagrin of the Austrian higher command who were present.

A few days later a treaty was signed in Turin between France and Piedmont – a document that was intended to remain secret in perpetuity and whose existence Cavour denied. One clause bound Napoleon to fight against the Austrians so long as the latter could be made by Cavour to seem the aggressor. Another clause formulated the aim of enlarging Piedmont to become a Kingdom of Northern Italy with eleven million inhabitants. In return, Victor Emanuel agreed to cede Nice as well as Savoy to France.

The agreement to surrender these two provinces was a particularly sensitive point, which Cavour had to keep absolutely secret from all but half a dozen of his closest collaborators. He could not afford to let his domestic opponents know that he was unconstitutionally pledging the country's honour to the cession of national territory; nor indeed could anything be said in the treaty itself about the parliamentary consent that, according to the *statuto*, was necessary. If Garibaldi had suspected that his home town of Nice was to be sacrificed, the patriotic front would have split irremediably and the war could not possibly have been fought. Moreover, the Savoyards were some of the best soldiers in the army and the government could not afford to let them know the truth.

Cavour was privately taxed on this issue by a parliamentary commission, but replied with an assurance that any suspicions about the surrender of territory were quite baseless. Two other clauses in the treaty which he strongly disliked yet had to accept were that the joint armies would be under French command, and that he would reimburse France for the full cost of the war. This latter undertaking was, as he well knew, quite beyond the country's means and would never be honoured; the former would effectively give their ally control over every major political and military decision during the war. Fortunately, however, these concessions were kept secret.

The treaty was sealed immediately afterwards by the marriage of Prince Napoleon and the Princess Clotilde. She was sometimes said to be sixteen but in fact was still some months short of her sixteenth birthday, and so unpopular was the marriage of this saintly girl to such a notorious *roué* and infidel that there was an embarrassing boycott of the court festivities celebrating the event. Cavour's chief press officer, Massari, called her the first casualty of the war. The marriage was not a success and for most of their remaining lives the two lived separately by mutual consent.

Cavour had a further proposal for Victor Emanuel to marry a Russian princess and so consolidate the plan for a Russian alliance. But the King, with the intention of making this impossible, told his ministers that he had at last decided to marry Rosina Vercellana, a lady who had been his established mistress for the past twelve years and by whom he had a second family: indeed he tried to persuade them, quite falsely, that the marriage had already taken place. Cavour had usually been most complaisant over the King's innumerable affairs, paying off his ex-mistresses, sending them into exile when necessary, finding jobs for their relatives and using the diplomatic bag to deliver private love letters. But he strongly opposed this *mésalliance* with a commoner whom he despised as a debauchee and suspected of interfering in politics to his disadvantage.

Already in 1856 he had made trouble over this liaison, and heated scenes now took place between him and the sovereign. He even tried to bribe one of the King's ex-mistresses to provide incriminating evidence against her rival. Once again Rattazzi's help was enlisted and the two politicians succeeded in postponing the proposed morganatic marriage until at least after the war. But Cavour, who was no courtier or flatterer, acted with excessive tactlessness. One of his wounding arguments to the King was that Rosina was unfaithful to him and had been observed by police spies taking part in orgies with other men. Victor Emanuel was absolutely furious – whether more with him or her is not clear – but the lady proved far the better diplomat when she replied that the monarch's sexual attentions were so constant and insatiable that they left her with no appetite or stamina for other men. The King was flattered and stood by her loyally, but also asked for the matter to be further investigated. Acting on a tip-off, the police surrounded her house hoping to catch her *in flagrante*, but were surprised to find nothing, and eventually an enquiry by Rattazzi came to the conclusion that Cavour's insinuations were untrue.

After a few weeks this particular storm subsided and the King did not marry Rosina until many years later. Cavour had to admit that he had been imprudent to risk a political crisis on such flimsy and delicate evidence, and those of his friends who had some intimation of what had happened, including Castelli, Farini and Minghetti, all agreed that he had been in the wrong to act as he did. The King sent him a note of reconciliation but in private spoke of having been on the point of challenging his Prime Minister to a duel, and the incident was never forgotten or completely forgiven, certainly not by Rosina herself who had a fierce sense of pride. Victor Emanuel wrote to the Pope apologizing for being prevented by politicians from legitimizing his liaison, and explaining once again that he was maturing plans to resume greater powers for the monarchy so as to halt the process of secularization.

This was a prospect which Cavour, had he known about it, would not have relished. Equally detrimental to his position was a widening split among the leading parliamentary liberals. He said he would never forgive Rattazzi for not supporting him more strongly over Rosina and would never again allow his former friend to join the Cabinet. There were no major political issues separating these two most prominent politicians in Piedmont; the main factor in their division was a calculation of political expediency, and in the second place there was a resentment on Cavour's part against someone who lacked his own political flair but who on this occasion behaved with greater tact and common sense.

The Prime Minister's unrestrained and testy behaviour can be explained by the great tension under which he was living, and the immense difficulties in the way of his overwhelming desire to start a war. Every aspect of policy depended on decisions that he alone could make. Only the main theme was clear: to provoke Austria into an excessive reaction that would give the French an excuse to fight. He had not only to create the complete illusion that peace-loving Piedmont was at the mercy of Austrian aggressiveness, but to compel the Austrians to start a war that he wanted and they did not. As well as equipping the army, he had to provide the money and the borrowing facilities; he had to set up a network of agitators through northern and central Italy and in the Balkans; and above all he had to manipulate the intricacies of diplomatic relationships so as to isolate Austria and find allies where he could.

By February 1859 the rest of Europe was growing seriously alarmed and the French were becoming less eager as their aggressive plans were partially exposed to public view. To Cavour's annoyance, the 'blindness', 'egoism' and 'pettiness' of England and other countries made them all too eager for peace. He told one army officer that if only England would join him 'we could together settle all the problems of the world'. But the official statements he continued to send to other governments were quite different: namely, that he was doing his utmost to prevent war and would never for one moment countenance the underhand and revolutionary intrigues of which others accused him.

Unfortunately for Cavour such statements were not believed in London or perhaps anywhere, and members of his own Parliament accused him of trying to start an aggressive war. Tories and liberals in London, though they both sympathized strongly with the regeneration or *risorgimento* of Italy, all agreed that a European war would be unthinkable except as an absolutely last resort. Palmerston, if only Cavour had realized, was ready to work towards the total exclusion of Austria from Italy, but both political parties in England were antagonized as they saw that war was being deliberately sought by Piedmont and would very possibly involve the rest of Europe. They were certain, furthermore, that its result in Italy would be to replace an Austrian master by a French Emperor who would be perhaps equally oppressive and certainly a greater danger to Europe. Memories of the first Napoleonic empire made the English determined to do all they could to prevent any repetition. One index of their reaction was the comment of Lord Cowley, the British ambassador in Paris, who now anathematized Cavour as an 'infamous' character, 'as un-principled a politician as ever existed', one whose word could never be trusted and who had 'ruined himself in the opinion of every honest man'. Lord Malmesbury could not but agree.

On 9 February, Cavour made a mollifying and flattering reference to the English in a parliamentary speech, but privately apologized to the French for the remark and explained that his real views were quite different. Massari heard him utter the improbable remark that he was resigned to fighting single-handedly against England and Austria combined; 'if Russia takes our side, we can laugh at England; we Italians have conquered the world before now and can do so again'. He was ready to 'set Europe alight', even to 'set fire to the four corners of the earth'. England, he said, could not oppose him without risking war with the United States and a rebellion in Canada and the West Indies.

John Daniel, the representative of the United States in Turin, would have been surprised to hear this last remark. Daniel's view of Cavour was of someone with an unjustifiable but irresistible urge towards violence and aggrandisement whose chief motive was personal am-bition. Cavour had made his country into a 'satellite of France', and according to this American diplomat, so much money had by now been spent on war preparations that the government would fall from power if its desperate gamble failed.

In addition to Cavour's difficulties over handling foreign diplomats, there were further problems with the different groups that made up public opinion at home. Above all there was the difficulty that he had to prepare to precipitate a revolt in central Italy, while at the same time preventing the mob riots and attempts at social reform that had antagonized the wealthier classes in 1848. Here was a dilemma that was almost insoluble. He had to encourage revolution, but not too much. He had to prove to Europe that ordinary people in Italy were desperate enough to rebel, yet in his anxiety to keep clear of the taint of 'mazzinianism' he laid himself open to Mazzini's criticism that he was far more interested in stopping rebellion than encouraging it.

The same ambiguity disturbed his relations with Garibaldi, because he needed to exploit the prestige and guerrilla skills of this ex-republican, yet could not offend the French or the Piedmontese military establishment by allowing such a potentially dangerous man too much scope. In another personal meeting, Cavour received confirmation of Garibaldi's enthusiastic agreement to train regiments of volunteers when the time for action arrived, but immediately afterwards the army commanders were reassured that this agreement was intended mainly for propaganda purposes. The government needed to recruit volunteers from other parts of Italy so as to prove the existence of a nationwide movement and dispel fears about Piedmontese aggrandisement, but at the same time it wanted their numbers to be limited. Everything must be under government direction. Garibaldi should take no personal initiative. Even when Luigi Mercantini wrote the 'Hymn of Garibaldi' that quickly became immensely popular, this was deprecated, and Cavour expressed his contempt for such unwarlike word-mongers and their useless verses.

The Piedmontese diplomatic representative at the Grand-Ducal court in Tuscany, Carlo Boncompagni, received secret orders on 20 January 1859 to take further steps to undermine the government to which he was accredited. His instructions were to encourage agitation and if possible prepare a mutiny among officers in the Tuscan army, but without letting people suspect any involvement by the embassy. Boncompagni was not happy at having to use his diplomatic immunity as a cover for revolutionary action, and may well have been glad when the Tuscan Liberals sent word that they disapproved of such treachery to their ruler.

Cavour spoke contemptuously of these cowardly 'Tuscan gentlemen' who were betraying the national cause by remaining passive at a time when he needed to find some evidence to convince Europe that Italy 'was in a state of complete disintegration'. He hoped for something better in the papal Romagna, where a previous history of revolutions suggested that the local 'race' was more vigorous. He was not anxious to challenge the Pope in Rome itself – that 'wasps' nest' as he called it – because the French would turn against him if the papacy called on the Catholic world for armed help; if, however, the Vatican wanted to fight against Piedmont he would accept the challenge, and had no qualms about 'risking the salvation of my soul in a patriotic cause'. In the Romagna, if nowhere else, some revolutionary activity must without fail take place, though he insisted that it must be as moderate as possible and divorced from the least hint of social or mazzinian-style insurrection.

Here was the same almost impossible dilemma: he was asking the rest of Italy to start revolutionary movements which were not to be too revolutionary, which were above all not social revolutions, and which should preferably involve only the *signori* or people of education and substance. Unfortunately these men had too much to lose to be eager for insurrection and were completely ignorant about how to start one. Their links with Cavour were generally through La Farina, who had made the National Society more of a propaganda organization than an instrument for instigating practical agitation. From Parma, Bologna, Florence and Milan arrived complaints that any communications arriving from Turin were confused and half-hearted, and indeed that the National Society was turning out to be more divisive than conciliatory, more cautious than venturesome, and more hostile than friendly towards the genuine forces of revolution.

Napoleon was disappointed that there was so little obvious sign in Italy of the disaffection that he had repeatedly been led to believe was almost universal. He knew that public opinion in France was strongly against fighting Austria, and had heard from General Niel, whom he sent to investigate in Turin, that public opinion there was hardly more favourable and even Lamarmora, the Piedmontese Minister of War, was unenthusiastic. Niel reported that 'with the exception of Cavour, Rattazzi and half a dozen other madmen, the whole of Piedmont is against war', and this French general ominously remarked that Cavour himself seemed to have 'completely lost his head'.

Early in March the Emperor therefore decided that the war had better be postponed to another year. His own diplomatic preparations had been a disaster – so much so that the Prussians, far from showing friendliness, were threatening to join Austria and force France to fight on two fronts simultaneously. Partly to blame were certain regrettable indiscretions in Turin; intercepted correspondence revealed that even Mazzini knew in some detail about the Franco-Piedmontese treaty that had been meant to remain absolutely secret, almost as though Cavour were trying to force Napoleon's hand by leaking information about French involvement. Instead of a coalition being formed against an aggressive Austria, France found herself accused of being the potential aggressor. Buol, on the contrary, explicitly stated that he had no intention of attacking, and even indicated that Austrian troops were on the point of being withdrawn from central Italy; whereas the Piedmontese were putting both themselves and France in the wrong by refusing to give a similar undertaking and by continuing to talk about an imaginary danger that no one else could perceive.

Cavour had in fact been informing his associates that he had implicated France so deeply that she was committed to fight, so this news of what he called French 'perfidy and bad faith' ruined his calculations and made his assurances look very hollow. He told the French ambassador that he no longer wanted Austrian troops to withdraw from central Italy, because that would eliminate one of the few remaining pretexts for war. It would be too great a loss of face for Piedmont to back down now that several thousand volunteers had already arrived in Turin from other parts of Italy. Rather than give way he would act like Samson and bring down the very structure of European society; he would start revolutions everywhere, and if he perished it would be in a sea of blood.

Such remarks were made in desperation, hoping to persuade Napoleon that even if France now left him in the lurch, war was unavoidable. To the British he spoke differently, saying that he could not match Buol's promise to remain peaceful, not indeed unless the Austrians withdrew their troops from Lombardy as well as central Italy. When Malmesbury promised not only to guarantee the territorial integrity of Piedmont against a hypothetical Austrian attack but to mediate in remedying any legitimate grievances that Piedmont might have, Cavour rejected the offer, knowing that mediation would ruin years of patient effort designed to bring about war. When the British promised to help him get liberal reforms in other parts of Italy the answer, as Massari explained to Hudson the British ambassador, had to be that Italy required not more liberalism but national independence, even if that meant forgetting about reforms and resorting to a military dictatorship.

Cavour made no bones about this. The national question superseded all others. No further discussion could be permitted, and he said he was obliged to impose a virtual dictatorship in which blind faith would be demanded from everyone. Fortunately Parliament, apart from isolated criticism by individuals, left him a free hand once again. Between 24 February and his request for full powers on 23 April he had to intervene only twice in debate, very briefly. After that the *camera* was closed for the next twelve months.

* * *

In every other field his activities were prodigious and tireless. He once wrote that none of his immediate collaborators except the trusty Costantino Nigra gave him unqualified support. Even Lamarmora continued to be full of doubt. But if other ministers were unanimous against him on any point – for instance when they collectively blamed his blind confidence in the good faith of Napoleon – he simply disregarded their views. So little could he rely on his colleagues that occasionally he was up most of the night personally deciphering despatches. Privately he confessed that he was worn out and felt like battering his head against a wall; yet he did his best not to show his anxieties or the frayed nerves, and it was noted that he lost neither his outward good humour nor his sleep. His appetite for food was undiminished: the King, as a practical joke, once gave him horsemeat for dinner calling it venison, and was amused when Cavour, perhaps diplomatically, commented that the venison was excellent.

Meanwhile the National Society was busy collecting money to help pay for the transport of volunteers from other Italian states. By the end of March nearly ten thousand of these volunteers had arrived and could be heard speaking all the various dialects under the colonnades of the Turin streets. Their presence was of immense moral importance. They were also very useful provocation against Austria because some were deserters from the Austrian army. Among the more notable refugees were two Neapolitans, Carlo Poerio and Luigi Settembrini, who had been released from gaol in Naples and exiled to America with sixty other prisoners; they had forced the captain of their ship to land in Ireland, after which their appearance in London – where they had become famous through Gladstone's pamphlets on the Neapolitan prisons – gave a great boost to the cause. When they arrived in Turin it caused some surprise that they looked so well-nourished after what patriotic propaganda had been saying about their torture and deprivation by the Bourbon government.

In the middle of March the Russians proposed, and France and England agreed, that a congress should meet to find some way of averting war; Walewski, mindful of the Paris congress three years earlier, did his best to insist that Piedmont as a second-class power should not be represented. This was terrible news for Cavour. He would no doubt have gained a good deal from an international conference, but in his view not nearly enough. He tried first to oppose the idea of a congress; then in desperation promised that, if only he were allowed to be present, he would renounce any intention of fighting; otherwise he threatened that he would ally with the revolutionaries and in six weeks' time would be ready to 'ignite the fuse of the great explosion'.

When this apparently empty threat was not taken seriously, he decided that his only hope was to make a quick visit to Paris to discover if any division of opinion existed which he could exploit. There was so much work for him to do in Turin that the possibility was raised of Rattazzi going to Paris instead, but Cavour objected: his rival lacked *finesse*, and someone who was ill-bred enough to spit on the carpet was, he wrote, too uncouth for such a delicate role. Before leaving for France, Cavour sent another vain plea to central Italy for serious agitation that would give substance to his promises and threats.

During six days in Paris he tried every trick and stratagem to make the French government abandon what he called their cowardly pacifism. He accused them of breaking formal promises. He said he would have his war whatever others might do, and also let it be known, whether discreetly or by deliberate indiscretion, that his belligerence had been entirely owing to Napoleon's instigation. He threatened that if necessary he would emigrate to America and publish certain documents in his possession that would incriminate the Emperor in the eyes of history and French public opinion. He also threatened that he was ready to punish the French by allying with England. He furthermore argued that at this late hour the dangers attending a refusal to fight were greater than those of war: indeed, if he resigned, the King would probably abdicate, and that would leave France with an Austrian satellite instead of a subservient client on her southern frontier.

The English ambassador in Paris said he had never seen Napoleon so indecisive or in such low spirits as after this multiple onslaught. Lord Cowley had a long talk with Cavour which reinforced the ambassador's impression that the Piedmontese minister was 'playing a treacherous game'. Italian liberty did not seem to be uppermost in his mind, but rather hatred of Austria, personal ambition and a thirst for Piedmontese aggrandisement; the Englishman sourly commented that 'surely twenty million human beings who considered themselves maltreated would furnish more than a few thousand recruits to swell the military ranks of the power which assumes to be their protector'. Cavour was desperate enough to tell Cowley that much of the blame should rest on the shoulders of Hudson, the British representative in Turin, who 'is a greater revolutionist than any Italian, and has egged on the Sardinian government to action from first to last, and his house is the regular rendezvous of all the disaffected'. These tactless and no doubt deliberate remarks nearly wrecked Hudson's career, and it was not the only time that Cavour tried to make trouble in London against this good friend of Italy.

Cavour left Paris appalled that almost everyone he met was angry with him for being so indiscreet and for trying to drag France into a war that would be seen as one of pure aggression. Dining in his hotel on the final evening he assumed an air of false bravado, hoping that this would be reported to the Tuileries by police spies, but in reality he was close to tears. He had found Napoleon to be as enigmatic as ever and in a 'state of deplorable uncertainty'. The war would happen one day, Cavour concluded, and almost certainly against Prussia as well as Austria; perhaps it would be in two months' time, perhaps next year, but only when his French ally thought the time was ripe. By then, as Cavour now realized belatedly, the Italians must be ready to field an army larger than that of the French, because Napoleon would never forgive them if France were left to carry the main burden of the war.

This was a matter which, preoccupied with so much else, Cavour had left on one side, with the result that there continued to be much careless optimism over military preparations. He boasted casually and more than once that with only fifty thousand French soldiers in support he could push the Austrians out of Italy and back to Vienna. But the two generals best in a position to know, Alfonso Lamarmora and Enrico Cialdini, when they finally realized what was expected of them, said that for the Piedmontese to launch an attack was quite out of the question; on the contrary, there was little chance of being able to stop the Austrians capturing Turin. Unsubstantiated rumours recorded scandalous and delusive examples of negligence – even of Piedmontese workers being attracted by high wages to cross the frontier and help the Austrians build their fortifications.

Most ominous of all was that King Victor Emanuel was so confident of his almost non-existent military prowess that he insisted on being allowed to take the supreme command, and was determined to leave the senior staff general, Lamarmora, with a merely subordinate and advisory function. Cavour ten years earlier had protested against an amateur such as King Charles Albert exercising the powers of Commander-in-Chief, but the official report on the war of 1848, with its stark revelations about the imperative need for a professional commander, had been kept secret; one reason had been to avoid giving offence on this question of the royal prerogative. General Dabormida, who had signed that report and who as *aide de camp* to the King in 1859 was in a good position to judge, foresaw disaster if Cavour refused to stand up to the monarchy on such a crucial issue, and the same apprehension was shared even by some among the more extreme royalists.

Unfortunately the Prime Minister felt himself in too weak a position to insist. At some point in April there were further angry scenes at court, suggesting that the quarrel over Rosina had not been forgotten. The King told others that he blamed Cavour for failing to find a solution at Paris and for sacrificing Clotilde to no evident purpose. He condemned his Prime Minister for being too easily discouraged, too prone to self-deceit and too eager to throw all the blame on the Emperor. Victor Emanuel said that Cavour had 'lost his way', to the point of sometimes seeming almost deranged; he had 'forfeited the confidence of serious and sensible politicians by momentary outbursts of uncontrollable fury and by the trust he has placed in incompetents'. The King rather looked to Rattazzi for advice, which suggests that he was again turning his mind to a possible change of government. He told an English acquaintance that at one point he almost put Cavour under arrest for shouting from the rooftops abuse of their French ally who alone could help them.

Such remarks may possibly have been one of the King's not infrequent distortions of the truth, but among those who could observe from close at hand there was a feeling that the Prime Minister was not in charge of events, or had taken on too much and permitted adventurousness to go too far. For instance, Cavour in Paris had found time to put the final touches to his scheme to use agents in Belgrade and Bucharest for smuggling shiploads of arms up the Danube to start a revolution in Hungary. He realized too late that such revolutions among the subject nationalities in eastern Europe could only antagonize Russia, whose help might have been far more useful. The idea was an extravaganza worthy of Mazzini, involving notes written in invisible ink to professional revolutionaries who had every interest in exaggerating both their capacity to act and their need for money. By mid April, news of the plan had begun to leak out. Cavour promised to send a hundred thousand rifles to the Hungarians, of which twenty thousand were despatched; but they arrived only after the war was over and were perhaps used for very different purposes from those he had in mind.

Victor Emanuel's view at the time, and he confirmed as much in retrospect, was that all this 'trickery and deceitfulness' had been a mistake. He thought that Piedmont should avoid putting herself in the wrong by overt belligerence and sharp practice. The war should be postponed for another year, especially as very real gains in central Italy could be expected from a congress. From England, Prussia and France came further pressure on the King to accept disarmament and an international conference, coupled with a hint that these other countries would in that case help him register some positive acquisitions. It was possible that a congress would accept the idea of forming a new Italian Confederation, which was precisely what Cavour had welcomed at Plombières. Such a solution would enable this small subalpine state to become effective master of Italy without firing a shot.

Cavour, rightly or wrongly, stood alone or almost alone in thinking otherwise. At one point the whole Cabinet was against him. From France and England came a formal request that he should show good will and disarm as the Austrians had already agreed to do, but his own view was that disarmament would seem to other Italians like dishonourable surrender on his part. He preferred to keep up the tension and confusion by giving the impression that he had concealed cards to play. He tried once more to persuade the French to hold fast, and threatened again that, if a congress met, Piedmont might desert them and ally with England. An attempt was made to confuse other countries by giving them further false information: he tried, for instance, to make others believe that Russia and Prussia were firmly on his side; and that France was not only determined to fight, but was advising him to refuse any concession; and that Malmesbury had given assurances that England would not object if he invaded Lombardy.

Cavour in fact had private information that led him to gamble on the probability that the Austrians could not hold out much longer. As he saw it, they must be assuming that the loss of Lombardy would trigger off the dissolution of their whole multinational empire and was therefore something they had to resist at all costs, if necessary by the use of pre-emptive force. They were known to be on the verge of financial bankruptcy, and partial mobilization of their army was said to be costing a million francs a day. Sooner or later some of the politicians in Vienna might lose their nerve and decide to exploit the general confusion by choosing war, hoping that other countries would recognize that Austria was in the right and Piedmont's machinations were dangerous and wrong. While waiting to see if this hypothesis was correct, Cavour was determined to give the impression of unshakeable confidence. On 16 April he said he would 'turn the whole world upside down' rather than back down. On the following day, when informed from London that an ultimatum was being drafted in Vienna, he expressed his conviction that Austria was about to attack and victory was assured.

Twenty-four hours later his confidence collapsed when a peremptory note from Paris insisted that he must give way and accept a proposal to disarm. Cavour was woken to hear this news in the early hours of the nineteenth, and his immediate reaction was that there was nothing left but to blow his brains out: 'the English have won; we have lost everything and Napoleon has abandoned us.' A desperate letter was sent to his nephew with instructions on what to do at his death. Later in the day, Castelli and Farini found him in his office having given orders to admit no one. They were sufficiently alarmed to force the door and discovered him busily tearing up and burning his papers. Cavour never again referred to his talk of suicide, and possibly it was one of those moments of *raptus* which, if we can believe the King, left him with no memory of what had happened. But Castelli burst into tears and never forgot this terrible scene; knowing 'the violence of Cavour's nature', he momentarily feared the worst.

The irony of the situation was that an apparent setback in fact marked the first step in the greatest triumph of Cavour's career, because by finally and very unwillingly accepting disarmament he embarrassed the Austrians and won the enthusiastic support of everyone in Europe who feared war. The Austrian politicians on the other hand, realizing that Napoleon must have withdrawn his protection from Piedmont, made the mistake of concluding that the moment had arrived for them to strike and end this continual succession of provocations. At any time during the next two days, Buol could easily have stopped short of war, especially when other countries offered to mediate. Even after an Austrian ultimatum was delivered on 23 April, Cavour had reason to be worried by what he called the 'perfidious' attempt on the part of England to prevent or delay the outbreak of hostilities.

He need not have been bothered, especially as the telegraph line between London and Vienna was partially interrupted – and this was possibly a decisive fact. He had succeeded against everyone by manipulating Austria into making him seem the injured party, thereby fulfilling his main obligation to Napoleon. Massimo d'Azeglio wrote from London with congratulations, calling it one of those lucky strikes that a gambler can expect once in a lifetime. Cavour's letters to his agent, Corio, reveal the sudden change from excitement to the depths of depression and back to euphoria. Before 19 April, since Leri was near the frontier, he had wanted his cattle sold before the Austrians began their invasion; on the nineteenth he cancelled this order as the prospect of war receded; but on the twenty-second he wrote again with advance news that war was certain, saying that stocks of wheat should be sold at once before the Austrians arrived to requisition them.

Buol gave him three days to reply to the ultimatum and this period was spent in speeding last-minute military preparations. Only at the last moment on the twenty-sixth was a formal rejection presented to the Austrian envoys who had been waiting in Turin, after which he turned to his colleagues and said in triumph, 'alea jacta est; we have made history, so we can now have dinner.' Parliament was hurriedly called upon to confirm the grant of full powers enabling the King to govern by royal decrees for as long as the war should last. Solaro della Margherita abstained from the vote on the grounds that the demand was unconstitutional; 110 deputies approved, 24 voted against, and in the senate there was unanimity. An amnesty was declared for all political prisoners and all political refugees – except, of course, Mazzini. Parliament then went into recess and did not meet again until the following year.

CHAPTER 15

The *Terza Riscossa*
April – July 1859

The war began in a very desultory fashion as though both sides, despite all their fighting talk, had been caught by surprise and without any plan of attack. Cavour had been hoping that the Piedmontese army would score some dramatic success before the French arrived. But it was strange that someone who had talked of marching on Vienna and fighting single-handed against both Austria and England had not done more to consider possible plans of campaign. The General Staff privately feared that the Austrian army with its greatly superior numbers could capture Turin in a matter of hours, but perhaps they kept this alarming thought to themselves. In fact the enemy made the great mistake of giving Cavour three clear days to answer their ultimatum – a mistake he did not make himself when he attacked the Papal States in 1860 – and then waited another three days before crossing the frontier on the twenty-ninth.

This delay was providential for him. He was momentarily worried that the slowness of the Austrian attack portended another intrigue by the English to halt the fighting, whereas in fact, by giving the French time to mobilize, it was his salvation. He arranged for a large area of country to be flooded to delay any invading force, but Napoleon was not prepared for the speed of events and let two weeks pass before arriving in Genoa. This left a period of considerable anxiety as the Piedmontese fought a gallant holding action.

Never in his life had the Prime Minister worked so hard. As well as the duties of Foreign Minister and Minister of the Interior, he had to take charge of administering the army and navy so that Lamarmora could be with the King at the front. He spent day and night in his office supervising every department of government, trying to organize revolutions in other Italian states, giving orders about arms production and police activity, writing war bulletins, and even taking responsibility for finance when the minister Lanza was absent. Inevitably, some decisions were bungled and he lacked time to keep in touch with diplomatic developments. Foreign ambassadors in Turin could not find him; his own ambassadors abroad were left without instructions or information on which to act; his Cabinet colleagues were also left partially in the dark, and so was the King himself.

As well as running the civil administration, Cavour was determined to have a say in military strategy. But Victor Emanuel, who disliked receiving advice even from his own General Staff, was offended at the additional intrusion of an amateur who was far away from the actual fighting and already had too much to do. The Prime Minister did not hesitate to criticize the tactics adopted at headquarters and sent urgent requests that the King should abandon any attempt at counter-attack so that the army could fall back to defend Turin. Nor did he give way until the French military authorities intervened to tell him that his suggestion might have spelt disaster.

These strained relations with the royal Commander-in-Chief continued throughout May, and intermediaries between the two men had to tone down their exchanges before delivery. Cavour had good reason to fear that the sovereign was intending to misuse his newly conferred dictatorial powers. King and Prime Minister therefore decided to go their different ways with a minimum of communication between them. Cavour was allowed to know so little of what was happening at the front that he sometimes had to wait for news about the fighting to arrive from Paris. He reached the point of saying that in normal times he would already have resigned and would certainly retire at the first moment when peace returned. But so accustomed was he to acting on his own responsibility that he allowed the King to know almost nothing of what was happening in Turin and elsewhere in Italy. This lack of co-ordination turned out to be a great misfortune.

At first he was hoping to persuade both the Grand Duke of Tuscany and the King of Naples to join a coalition against Austria in return for his guarantee to support them against any threat of a revolution. He tried to convince them that he wanted not the preponderance of Piedmont but rather to link the equal and autonomous states of Italy in a common cause. But Boncompagni in Florence had secret orders that, if this attempt at persuasion failed (as indeed it did), he should again encourage a *pronunciamento* by some of the senior officers in the Tuscan army. The Grand Duke was in fact chased into exile on 27 April, but this was the result of one of those mass popular demonstrations which Cavour so greatly feared and which were sometimes a decisive factor in the *risorgimento*. The Piedmontese government at once asked Napoleon for permission to control the situation by sending troops and setting up a military dictatorship in Tuscany, but received a negative answer. The Emperor would not permit anything that might lead to Piedmontese annexation of central Italy, and preferred to send a French occupying force to support and supervize the revolutionary government in Florence.

With regard to Naples, too, the first intention at Turin was to lure or force King Ferdinando into joining the national movement, because if this kingdom of nine million Italians remained an ally of Austria, foreigners might think that national independence was wanted only by a minority of the nation. In May, when Ferdinando died and was succeeded by his young son Francesco, Cavour sent one of his most trusted aides, the Count de Salmour, to repeat this advice in Naples. Salmour was hoping that he would not have to use his ambassadorial position as a cover for starting a revolution, and in fact Cavour was too little concerned about this area of Italy to contemplate anything so drastic.

Another problem was posed by the presence in Turin of Garibaldi, who had been gazetted a general in the Piedmontese army so that he could train volunteers for a diversionary movement in Lombardy. Victor Emanuel had informed the Prussian ambassador that two hundred thousand volunteers would at once rally to the Piedmontese flag when hostilities began. Others put the figure even higher; but there were political dangers and logistic difficulties in arming so many civilians. Perhaps as many as twenty thousand volunteers eventually arrived in the hope of joining the army or forming some kind of foreign legion, but nowhere near enough arms and uniforms were available for even this reduced number, and little more than three thousand volunteers ended up under Garibaldi's command.

Part of the trouble was that the regular army disliked and despised these irregulars as untrained, undisciplined and politically suspect. Often they were treated badly and some of them later remembered how their patriotic idealism was scorned with incomprehension or ridicule.

Garibaldi complained that every kind of obstacle was placed in his way, but dutifully obeyed orders and made the best of an unpromising start to the great upsurge of national feeling that he had hoped to stimulate. He appreciated that Cavour was in difficulties not only with the military establishment, who had not been trained to appreciate guerrilla action, but equally with the political conservatives who feared any association with popular movements. He may also have guessed that there were further problems with the French Emperor, to whom a promise had in fact been made by Cavour that these irregulars, since they were required merely as an indication of popular enthusiasm, would be given a minimal part to play once war began.

Garibaldi was the single outstanding military leader in Italy, and with a larger and better armed force might have raised a general insurrection throughout Lombardy that could possibly have been decisive for the campaign. But Cavour was caught in his old dilemma. On the one hand he wanted Garibaldi to organize a wholesale insurrection in order to show the French the extent of patriotic feeling. On the other hand the government had to send what amounted to counter-instructions, because there must be no 'disorders', no popular movement that might get out of hand and no further recruitment of irregulars in territory that Garibaldi succeeded in occupying.

With this degree of discouragement, most leaders of opinion among the patriots in Lombardy and central Italy preferred to wait until the French or Piedmontese armies arrived, and only then manifested their patriotic sentiments. Garibaldi did excellently with his limited resources, as Cavour handsomely acknowledged. The small force of volunteers scored some immediate victories and held down greatly superior forces when sent into Lombardy ahead of the regular army, but were given insufficient support or equipment and were consistently kept well away from the main fields of battle.

Cavour was understandably disappointed that his supporters in the National Society were unable to start the 'spontaneous' but 'moderate' insurrections that he had promised the French. The organizers of the Society had given precise orders for a general rising as soon as the war started, and talked of as many as four hundred thousand men being ready to fight, but not much happened. Their leader, La Farina, was dismayed that, in strong contrast to what happened in 1848, no movement took place in Sicily or Calabria or Milan, and an insurrection in Parma that he had carefully and confidently prepared against the ducal government received almost no support at all when he gave the signal to rise. Evidently this society was less strong and less well organized than he had led the government to think or perhaps than he himself imagined.

In Florence, on the other hand, the popular demonstration of 27 April was inspired by people closer to Mazzini's Party of Action and was a great success. Cavour briefly hoped that it would enable him to proceed towards annexing Tuscany, but this would have been contrary to what had been agreed at Plombières, and he desisted as soon as he realized that it would cause considerable annoyance in Paris. Another grave disappointment was the behaviour of the leading liberals in Florence. These men had refused to associate themselves with the popular demonstrations that led to defenestration of the Grand Duke on 27 April. Subsequently they succeeded in taking over the provisional government, yet most of them were quite as anxious to keep their regional autonomy as they were to be annexed by Turin.

On 4 June the Austrians suffered a major defeat at Magenta. Unfortunately, owing to what seems to have been a series of misunderstandings, the Piedmontese army failed to arrive at Magenta until nightfall, otherwise the enemy might not have been able to recover and the war would have been virtually won. But Napoleon's victory at least made possible the occupation of Milan as well as Parma and Modena.

Cavour had hurriedly appointed a commission to make recommendations about setting up a provisional government for Lombardy, and now nominated a distinguished Piedmontese lawyer to be Governor of this region. His orders were to conscript a new army in the province – something that the government had tried to stop Garibaldi doing – but also to allow no public discussion of politics, to listen to no local advice, and to permit only a limited freedom of the press. A main objective quite clearly was to avoid autonomist movements such as those which had taken place in Milan during the previous revolution of 1848 and which were already becoming entrenched in Florence.

On 12 June, as a result of their defeat at Magenta, the Austrian garrisons withdrew from Bologna and Ancona, leaving these provinces of the Papal States wide open to revolt. Cavour had great hopes that the Austrian withdrawal would be followed by widespread patriotic demonstrations or even a declaration of independence from the papal administration. He had been assured by Farini and Minghetti – both natives of the area – that there was unanimous feeling for annexation to Piedmont, and he had so informed Napoleon. Probably he did not appreciate that Farini and Minghetti represented a small minority of educated and well-to-do liberals who were mostly too timid to take to the streets. The masses, with no Garibaldi to arouse them, remained inert even after the Austrians departed, while the liberals were waiting for more material aid from Turin, or at least for more precise orders about what they were expected to do. As a result, any insurrections that took place were late and half-hearted; and as soon as the insurgents realized that Cavour was either militarily unable or diplomatically unwilling to come to their aid, enthusiasm waned or disappeared. The unpalatable result was another bull of excommunication against everyone involved; furthermore, doubt was inevitably thrown on the claims of the National Society about the extent of patriotic fervour.

Worse still, the French were irritated by what seemed to them to be another piece of deceit. While they could have welcomed an insurrection directed against the retreating Austrian army, a subsequent rising against the Pope would greatly displease the Catholic population of France. Moreover Napoleon had invaded Italy on the understanding that there would be general rising in his support, only to find a surprising amount of indifference. The Emperor complained to Cavour with some indignation that 'only by showing one is ready to fight can one prove one's worthiness to become a nation', and the phrase expressed a sense of bitter frustration and disillusionment in Paris that at once acquired political implications.

Stung by the reproach, Cavour changed direction, and instead of expressing anxiety about the volunteer movement as he had hitherto, demanded further recruitment in order to prove that he was fighting a truly national war and not one of ambition and conquest. But it was too late to organize anything significant. No one could accuse the Italians of lacking military ardour: indeed, observers noted that the many Italian soldiers in the Austrian army fought as well and enthusiastically as those in the Piedmontese forces. What was wrong, wrote Cavour, was rather that 'patriotism has so far produced very feeble results', and in desperation he blamed Farini for giving the lie to all the promises he had made to the French. Perhaps only now was he able to see what Mazzini pointed out: that this failure arose in part from his own ambivalent attitude towards all popular uprisings and in particular Garibaldi's irregulars.

In particular he complained that the Tuscan aristocrats who now ruled in Florence continued to show little interest in contributing men and money to help the war in Lombardy. Fear of revolution made these admirable but over-fearful men unwilling to arm their peasants or even to recruit a civic guard. Instead they had the effrontery to ask for Piedmontese troops to be taken from the field of battle and sent to Florence in order to keep the local population under control. Cavour was contemptuous and also greatly disheartened when dozens of other towns, instead of sending recruits, begged him to let them have Piedmontese policemen for this same purpose.

In the streets of Milan too, although the French were received with great public enthusiasm, under the surface there was nothing to compare with the much more active patriotic excitement that had accompanied the spontaneous and extremely successful civic revolt of March 1848. Among the peasantry in the Lombard countryside and even among the urban aristocracy, there were occasional inexplicable but unmistakeable signs of opposition to the Piedmontese and fraternization with the Austrian oppressor. Evidently patriotism had not had time to become generally felt and understood. Karl Marx, in a contemporary newspaper article, commented that the small state of Prussia in 1813 had produced more enthusiasm and more volunteers against France than had the whole of Italy in 1859 against Austria.

The second great battle of the war, at Solferino, was fought on 24 June. Before this, however, there were already clear signs that Napoleon was wondering how he could bring the war honourably to an end. Not only was he upset by the lack of popular support in Italy, but the Piedmontese had broken some of their engagements to him. Fortunately he did not know that Cavour had already begun asking the English government to help in countering the preponderant influence of France in Italy; but at least he knew by now that an enlarged Piedmont was unlikely to be the subservient French protectorate he had hoped. The national interests of France would not be served by the clear intention in Turin to annex not only Lombardy but also Tuscany and a much larger part of the Papal States than had been stipulated; even Canton Ticino in Switzerland was becoming an objective of annexationist propaganda. After the Pope's bull of excommunication the Emperor could hardly associate himself with the projected invasion of the Romagna. Not only was Cavour intending to proclaim the total abolition of the Pope's temporal power, but from an intercepted letter it was by now known in Paris that the people of Bologna were being wrongly informed from Turin that Napoleon secretly agreed with this intention.

Victor Emanuel was exceedingly annoyed to discover that his ministers had thus been imperilling the French alliance on which so much depended. Cavour, as the King wrote once again on 20 June, seemed to have lost his head: insufficient care was being taken over supplying the army with food and munitions, while far too much attention was being given to conspiratorial intrigues that were ineffective and simply made more enemies. The King put this down to mere clumsiness and inefficiency. Cavour had chosen to take so much responsibility on himself that his friends wondered how much longer he could sustain the burden. The Prime Minister believed that he alone was able to direct the whole field of policy-making, that he alone had the strength of will and disciplined intelligence to supervise all the different departments of government.

The results were unfortunate. For example, he had promised the French from the very beginning that he would support them with a hundred thousand soldiers, and later went so far as to say that the Piedmontese army must carry the main burden of the campaign; but such expectations were far removed from reality, and only some fifty thousand soldiers were in the field apart from twelve thousand volunteers. Even for this very much smaller army there were insufficient guns and transport, with the result that the normal process of recruitment had to be slowed down. Cavour talked casually of capturing Vienna, but was unaware that his generals, despite ten years of preparation for just such a war as this, had inadequate working maps even of Lombardy. By the end of June the allied armies were held up because supplies of food were disorganized. Cavour had worked immensely hard to provide what was needed, but traffic was piling up on the railway owing to unforeseen difficulties in repairing war-damaged track and co-ordinating the movement of trucks.

These deficiencies explain in part why the difficult French victory at Solferino and the even more difficult Piedmontese victory nearby at San Martino could not be exploited, and why the war came to a premature end soon afterwards with the Austrians still firmly entrenched inside Lombardy. Cavour visited the scene of these battles and received a vivid impression of the horrors of war: with only one doctor for up to five hundred casualties, and with some of the wounded brought to field hospitals after four or five days lying in the open under a hot sun, it is easy to understand why the French were losing their eagerness to continue fighting.

Napoleon's major worry was that the Prussian army was being mobilized menacingly on the Rhine where it outnumbered those French troops that had been left behind on garrison duty. Although many Prussians sympathized with the aspiration towards Italian unity, their main concern remained that Napoleon might be aiming to defeat Austria so that he could then challenge them in northern Europe. Inevitably their anxiety grew as the fighting came closer to the southern frontier of the German Confederation and its Mediterranean port of Trieste. By now it was no longer a secret that the Piedmontese were attempting to start an insurrection in Hungary, and the Prussian ministers gave an ominous warning that such a revolution would be the signal for their own intervention against him on the Austrian side.

By early July Cavour was in a state of increasing agitation as his plans were going wrong. Not only Prussia and England, but also Russia, on whose active help he had counted, were trying to bring the war to a close. In addition the French alliance, which was an indispensable basis for his policy, was showing signs of fracture, and on 3 July the French formally complained that his ambitions in central Italy were damaging the alliance and diminishing the chances of allied victory. One further problem, as Cavour had to agree with Napoleon, was the King, for Victor Emanuel was proving to be an incompetent general who even at this late hour would somehow have to be removed from any effective command. Some people were alarmed and discouraged to hear Cavour talk not just against the King but also once again of wanting to capture and execute Mazzini. On top of everything else his political base in Turin was being undermined, as he must have realized when Rattazzi was twice summoned to military headquarters for private consultations with the Commander-in-Chief.

The one remaining chance of success was for the allied armies to continue their advance into Venetian territory, and this would be very dangerous so long as two powerful Lombard fortresses at Mantua and Peschiera remained in Austrian hands. Napoleon allocated the assault on Peschiera to the Piedmontese, but although Cavour had told the

American Charles Sumner that this would present no great problem, the necessary siege artillery purchased from Sweden was still in Turin, and somewhat late in the day it was discovered that three weeks would be needed to move these guns into place. Cavour blamed the delay on military headquarters, though he himself, as acting Minister of War, was to some degree responsible.

On 5 July, after this unexpected obstacle was explained to the French, Napoleon decided to ask for an armistice. The next day the Emperor gave his reasons to Victor Emanuel, who concurred so long as the intention was to provide time for regrouping their forces and bringing up the artillery. The King was seen to be quite pleased with this arrangement and gave his consent without waiting to consult anyone, let alone the Prime Minister. Despite later denials, the King said at the time that he was sure the advantage of a cease-fire would lie with the allies and not with Austria. His only objection was that Franz Joseph refused to meet him personally because the Austrians would not admit that they had been beaten by Piedmont and would therefore negotiate only with the French.

On 8 July a five-week truce was agreed by all three belligerents and Lamarmora sent this information to his ministerial colleagues in Turin. Cavour already knew that there was considerable pressure from other countries in favour of peace, but, deeply shocked at the news of an armistice, set out for the front and arrived early on Sunday the tenth. By that time the King had persuaded himself that this might be a good occasion to arrange not just an armistice but an actual peace, and had therefore authorized the French to negotiate a settlement on the basis of the cession of Lombardy to Piedmont. French and English observers at headquarters agreed that the prospect of peace seemed, if anything, to please Victor Emanuel even more than Napoleon.

Cavour, when he arrived and heard of this development, was astounded and could think of no other solution than that, if France wanted to back down, Piedmont should continue the war alone. This was an absurd but perhaps understandable reaction. There was little point in his discussing the matter at length with Napoleon because he knew that the French were now strongly critical of his attempt to annex central Italy. The King therefore went to discuss the French proposals without his ministers, and returned that evening with the news that the two Emperors were to meet the next day at Villafranca to draw up preliminaries of peace.

Early on the eleventh these two met for an hour without any Piedmontese representative and confirmed that they should end the fighting. The general principles of their agreement were conveyed to Victor Emanuel, who according to several witnesses still did not seem displeased. Nor did he raise any objections or suggest alterations when Prince Napoleon was sent the same afternoon to the Austrian camp at Verona, whence he returned with a signed document containing a more precise outline of the terms of peace.

This document was then countersigned by the King 'so far as concerns me'. He later gave several not easily reconcilable versions of his state of mind, but after hearing Cavour's reaction he was less happy with the outcome than before. Indeed he told one general of his chagrin that his father, ten years earlier, had won more and without foreign help. The two Emperors had agreed that there should be an Italian Confederation, of which Austria would be a member because of her continued possession of Venice. Piedmont was not to annex Modena or Parma, nor even the part of Lombardy around the fortified towns of Mantua and Peschiera. The Austrians surrendered most of Lombardy, but only to the French, who undertook to cede it subsequently to the Piedmontese. Napoleon said he would forgo his claim to Nice and Savoy, but still expected to be reimbursed for the cost of the war.

About midnight this greatly disappointing settlement was presented to Cavour, who resigned after making a terrible scene. He was purple in the face and breathing with difficulty, so that an apoplectic stroke was feared; he 'seemed almost to have lost his mind', according to one newspaper correspondent who saw him a few moments later. The King sat quietly smoking a cigar as his Prime Minister tried to insist that they must renounce the offer of Lombardy and continue fighting alone; to which the reply was that to give up this region would be dishonourable and to continue the war alone quite impossible. Victor Emanuel told other people how Cavour insulted him at this meeting and called him a traitor: the King could think only that 'vanity and pride had turned his head', but 'I believe his reason forsook him in those moments'. Cavour gave no detailed account of what happened, but later recalled that he had been less trenchant and censorious than on previous occasions when the two of them had quarrelled.

The general reaction to Cavour's resignation was muted by the shock and despondency of seeing the patriotic movement brought to a halt in such a sudden and dramatic manner. The King, however, was not too dejected; he looked forward to taking a predominant position in the Italian Confederation that Napoleon was hoping to create, and talked with some pleasure of the possibility that Cavour might be pensioned off to go and live in America. Massimo d'Azeglio, the man whom Cavour generously acknowledged as 'the father of the Italian question', had mixed feelings. Azeglio had buried his personal disagreement over policy and rallied to support the government during the war, but now feared that the national cause might suffer because of events in central Italy and because of Cavour's growing reputation for secret intrigues and bad faith.

Few can have failed to recognize that the resigning Premier was by far the ablest politician in the country, and there was widespread expectation that his resignation could be only temporary. But strong criticism was voiced in some opposition newspapers. He was said to have brought his downfall on his own head by trying to centralize all power in himself and failing to see through the adulation of subordinates who were too often mediocre if not inept. John Daniel, the United States minister, was not entirely wrong in ascribing his fall to the self-delusion that he could outwit the French into sacrificing their own interests to those of Piedmont: 'artful, adroit, unscrupulous and audacious as he is', wrote Daniel, 'he has been used, outwitted, played with, and made a tool of by one more artful, more unscrupulous, more audacious, and very much more profound than himself.'

Cavour was soon referring to his resignation as having been a personal sacrifice made in the general interest of the country. He knew he was a *bête noire* in the eyes of European diplomats and would therefore have been poorly placed to win any concessions at the eventual peace settlement. Before the end of July he was nevertheless wondering whether he might be appointed to represent the country at the congress that was due to discuss the formal peace treaty in Zürich. In the meantime he helped Lamarmora and Rattazzi form a new government, after warning them that he was handing over a desperate situation and a thankless task which was bound to make them unpopular.

Some of his close acquaintances thought that the setback at Villafranca finally turned Cavour against the idea of a federal Italy and at last brought him close to Mazzini's ideal of national unification. It

CAVOUR

was certainly a very important moment for him and for the country. A few days afterwards he was regretting his momentary lapse of judgement and saw plenty of hope for the future. Lombardy had been acquired. Independent provisional governments were being set up on his advice in Modena and Parma to prevent the former dynasties returning, and later these joined the Romagna to form a single provisional state with the ancient name of Emilia. Representative assemblies were then summoned in Emilia and Tuscany to request annexation by Piedmont. Cavour was delighted with these developments. Even though a French veto prevented any territorial change for the moment, the idea of annexing central Italy was being strongly supported by the English government, and Napoleon eventually said he was ready to renew the war against the Austrians if they used force to restore the deposed dynasties. These elected assemblies were at last proving that a substantial number of Italians were ready to win independence by their own spontaneous decisions and without having to rely on an imposed settlement by a foreign army. Here was a major success.

CHAPTER 16

Out of Office
1859 – 60

For the second half of 1859, Cavour was out of office. At first he was relieved to be free of the cares of state, and in six weeks did not so much as open a newspaper. But idleness came as an anti-climax after three years of 'almost superhuman effort' during which he thought he had had to work perhaps harder than anyone ever worked before. In this new mood of dejection he wrote to his mistress, Bianca Ronzani, that he was exhausted, discouraged, even embittered at the way events had gone. He felt he was moving into a premature old age, leaving others to complete the great achievements he had hoped for.

He considered travel, but thought that after recent events it might be invidious to visit France or England; and despite frequent talk about going to America he now made the excuse that he suffered too much from seasickness to contemplate crossing the Atlantic. Part of the summer he therefore spent in Switzerland, where he told de la Rive that southern Italy might provide the next stage for the national movement. Since diplomacy and the French alliance had failed him, he feared that he might have to spend the rest of his life as a conspirator; but he also explained that it was now England's turn to help Italy. Back on his farm at Leri he read and took notes from *The Prince* by Machiavelli, an author who he thought might help to provide some of the political lessons that the times required.

The King had been voted full powers by Parliament before the legislature went into recess at the outbreak of war, and now wrote to tell his daughter that he had purposely appointed a weak Cabinet under General Lamarmora so that he could govern personally. Without Cavour looking over his shoulder, Victor Emanuel 'seemed like a schoolboy on holiday', commented de Reiset, a French visitor. The monarch was full of ideas, even if they were largely unrealistic. He had thoughts of annexing Sicily and purchasing Venice from Austria; alternatively he wondered whether another war against Austria might be possible in the spring of 1860. He also asked the Prussians if there was any chance of their helping him to acquire Mantua and Peschiera. If only Piedmont could annex Venice and Parma, plus possibly the Romagna under the Pope's nominal sovereignty, he was ready to renew his offer to cede Savoy and Nice to France, and would also allow the deposed dynasties to return in Tuscany and Modena.

Lamarmora was not a strong Premier. He accepted the post only when pressed by Cavour, and in September told Cavour and Azeglio that he would be happy for either of them to take his position. Both refused, and without any doubt the King felt happier with more pliant ministers. As October came and went, Cavour watched his successors floundering in a sea of difficulties, and began to show increasing irritation with a life of inactivity. Parliament was not recalled, but he agreed to prepare for its recall by presiding over a commission for electoral reform. Rattazzi and Lamarmora asked his advice on a number of points, and he gave it freely. On at least one occasion he was invited, with Azeglio, to attend a Cabinet meeting. But the more he saw, the more he was upset to find that the new Foreign Minister, Dabormida, was too anxious to know Napoleon's views before taking any initiative in foreign affairs. He had himself been accused in the past of doing the same, and would be so again, but for the moment he thought that something more virile and less subservient was needed.

By November it was clear that the Italian Confederation arranged at Villafranca would never come into existence, because both England and France realized that the inclusion of Austria would make it unworkable as a solution to the Italian problem. This fact, together with the continued demand in central Italy for annexation to Piedmont, convinced Cavour that the time was coming when his own presence at the head of affairs would again be possible and advantageous. Lamarmora's government, under pressure from London, asked the former Premier to be its delegate at an international congress where these matters could be settled, and he said he was prepared to sacrifice his *amour propre* and accept, but was irritated when the King kept on delaying any formal appointment. Still more humiliating was that the French tried to discourage the choice of such a strong personality whose independence of mind they already knew well.

Cavour's resentment was concentrated, somewhat unfairly, on Rattazzi, the Minister of the Interior, who was the leading personality in the government. He even convinced himself that the motive behind the armistice in July must have been a deliberate intention to get rid of a government that the King disliked. It also occurred to him that Rattazzi was perhaps exploiting the back-stairs influence of the King's mistress in order to keep the conservative liberals out of power and shift the political centre of gravity further to the left. One sign of this shift, against which Cavour protested, was the nomination of Valerio and Depretis to provincial governorships. There was also good evidence that Brofferio and others on the radical left were taking money from the King to launch a new political movement aimed at increasing royal power and delaying the return to parliamentary government. Most ominous of all was the reappearance in Turin of Garibaldi, who was seen to be closely in touch with Brofferio and mysteriously had plenty of money for collecting guns and recruiting volunteers.

Cavour's friend and secretary, Isacco Artom, found him in December full of pleasurable excitement at the possibility of returning to power before long. Until parliamentary elections could be held, no one could be sure how public opinion would react to recent political developments, but Cavour was pleased to note that conservative newspapers, even those that had strongly opposed his own administration, were genuinely alarmed by the inexplicable activities of Garibaldi and hence were actively searching for a safer and less radical alternative. One symptom of growing discontent with the government's policy was that the Whist Society, the club of the conservative aristocracy who had been suspicious of Cavour ever since his *connubio* with the centre-left, now elected him their president, for which he expressed his gratitude.

One other highly advantageous development was that the weakening of French influence in Italy after Villafranca had revived in English public opinion a much more positive interest in Italian affairs. Palmerston, who was now Prime Minister in London, again proclaimed himself in favour of trying to expel the Austrians from Venice. The British Foreign Minister, Lord John Russell, advised Victor Emanuel that Cavour ought to be brought back into the government, and added that Piedmont could proceed to annex central Italy with English support and without the need for either revolution or further war. Russell and Palmerston were both coming round to the view that, if all else failed, England should be ready to take arms for the 'aggrandisement of Piedmont' in the interest of a more durable European settlement. This was a major change full of promise for the future, even if other politicians in London were less enthusiastic.

Another dramatic event in December was that Napoleon, after months of apparent hostility to any further change in Italy, suddenly made the wholly unexpected suggestion that the papal government in the Romagna should be secularized. If this meant that France as well as England was recommending an end or a partial end to the Pope's temporal power, there was all the more need for a strong government in Turin that could make the best of a complex and rapidly changing diplomatic situation. Cavour told the French ambassador that if in July he had conceived for a single moment how the armistice arrangements could have permitted this sequence of events, he would never have resigned.

A further development was Napoleon's remark to Dabormida that he wanted to annex Savoy and Nice if a good bargain could be struck. Dabormida's immediate reaction was that Piedmont must avoid any surrender of national territory and should rely instead on the promise of English help to annex central Italy; but other ministers were less optimistic, and Rattazzi raised with Cavour the suggestion that they should jointly agree to a compromise that would give up the single province of Savoy in exchange for the annexation of Emilia and Tuscany. Cavour at first seemed favourable but then backed down, and Rattazzi concluded from this change of attitude – whether fairly or not – that Cavour's friends were intending to sacrifice Nice as well as Savoy in a bid to win Napoleon's agreement for their return to power.

During the first two weeks of January 1860 these various indications suggested that a new chapter was about to open in Italian history, and the main question was who would be in the post of command. The King had no doubts on this score and was determined if possible to hold on to his almost dictatorial position for as long as Parliament could be kept in abeyance. He continued to speak with great asperity against Cavour, the one politician who was a personality strong enough to stand up to the monarch; and the King now confessed that summoning Garibaldi to Turin had been part of his plans for another war in the spring.

Such a blatant and irresponsible alliance of the monarchy with the radical left was too much for Lamarmora, and several ministers backed him in threatening to resign. Their resignation would have left the way open for Cavour's return to government and was thus a very effective threat: as the King told one of his surprised courtiers, 'rather than Cavour, I would prefer Garibaldi as Prime Minister.' But Victor Emanuel decided under pressure to back down and accept Lamarmora's more moderate policy, especially when it was reinforced by the direct intervention of Hudson, the British ambassador. A few hours later, Garibaldi's recruitment of volunteers stopped as mysteriously as it had begun and he disappeared from Turin.

Castelli was one of a number of people who were trying hard to reconcile Cavour and Rattazzi, the two most experienced and proven liberals in politics. But Cavour would have none of it, and insisted against all Rattazzi's denials that King and ministers were acting with no higher motive than to keep him out of office. In a series of private meetings with them he was quite exaggeratedly offensive, questioning not merely their ability, but their patriotism, morality and personal honesty.

Even General Lamarmora, who had been in office longer than Cavour, and whom Cavour had called the one indispensable man in politics, the one from whom he had no secrets, was denounced in the presence of third parties as being a contemptible place-hunter. Rattazzi was told to his face that he was a useless, envious, vulgar nonentity who had been a disaster for the country. Dabormida and Lamarmora, both of whom had more than once offered to make way for Cavour's return to power, thought as they heard these aggressive remarks that their former colleague must be out of his mind as 'blinded with self-conceit he beat his fists on the table.' Lamarmora had witnessed such scenes before and knew that in moments of passion Cavour could unexpectedly change from exaggerated expressions of love and admiration to equally exaggerated contempt, treating former friends with inexplicable brutality and then acting the next day as though nothing had happened.

Cavour was evidently determined to force the government's collapse – and not from what his opponents called 'a miserable lust for power'. He was rightly afraid that the ministers were unable to control the monarch, who was bent on provoking another war with Austria that might ruin any hope of profiting from the novel signs of goodwill in

France and England. Parliament should therefore be recalled. The ministers agreed on this point and differed from him only on the matter of timing. By the terms of the electoral law it would be impossible for elections to take place in time for Parliament to meet before the last week in March, whereas Cavour demanded that the legal formalities be set aside so as to permit an earlier meeting before any irreparable damage was done.

Another threat to the continuance of Lamarmora's government was that the Minister of Education, Senator Casati from Milan, was on the point of resigning over the speed with which Piedmontese institutions were being forced upon his own province of Lombardy. The annexation of this province was justified by the plebiscitary vote of 1848, but that vote had been specifically conditional on the summoning of a Constituent Assembly to determine any changes that might be needed in the existing Piedmontese constitution, and such a Constituent Assembly held few attractions for Turin. Casati thought, as did others, that Lombardy possessed its own traditions and laws which might in some respects be worthy of adoption by the new kingdom. In particular he spoke for the landowning classes in accusing Rattazzi of appointing too many local government officials who did not belong to this class and who, perhaps for that reason, were talking provocatively about the need for social reforms. Casati had protested against this in the Cabinet and been outvoted, but was now ready to provoke a government crisis over the issue. Other Lombards complained that their region was being treated not as an equal partner in a new state, but almost as a conquered colony.

The final push was given by Sir James Hudson, who Azeglio blamed, perhaps wrongly, for his own fall from power in 1852. Hudson was an admirer of Cavour, an enthusiastic supporter of the patriotic movement, whose influence behind the scenes was at certain moments very considerable. He was a handsome, elegant bachelor and a notable art collector, who had travelled a great deal in Italy and had many friends throughout the peninsula. Cavour did not entirely trust him but often asked his advice and sometimes engaged his help. In the first two weeks of January, Hudson intervened actively, speaking three or four times personally with the King, trying to bring Cavour back into politics, and concerting a move with Italians from other regions to force the recall of Parliament. After carefully calculating the risks, he reported to London with some bravado on 9 January that 'to upset this government by a strong, rough effort would not be difficult.'

On the sixteenth, the ministers at last decided to resign and advised the appointment of Cavour to succeed them, but the King still held out against a manoeuvre that would bring his period of personal government to an end. Meanwhile Cavour went to see Hudson, by whom he was reproached for creating too many difficulties and for holding out over the relatively minor point of when Parliament should meet. In the middle of their discussion, General Solaroli arrived with an olive branch from Lamarmora, and Cavour finally agreed that he would collaborate with the government provided only that the elections were held in March. A note was drawn up to this effect, and, since Cavour said he was too tired, Hudson wrote it at Cavour's dictation. This note in Hudson's handwriting, whether or not the result was intended, gave Lamarmora an excuse to insist finally on resignation, since it could be called evidence of an improper intervention by a foreign ambassador in the country's internal affairs.

In the evening of the same day, as Cavour was getting into his carriage to return to Leri unaware of this new turn of events, a message arrived from the Palace inviting him back as Premier. The only conditions imposed by Victor Emanuel were that General Fanti be appointed Minister of War, and that Cavour promise never to interfere again in the King's private life. Cavour agreed to both conditions. As a guarantee, Castelli was summoned as a witness to hear Cavour apologize for letting the matter of Rosina come between them, and an undertaking was given never to raise the subject again. On the twentieth the new government was installed, and the next day a decree announced that elections would be held.

CHAPTER 17

The Mature Statesman: Private and Public Life

At the time he returned to office in January 1860, Cavour was at the height of his powers and had achieved a considerable international renown. In character he still seemed to possess the same mixture of almost contradictory qualities that had presented such a puzzle in his youth. Sincerely held conservative beliefs appeared to conflict with a readiness for radical reforms and a surprising resort to revolutionary action at crucial moments. As well as being judicious and prudent by temperament, at some moments he could be passionate and violent; he was usually cautious, but on occasion breathtakingly audacious; a man of ideals and high principles, he could also be matter-of-fact and even coldly cynical. Along with personal kindness and generosity there was from time to time a surprising ruthlessness; in addition to being enormously ambitious and energetic, he usually succeeded in giving the impression of a man who was relaxed, easy-going, and essentially a middle-of-the-road moderate.

Because of these apparent contradictions, and because it was occasionally hard to distinguish the genuine Cavour from the appearance that he wanted to convey, some acquaintances found him hard to fathom. His young cousin William de la Rive had to admit that, in the last years of Cavour's life, the charm and the smile might be no more than skin deep; and, just as with the first and greater Napoleon, it was difficult to find some 'human feeling by which to lay hold of him'. 'Far from being a reed painted to look like iron', wrote de la Rive, appearances were deceptive and in fact 'he was an iron rod painted to look like a reed.' Underneath the polished surface of affable good nature there was an increasing inscrutability as the years went by; even a sense of menace. Consumed with ambition for his country, and also quite naturally for himself, his face could sometimes betray the implacable severity and iron will of a conqueror.

Political opponents were not always generous or very subtle in their interpretation of Cavour's character; but their criticisms, even when unfair or exaggerated, are a fact of history that cannot be disregarded. Brofferio and the Sardinian ex-priest Giorgio Asproni, who both watched his conduct day by day in Parliament, called him vain, mendacious, overbearing and inconsiderate; they believed that he lacked moral sense and was a corrupter of politics as well as being insatiable for power and money. From a greater distance and a higher standpoint of principle, Mazzini and Garibaldi looked on him as an aristocrat out of touch with the common people, and as a Piedmontese who, misunderstanding the rest of Italy, was moved by a pragmatic desire for Piedmontese aggrandisement rather than by an ideal vision of a new Italian nation. Mazzini talked scornfully of his 'paltry, hateful programme of expediency', and condemned as unjustifiable any patriotic movement that had to depend on foreign armies and an alliance with despotism. Carlo Cattaneo and Giuseppe Ferrari, two liberals of a radical and federalist stamp, thought that Cavour's scale of values was becoming perverted in his search for personal and national power: in their view his overriding objective of defeating Austria was in practice damaging or excluding other nobler objectives such as the liberties of the subject and the moral education of the nation.

John Daniel, the American minister in Turin, was someone else who noted a vanity, a lack of sincerity or moral principle, and a disdain for other people and their views. Cavour, he said, was 'one of those domineering, grasping men', who had 'a radical contempt for all law but their own will'. Daniel's views were no doubt conditioned by the fact that he did not fit easily into the aristocratic world of this small provincial capital. He wrote in January 1860 that Cavour 'is a Voltairian in his philosophy and wholly unscrupulous in his words and actions – a fact which should not be regarded as a fault in him, for were it otherwise he would be wholly unfit for and incapable of the government of an Italian people. He loves money and has made a large private fortune while attending to the affairs of his nation, and he dearly loves *power*. Of this he can never bring himself to partake with any other: nor can he brook the least opposition from any quarter great or small.'

* * *

After the death of his parents, Cavour continued to live in the family palazzo where his widowed brother presided over what was often an unhappy and sometimes a melancholy household. Gustave was a devout Catholic who, especially on ecclesiastical matters, often disagreed strongly with government policy; occasionally he made the younger man feel almost a stranger in their joint home, uncharitably protesting at the latter's 'unchristian' life and mismanagement of the family properties. For some years after 1854, Gustave suffered from a mysterious depressive illness that left him slightly unbalanced. What made this worse was that his surviving son, a bachelor who lived with them, was a morose and highly neurotic person who was often at loggerheads with his father and sister. Moreover the major domo, who managed the household and on whom Gustave depended absolutely, disliked Camille and was heartily disliked in return, which all added to the general gloom and discomfort.

One cause of resentment was the official entertaining that, albeit generally at government cost, sometimes had to take place in the Palazzo Cavour. Gustave was miserly as well as puritanical and became quite unreasonably worried that the family inheritance was being squandered on such wordly expenditure. In addition to all his political labours, the Prime Minister was therefore obliged to draw up a quarterly balance sheet to prove to his brother that, instead of being extravagant, he was painstakingly paying off the family mortgages. Over half a million *lire* of these mortgages were discharged in the course of ten years. Gustave had no inclination and Camille no time to keep fully abreast of the developments in agricultural techniques, but the average income from Leri increased fourfold during this period, in large part owing to the careful administration of their agent and partner Giacinto Corio.

Occasional rumours circulated in Turin that Cavour had it in mind to take a wife, but none of them were true. He himself confessed that by temperament he might be incapable of real love; or, put differently, he set great store by personal independence and deliberately chose to eschew the encumbrance of any settled sentimental attachments. He once told Corio that he was shy of giving too much affection even to an animal pet because its death might prove upsetting. To Salmour, who was convinced that marriage might have kept him alive much longer, he gave a further reason that a wife left on her own by a busy husband would expose him to gossip, scandal, and hence ridicule. He had always been peculiarly sensitive to the threat of ridicule, and Garibaldi's matrimonial discomfiture thus afforded him a good deal of merriment. He himself had cuckolded too many husbands to want his own reputation put similarly at risk.

Cavour did not forget his early attachment to Anne Giustiniani, and in 1858 took money out of the secret funds of the police to make a gift to her son in Geneva who seems to have been in financial difficulties. From 1856 onwards he kept another permanent mistress to whom he was sincerely attached. Bianca Ronzani was a lady who had been employed earlier in the same role by the King. She was a young ballerina of whom no one else seems to have had much good to say. Her husband was in charge of the Theatre Royal in Turin until his debts became so considerable that – probably with financial help from his wife's new protector – he departed for South America. Cavour almost never mentioned Bianca to anyone and never escorted her in public, though the existence of their liaison was commonly known and much disliked by his own family. She lived in a comfortable three-storey house that he bought for her on a hill overlooking Turin. Many of his private letters to her she subsequently sold on the international market. Costantino Nigra, after locating some of these letters in Vienna many years later, persuaded the King that they should be re-purchased and destroyed, because their contents were too shocking and would certainly damage his reputation if they became known to the general public.

No one ever denied that Cavour was immensely industrious, and he told an English acquaintance that no amount of work would ever cause him fatigue. Sometimes his day began at 5.00 a.m. or even earlier, when he would receive visitors in his dressing-gown and tasselled velvet night-cap. They might find him reading the London *Times* by candlelight and smoking a cheroot. Oddly for such a methodical person, his room was in complete disarray, full of books, newspapers and piles of letters, in such disorder that he could mislay documents altogether. By breakfast-time some of the most urgent business was finished, after which he would walk the short distance to the ministerial offices in Piazza Castello. Usually returning home for a quick lunch, he would then stroll under the porticos of Via Po, accessible to anyone who cared to accost him. The afternoon was for Cabinet meetings and Parliament; the evening for further private work. He also liked to attend the State theatre, where foreign diplomats all had their private boxes in which they expected to transact a substantial amount of official business.

Cavour said he was never bored and clearly was never idle for a moment. He had a singular gift for passing quickly from one subject to another, never objecting to interruptions and always able to resume the thread at the point he had broken off. He had found earlier that the Finance Ministry took most of his official time – so much, indeed, that the burden could not be supported for more than a short while. He used to say that he worked fourteen hours a day, of which Foreign Office business took only two. He preferred to answer all letters at once. Hating red tape of any kind, despising all routine, he used to cut through forms and regulations, explaining in the words of St Paul that 'the letter kills but the spirit gives life.' Of course someone who took upon himself minor as well as major matters, even down to settling the nation's railway time-table, had insufficient time to supervize the whole field of government, and outside the areas of finance and diplomacy a lack of attention to the great bulk of administrative detail remained in some people's estimate a weak point in his many accomplishments.

As a young man Cavour had been criticized by his father for being too much attached to theory, but the exercise of administration made him more and more a pragmatist and opportunist who boasted of his lack of system and was always on the alert to take an alternative path if it seemed more expedient. Rattazzi said of him that he perhaps never conceived any great long-term project but was concerned rather with living from day to day, and indeed one of his stronger qualities was the adaptability needed to make the best of circumstances not of his own choosing. As Hudson remarked at a crucial moment in 1860, 'he has no plan: he is a waiter upon providence and the chapter of accidents.'

His writings and speeches abound in remarks that show this pragmatism to have been consciously adopted as an absolutely cardinal political principle. He used to say that in politics there were no universal laws and hence one should disregard 'absolute ideas and preconceived schemes'. The chief skill of any politician was, in his view, to know what was feasible, in other words how if necessary to make the best of a bad job. He once referred to this as *le tact des choses possibles*, which made it imperative to avoid that most damaging of all criticisms – the accusation of being utopian or doctrinaire. History, he used to say, 'is a great improviser'. Often one might have to rest content with possessing no long-term aim; the best to hope for might be that what he called some accident or 'hopeful chance' might indicate how to circumvent an immediate difficulty and so take a problem one stage further towards a solution; because 'the world must be accepted as one finds it and not as one might wish it to be'.

Highly intelligent though he was, Cavour could not be called a conventional intellectual and his interests outside politics and economics remained fairly limited. He pointed out to the French diplomat d'Ideville that he possessed no pictures in his apartment because he had still not developed any affection for art, and he once told Rattazzi that all poetry was insipid frivolity. People were nevertheless surprised to hear him say that he kept abreast of the latest novels from England and France, and to the end of his life he read the London *Times*, and *Morning Post*, and especially the *Economist*. Rémusat, another French visitor, noted in 1860 that he seemed to have no interest at all in philosophy or literature, and 'as with Englishmen his conversation never rises much above practical matters and political economy.' In this latter field he once declared that he thought John Stuart Mill to be the leading contemporary authority. In July 1858 an English railway engineer found him reading Macaulay's *History of England* and heard him call it 'as exciting as a champagne breakfast'. The following month he finished the first volume of Buckle's *History of Civilisation in England*.

The debates in Parliament were his chief intellectual stimulus, and during sessions he generally devoted four hours a day to one or both houses. While discussion was in progress he usually affected to be paying no attention – a fact which greatly annoyed some opponents – but he missed nothing and was prepared to intervene at almost any moment on almost any subject. His use of the Italian language still caused offence, especially to the purist Tuscans, but he was sufficiently proficient to be able to avoid reading his speeches and liked to use notes only when a debate required statistical evidence. In later years he sometimes tested the effect of a major speech by practising it first on his secretary Artom. He used to explain his unusual ability in the presentation of a theme by recalling that as a young man he had learnt to keep a long series of difficult theorems in his head and 'arrange them mentally in order of battle.' He took special care over preparing the conclusion of a speech so as to leave a striking image on the minds and imagination of his listeners. Though he lacked eloquence and his delivery remained stilted and awkward, he retained his early reputation of being the most logical speaker in Parliament.

Sometimes he confessed that his irrepressible love of controversy and struggle might be a defect, but had to admit that no achievement had much attraction for him unless obliged 'to fight and win it at the point of my sword'. He used to say that he took a genuine pleasure in difficult situations and always welcomed opposition, because 'without struggle there is no life and no progress'; but what he chiefly liked was not so much fighting as winning. Although he said he positively needed the challenge of clerical and republican opponents and was sure that they would be less dangerous inside than outside Parliament, nevertheless the election of 1857 showed that in practice he went to some lengths to exclude them and to act illegally in muzzling their newspapers. Preferably he wanted just enough parliamentary opposition to prevent his broad coalition from dissolving; anything larger might develop into a possible alternative government, and that was something he did his best to avoid by slightly shifting the centre of gravity of his coalition to right or left in conformity with the movement of public opinion.

Cavour sometimes said that he disliked the exercise of power and was eager to return to private life, but few people believed him. On the contrary, he was not infrequently attacked for going out of his way to concentrate too much power in his own hands. In his early days as a minister he admitted that a single executive department took so much of his attention that he lacked the time to carry out all the changes he would have liked, but with experience he became more self-confident; he also learnt that it might be politically advantageous to direct two or three ministries simultaneously in addition to his position as Premier. The justification he gave for this pluralism was that, by so doing, he would avoid unbalancing the equilibrium of the governmental coalition; but critics said that he was merely trying to monopolize power and avoid being outvoted or challenged inside his own Cabinet.

The other ministers were in any case treated as junior assistants rather than full collaborators, and John Daniel was not alone in reporting that they were all 'insignificant men who are in fact nothing but his secretaries'. Important information was concealed from them, and regularly they were told of decisions only after the event. The war against Russia in 1855 was imposed on Cavour's unwilling colleagues at the last moment, and during the peace congress of 1856 he ordered that crucial despatches should not be shown to them. Nor did he ask their approval or even inform most of them before going to the vital meeting at Plombières in 1858. In January 1859 he single-handedly negotiated the treaty with France, and in July resigned without seeing any need to consult with anyone.

This attitude of self-sufficiency and almost of condescension explains why he found such difficulty in belonging to the same Cabinet as the other leading Liberal politicians of the *risorgimento*. It is a significant fact that he broke in turn with Balbo, Azeglio, San Martino, Rattazzi, Lamarmora and Ricasoli, all of whom were politically close to him and shared perhaps most of his views, but all of whom came to regard him with considerable suspicion and impatience.

Cavour once said that he would repudiate any national movement that was not also liberal, but his definition of liberalism permitted a policy of forcing people to be free, and de la Rive reached the point of wondering whether his notion of liberty was more an expedient than an ideal concept. Agostino Depretis (himself a future Prime Minister of Italy) went so far as to say that an insufficiently liberal policy at home made it hard to accept that the government's foreign policy could be sufficiently Italian and patriotic. As a realist, Cavour did not quarrel with the fact that, to use his own words, 'national sentiment in Italy is stronger than a feeling for liberty', and he might have added that the great mass of the population had very little interest in either patriotism or liberalism. His great achievement was to triumph over such unpromising facts and, despite national wars, civil wars and violent conflict with the Church, to develop and extend constitutional practice.

His own variety of liberal pragmatism was far from clear-cut and by no means universally understood and approved. He himself confessed to being 'less liberal than the Americans': and the French ambassador, de Guiche, was able to report from Turin that the outward vestiges of constitutional government were in part 'an agreeable illusion' to cover a reality of uncontrolled personal authority. Likewise, both the English and American ambassadors were sometimes worried that the Piedmontese, in the process of pursuing their patriotic goal, would require an increasing concentration of powers that might put their domestic liberties at risk. But it was also an important truth that Cavour continued to derive his great authority from the explicit or tacit consent of Parliament. Without parliamentary support he would have been powerless against the revolutionaries, the extreme monarchists or the Catholic establishment.

Among his supporters there were some who, intending it as a flattering judgement, likened him to Cromwell – another man who, while theoretically condemning dictatorship, accepted and indeed welcomed the exercise of dictatorial powers. Cavour himself told de la Rive that Cromwell 'possessed in the highest degree the genius of government'. But while some admirers were delighted by the comparison between these two men, others made it a matter for lament. Deputies grumbled that they were increasingly treated as children or automatons whose views were taken for granted, and the Tuscan lawyer Menichetti heard Cavour say that members of Parliament could be illiterate for all he cared, so long as they attended sessions and voted whichever way they were told.

From the sparse ranks of the radical opposition, the brilliant but erratic Brofferio never tired of lampooning the disciplined ranks of the parliamentary *claque* who shouted in unison whenever derision or applause was officially indicated. Moreover, the Prime Minister's cynicism in such a matter was sometimes taken for granted, and in contemporary cartoons he was shown distributing titles and decorations by the sackful as a reward for political services. He himself affected an aristocratic disdain for the 'baubles' and gaudy uniforms which he sometimes had to wear, and once said in sardonic jest that there ought to be a law conferring on everyone the insignia of a *cavaliere*, exempting only those who had a genuine claim to honour and distinction.

Other critics pursued the argument that constitutional government was endangered by the lack of a clear separation of powers: they said that only if there existed a balanced allocation of responsibility between *camera*, senate, Cabinet, monarchy, magistracy and bureaucracy, could there be an adequate brake or corrective on the supreme authority of one man who virtually embodied executive and legislature in his own person. But to complain that Parliament had no individual initiative of its own was too sophisticated a view for the majority. Massari perhaps spoke for most members of the lower house when he called Cavour 'a necessary man' whose practical 'dictatorship' was something glorious for the State. Such a view was based on the argument that a deeply divided society in an emergent nation required single-party rule, at all events so long as the second largest political group had insufficient interest in either parliamentary government or national liberation.

Some of those who believed this, including Massari himself, agreed that what might be necessary might also be very dangerous; and the potential dangers became more obvious after Cavour's death. Even those who did not blame him for the absence of a 'loyal opposition' could nevertheless deplore the fact that by 1860 there still existed no other group which, while sharing his belief in constitutional government, was also strong enough to challenge his administration or criticize the methods he chose to adopt; and some argued that in the heat of the moment Cavour went to excessive lengths in obstructing the genesis of such an oppositon. According to Lamarmora, parties had virtually ceased to exist; or at least the only serious divisions were over mere trivialities or 'personal questions'.

One perceptive and moderate critic, Francesco De Sanctis, served briefly as a minister under Cavour and was one of the more judicious of contemporary political theorists. De Sanctis did not believe in any simplistic notion of a two-party system, but pointed out the inherent disadvantages of a centre coalition to which there was no alternative and hence no adequate check. He also pointed out that this centre coalition, for the very reason that it included people with quite strikingly different opinions on many issues, was moved by an instinct of self-preservation to shy away from discussion of questions on which there was internal disagreement: and these questions, almost by definition, were among the most important of all. Another criticism by De Sanctis was that Cavour became excessively authoritarian in order to conceal errors and cover arbitrary actions – something that might be necessary in an emergency but was inexcusable as a norm. One example was the lack of generosity shown towards Mazzini and Garibaldi, to whom De Sanctis thought that Italians probably owed as much as they did to Cavour.

One unfair criticism was that the Prime Minister remained essentially 'Don Camillo', the titled aristocrat who had not yet succeeded in throwing off the class allegiance and conservative label that had once made him unpopular. As late as November 1857 another cartoon in the satirical paper *Fischietto* showed him still with an attenuated *codino* or pigtail, suggesting that in the eyes of the public he had not entirely cut himself off from the reactionaries. But although he had once believed that aristocrats were inherently superior to the middle ranks of society, in time he changed sufficiently to be sometimes called, as in his youth a traitor to his own class. Experience of government, on top of the lessons he had learnt in Switzerland and England, taught him that 'an irresistible force is driving all classes towards equality'; and in his idealized liberal society, along with protection for minority rights, 'the interests of the majority must ultimately prevail'.

Of course he could not escape from the fact that society in Turin remained essentially aristocratic, nor from the fact that some elements in that society possessed only a qualified loyalty to the constitution of 1848. Cavour complained that few younger aristocrats showed much interest in entering active politics, and yet the elections of 1857 proved that some of them were learning the desirability of standing for Parliament. Although many of these nobles remained opposed to his ecclesiastical policy and some were slow to accept the idea of Italian patriotism, their presence in the *camera* was an indication that former social barriers were beginning to break down. The process none the less had a long way to go. Both Costantino Nigra and Giuseppe Massari, two of his closest aides, were still complaining in 1860 that whereas in Paris and Milan all doors would be open to them despite their status as commoners, in Turin they were rigidly excluded from fashionable society.

This degree of class distinction did not greatly trouble Cavour, and when in 1860 the French embassy asked him about the propriety of inviting his favourite colleague Nigra to dinner, he discouraged them as though it would be a social solecism. He confirmed to Massari in 1860 that he was far from favouring the 'democratic principle'; and another friend who saw him often in his last years, the Swiss Abraham Tourte, thought that to the end he remained 'more aristocratic than liberal'. Unable to deny his own past, he continued to employ the familiar mode of speech only when addressing other aristocrats – whereas to Castelli, Massari and Nigra he used *Lei* or *vous* instead of *tu*, and the very cordial letters he regularly wrote to his partner at Leri, Corio, kept to the strictly formal level of *Pregiatissimo Signore*. Since 1848 he had increasingly dropped the full signature *Camille de Cavour*, omitting the aristocratic *de*, but to some of his most friendly correspondents he retained the old form: the distinction related not to the degree of friendliness but to their social rank.

In the last year of his life, Cavour's 'extreme simplicity of manner' and his sense of 'frolic and fun' were still noted by Sir Henry Layard, but for someone so sociable and of such an affable and amiable disposition it is interesting that he also earned the reputation of always stopping short of real intimacy. It remained true that he did not easily make irreconcilable enemies, and he at least attempted to keep on personally friendly terms with opponents who were not greatly to be feared, for example Brofferio and the clerical newspaper editor Don Margotti. But often he could be unexpectedly harsh even to friends, and in moments of excitability was prone to make brutally sarcastic and truculent remarks that were hard to forgive.

A number of close acquaintances were surprised to observe from time to time this sudden almost inexplicable change in his affections. Deputies on the left complained in later years that he no longer came over to their benches in the *camera* for a friendly talk as he had done when he needed their support, and what was almost worse, no longer stayed to listen to their speeches. With the easy-going Azeglio he was for some years barely on speaking terms. Salmour, Lanza and Farini – all of them his friends – were upset when he suddenly seemed to have no further use for them. To his closest ministerial colleagues, Rattazzi and Lamarmora, he latterly became positively and almost unforgivably offensive. Even Castelli, who some thought to be closest to him of all, complained of being thrown away like a squeezed orange when no longer needed, and others employed exactly the same metaphor on other occasions.

Cavour justified such behaviour, explaining that when politics required a change, one's best friend might have to be sacrificed. Others gave a less charitable interpretation, maintaining that he could not abide potential rivals or subordinates who questioned orders and offered unsolicited advice. Often the complaint was made that he was not a good chooser of men, and kept to a narrow circle of un-distinguished assistants whom he chose because they would do what they were told. One obvious example was that he kept the Marquis di Villamarina for eight years in the Paris embassy, perhaps the most important diplomatic post of all, though this man was someone he himself called a complete incompetent. Villamarina's successor, Nigra, was a much more effective diplomat, but it is interesting that Cavour's confidence in him began to change when the younger man showed signs of wanting to act on his own initiative.

* * *

Another persistent criticism described Cavour as a man of deceit and intrigue who had no qualms about believing that a good end justified immoral means. He sometimes told people that this accusation caused him much amusement since in his own estimation he was far less *rusé* than others imagined. Far from wanting to be artful, he liked to explain his conviction that on the contrary one needed complete frankness in politics; also that political immorality was wrong, if for no other reason than that it was ineffective because it would damage a politician's credibility. He tried to insist that his own conduct was invariably sincere and open, his word being his bond, and indeed that duplicity and double-talk were abhorrent. Sometimes he condemned others for political immorality – for instance he did this of both Rattazzi and Malmesbury – but he succeeded in convincing Massari, who saw him almost every day, that he himself would never stoop to using immoral means, no matter how worthy the end.

He was protesting too much, and perhaps the main interest of the accusations of immorality is that he was so anxious to refute them. His true beliefs were perhaps those found in his youthful diary where he accepted as inevitable that all those who aspire to political power must be to some extent corrupt. In his early essay on Ireland, too, he was at pains to demonstrate that the dishonest methods employed by his great hero Pitt were sanctioned by public opinion which knew the difference between private and public morals. Again, speaking and writing in 1848, Cavour made it quite clear that he saw little place for philanthropy or gratitude in politics; on the contrary, the use of odious methods might be necessary and in that case they should be exercised without any restraint, since success was the one vital criterion and improper means were justifiable if they succeeded, but not otherwise.

The real test of his behaviour came when, as Prime Minister, he could take obvious pleasure in deceiving others, while being righteously indignant against the unprincipled conduct of those who paid him back in the same coin. The French desertion at Villafranca he called an outrageous breach of promise, whereas he never conceded that this armistice might have been caused in part by broken promises of his own. English politicians were called iniquitous for claiming to be liberal at the same time as they allied with absolutist Austria, but in April 1858 he told Parliament that the same judgement did not apply to the alliance of liberal Piedmont with absolutist Russia. Likewise he expressed horror when the Vatican tried to discredit him by leaking confidential information, though he himself was skilled at betraying confidences that he had promised to keep secret. Piedmontese ambassadors in foreign capitals were sometimes expected by him to give covert encouragement to local revolutionary groups, and when others reproached him for such double standards he privately admitted to a lack of scruple in matters of conscience so long as the political gains were sufficient.

Despite Cavour's public protestations about his own candour and honesty, a well-known southern journalist, Petruccelli della Gattina, described him as 'a cross between Sir Robert Peel and Machiavelli', and the remark was perhaps intended ambiguously as both praise and blame. The faithful Castelli more than once tried to discover how justified was his reputation as a cunning intriguer, and confronted Cavour with examples of apparent mendacity; to which the latter replied with a jocular admission that of course he had been deceitful – and even confessed that it was his practice 'never to put into public statements what I am thinking in private'. To Azeglio, Cavour went so far as to admit that 'if we did for ourselves what we are doing for Italy we should be real scoundrels'.

Azeglio's objection to this was partly on grounds of abstract morality, but also because such conduct was likely to produce the reverse effect of that intended. Using almost the same words employed by the radical Brofferio, the conservative Azeglio commented that 'disloyalty, lies, corruption and sleight of hand are no way to make a nation, nor indeed to make anything worth while'; and the sad conclusion he drew was that 'no one any longer takes Cavour's pledged word seriously, because people have learnt to believe almost automatically the very opposite of whatever he says.' Daniel similarly criticized him for being an 'arch-intriguer'; Tourte liked him immensely but would never take his words at their face value; and one French minister, Baron de Talleyrand, remarked after a long talk that Cavour's 'genius for intrigue is of quite heroic proportions'.

This reputation became a serious handicap only in the years 1860–61. Not only the French, but the English government – whose support was equally crucial in these last two years of his life – came to think him thoroughly untrustworthy however much they wanted to further the

Italian cause. Likewise, the Swedish envoy in Turin, despite strong sympathy with the *risorgimento*, was antagonized by what appeared to be dishonesty if not sharp practice. These were his friends. His enemies were more numerous and much more outspokenly critical. But in the course of 1860 he confounded all of them, friend and foe.

CHAPTER 18

Central Italy
January – April 1860

On 20 January 1860, Cavour returned as Prime Minister for what would be the last eighteen months of his life. He was simultaneously Foreign Minister, and for a while also kept the Ministry of the Interior so that he could supervise and influence the parliamentary elections to be held in March. The general policy of his new government was summarized as being one of conservative liberalism in domestic matters and, in foreign affairs, moving as fast as might be possible towards the liberation of Italy from Austrian dominance.

One great advantage was that a few days before his appointment, the English government had made a strong appeal for other countries to observe an attitude of non-intervention and leave Italians free to decide their future for themselves. This appeal, together with the greater friendliness of France after Walewski was succeeded by Thouvenel in the French Foreign Office, made Cavour think that 'in the not too distant future' a union of all Italy from the Alps to Sicily might at last be within the reach of possibility. The first step in this process had been completed when in November 1859 the annexation of Lombardy was confirmed by the Treaty of Zürich. The next logical move would be the annexation of the smaller central Italian duchies, and this was something that was already accepted in principle by the French and English governments before he returned to office. The main problem was Napoleon's attempt to stipulate once again that Savoy and Nice should in that case be given to France.

Cavour had offered a year earlier to cede both these regions and only the premature armistice of Villafranca saved them. In January 1860 there were those who thought that central Italy could still be annexed without the obligation to renew this earlier offer. The English government believed that the cession was unnecessary and feared that giving France such an extension of territory – including the internationally neutralized zones of northern Savoy – might upset the European balance of power. Lamarmora and Rattazzi therefore resisted French pressure before Cavour returned to power, and continued to maintain that to surrender the undoubtedly Italian territory of Nice would be dishonourable. There was also a very real danger that if France controlled the Alpine passes close to Turin, Piedmont would be left militarily vulnerable and politically dependent on her powerful neighbour.

When Cavour reviewed the matter he came to the conclusion that although he might be able to acquire Tuscany and the Romagna without making territorial concessions, it was wiser to play safe and purchase the active complicity of France. He accordingly let the French know that he would allow the cession of Savoy – the 'Ireland of Italy' he called it in some distaste when talking to visitors from England – and perhaps that of Nice; but this must be conditional on a clear vote of approval by the population of these two areas, and only as part of an agreed package that let him annex Modena, Parma, the Romagna and also Tuscany. For the next six weeks there followed complicated negotiations on this last point because Napoleon hoped to exclude Tuscany from the bargain: the Emperor wanted to avoid having too strong an Italy on his southern flank or anything that resembled Italian unification, which he denounced as the policy of his hated and feared enemy Mazzini.

What Cavour did not say was that he had another secret project to bring pressure on the Pope to surrender not merely the Romagna but also Umbria and the Marche. A message was sent to Rome suggesting an expedient by which Victor Emanuel might govern these regions as a papal vicar under the Pope's purely nominal sovereignty, leaving only the immediate area round the city of Rome under direct papal control. The reaction of Pius ix was that to renounce his divinely ordained sovereignty in favour of a secular state would be sacrilege, especially since Piedmontese anticlerical legislation would presumably be extended to an area which for centuries had formed an integral part of the Church's patrimony. The King was reminded by the Vatican that he was still under a papal ban and that to proceed further with this plan would automatically involve him in the penalties of another major excommunication.

Victor Emanuel was far from eager to face that prospect, especially as the other Catholic powers would almost certainly side with the Pope; nor was he enthusiastic about giving up his family's ancestral domain of Savoy; and he was in no doubt that the surrender of Nice would infuriate most Italian patriots. Cavour was thus courageously challenging a powerful but disparate opposition ranging from the monarchy and the papacy to the patriots. His policy was also bound to cause trouble in England where it would be taken as evidence that the French intended to round off their 'natural frontiers' not only in Savoy but also in Belgium and Luxembourg: a French occupation of Antwerp would certainly precipitate another European war. On the other hand Cavour did not want to antagonize his patron in France, at least not yet; and since he was intending to base his claim to central Italy on the results of a popular vote, it might be thought illogical if he refused the same right of self-determination to the inhabitants of Savoy and Nice.

In this finely balanced predicament, he had to feel his way and cover his tracks as he decided what alternatives were available and whose friendship would be most valuable. When communicating with foreigners he invented an absurd story that the King had tied his hands by having already committed Piedmont to surrendering Nice and Savoy. He continued to deny the existence of his own secret treaty of the previous year with France in which he had himself accepted this surrender, perhaps unaware that Napoleon had already told the English government about it. In precise statements to the Prussian and English ambassadors he protested that he would never cede an inch of national territory, and in particular promised that he would regard an exchange of Savoy for Tuscany as contemptible.

These various attempts at deceit were a gamble that could hardly succeed. He was still liked – even admired – in England, where there was support for his annexation of all central Italy, but recent events had rekindled a belief that he could not be believed. By now he was known to be secretly intending to give up Savoy, despite his denials and despite the treaty settlement of 1815 to which Britain was a party. He was increasingly seen by politicians in London as a pliant auxiliary of French imperialism, and hence might be not merely untrustworthy but a potential and dangerous enemy to the cause of peace.

During February he became increasingly desperate as he found himself enmeshed in a brave but intricate policy of deception. He pretended to a number of foreign diplomats that Piedmont, if necessary alone, might have to renew the war against Austria, and he gave the not entirely plausible reason that it would be more honourable to go down fighting than renounce his plan to annex Tuscany. Several contingents of the army were mobilized and he ordered large calibre artillery from Sweden and Belgium. Once again he talked of marching on Vienna, which astonished those in his entourage who remembered how near Austria had been to capturing Turin in April 1859. To the Swiss he offered the inducement that they could annex Austrian territory in the Vorarlberg if they agreed to take part. Even more incredible was that on 10 February, he asked the Prussian government if it would be ready to join him in a war against Austria, or alternatively in a quite different war against France. A few days later, nevertheless, he was telling Napoleon that he was prepared to fight alongside the French against Prussia, and specifically offered military help in winning for France a frontier on the Rhine.

These astonishingly belligerent proposals are impossible to interpret as part of a coherent policy, unless they were designed to keep up a general state of alarm and divert attention from Cavour's immediate ambitions in Tuscany. He was trying to persuade Ricasoli, the Governor of Tuscany, to arrange a second vote which he could present to other countries as conclusive proof that the Tuscans wanted to join Piedmont. Preferably this vote would be by an assembly summoned on a limited franchise. He was hoping if possible to avoid a popular plebiscite, in the first place because a democratic vote might give the wrong answer, but also because it might one day be invoked against him as a precedent by political enemies with greater mass appeal, whether they were clericals, republicans or federalists.

On the other hand Napoleon had come to supreme power in France by means of a plebiscite, and had shown how easily a popular vote could be manipulated to give the required result. Furthermore, the Emperor could hardly reject in Tuscany a procedure on which he based his own authority at home. A plebiscite by 'universal suffrage' could also be used to invalidate the criticism of those who were arguing that only the upper classes or *signori* in Italy were patriots, while the masses were indifferent or hostile. In normal circumstances, Cavour would have preferred a vote on a narrowly restricted franchise to elect an assembly representing owners of property, but on this occasion he had to recognize that an appeal to popular sovereignty might for these various reasons be more expedient.

Plebiscites were duly held in Emilia and Tuscany on 11–12 March. Cavour took care to promise the voters beforehand that annexation would not mean the end of local autonomy, and he specified that each region of Italy would retain all its former independent powers except in the fields of finance, foreign policy and military affairs. This promise must have helped to sway the vote, though he later changed his mind and had to agree that regional autonomy would be wrong. In any case he treated the results of the vote as a foregone conclusion, even arranging ahead of time for deputies from central Italy to be summoned to the Turin Parliament. A month before the plebiscite a new coinage was circulating at Bologna carrying Victor Emanuel's head, and examples were proudly demonstrated at Turin to any interested visitor.

He was right not to worry because both plebiscites almost unanimously opted to join Piedmont and Lombardy. The voting was well organized, in Tuscany by Baron Ricasoli and in Emilia by Dr Farini. One observer from England watched the vote at Pisa and called it an 'absurd farce'. Nevertheless, the intention was not so much to discover the will of the people as to demonstrate an overwhelming and incontrovertible majority. Landowners were instructed to march their peasants to the polling booths with bands playing and flags flying. Free wine was distributed. Voting was public, and no one was greatly worried if in some areas there were more votes for annexation than there were names on the electoral lists, or indeed if in some districts no opposition propaganda was permitted and no one dared to register a single contrary vote.

The result gave considerable satisfaction in London, partly because there had been some doubt which way the vote would go, but also because it was hoped that after so convincing a victory there would no longer be any need for an exchange of territory with France. Palmerston welcomed the birth of a new nation that was strong and free, and publicly expressed the wish that 'Italy may a third time rise to the eminence in the civilized world which she occupied in the days of the Roman Emperors'.

What partially marred the results for Cavour was the austere and unyielding character of Ricasoli. This future Prime Minister of Italy was far from having Farini's pliable and subordinate personality; on the contrary he was one of the few liberals who dared to stand up to the Turin government and assert ideas of his own. Massari described more than one occasion in the following week when Cavour was distraught and beside himself with anger over such a claim to independence. Ricasoli's recalcitrance eventually led to the realization that, despite governmental promises about the preservation of Tuscan autonomy, Italy could not afford rival policies or an alternative source of power.

Another difficulty was that the Pope issued a bull of excommunication against all who had advised or even accepted the plebiscite in the Romagna. As on previous occasions, no one was mentioned by name, but both King and Prime Minister were deemed henceforward to be outside the faith. This made their task harder, but it was too late for compromise and neither side was prepared to give ground. The anticlerical laws of Piedmont were imposed on the Romagna, and bishops who refused to cooperate suffered imprisonment. Cavour condemned the 'excessive' religiosity of those who continued to believe in the Pope's temporal power, and spoke scornfully of the 'rule by priests which is perhaps as damaging for Italy as the Austrian dominion over Venice'.

The French government was unhappy over this breach with the Church and even more unhappy that the plebiscites took place before any binding promise had been made to surrender Savoy. But Cavour precisely judged the necessity to move fast and with a minimum of consultation or publicity. Though he was fairly sure that most Savoyards would want to join France, he told a number of people that Nice was essentially Italian and, even more important, that its population would vote clearly in this sense. He was still firmly of this opinion as late as 7 March, but the following day Napoleon, fearing to be outmanoeuvred again, wrote to insist that the sacrifice of Nice must be determined in principle and irrevocably before France could agree to sanction any changes in central Italy.

On 12 March, Cavour therefore had to sign another secret agreement pledging himself to give up Nice as well as Savoy. Because they did not trust him, the French insisted that he must sign before the matter could be brought before Parliament in Turin, though he pointed out that his signature would be an unconstitutional and even treasonous act. But he bravely took responsibility for what could not be avoided, and said that he would make Parliament agree retrospectively so long as this compromising document could be kept secret.

It was a sad decision to take. He still secretly hinted that he would like help from London in keeping Nice, and some of the Italophile population in this province asked the British for money to compete with the lavish expenditure by the French government in buying votes. Fearing, however, that if the vote in Nice went against the French they would become a dangerous enemy, he finally gave way and ordered local authorities in Nice to secure a vote favouring secession. For a few days this unwelcome necessity made him feel physically unwell and Castelli discovered him in a state of angry confusion. In public he now had to argue, against all he had said in the past, that this town was not Italian and never had been; only in private did he confess that he was speaking against his true convictions.

On 21 March the French tried to commit him still further by warning him that they intended to publish the terms of their joint agreement, to which he replied that it must be altered before publication so as to disguise the fact that he had pledged away a large area of the kingdom without constitutional authority. Napoleon then insisted, in order to make doubly sure, that French troops should be present in Nice and Savoy when the plebiscite was held, and Cavour persuaded a reluctant Cabinet to agree to this humiliating demand on the understanding that no record of their agreement remained in the archives. One minister registered a protest that the presence of French soldiers would show the whole of Europe how unfree was the vote. General Fanti, the Minister of War, repeated that Nice was clearly Italian by nationality and ought to remain so, quite apart from the fact that it was strategically necessary for the country's defence. Outside the Cabinet, Rattazzi and Ricasoli said the same, and the King was reinforced by their criticisms in his belief that Cavour was giving away more than necessary.

At the end of March the parliamentary elections were held – a few hours before the decision to cede Savoy became public knowledge. This timing must have helped to make the results a great victory for what Daniel now called 'the Cavour party'. The Prime Minister personally won in eight different electoral colleges, and almost no one on the extreme right was elected – not Solaro della Margherita, nor even the more moderate Revel. On the left, Brofferio, the tribune of the plebs, lost his seat. Garibaldi was elected in his home town of Nice despite strong governmental pressure, and in Lombardy so were Cattaneo and

Ferrari, the two leading champions of federalism. Supporters of the government had campaigned fiercely against anyone who wanted a federal Italy or who put the development of internal liberties above the need to create a strong centralized state: according to La Farina who was Cavour's chief campaign manager, even the abominated but 'unitarist' Mazzini was preferable to Cattaneo, but some constituencies evidently disagreed.

There was another irritating setback when the *camera*, after the news about surrendering Savoy and Nice became known, put up a fight against the election of Giovanni Lanza who was the Government's choice for Speaker. The majority of Piedmontese deputies would have preferred to choose the most prominent figure on the opposition benches, Rattazzi, to defeat whom Cavour had to rely on representatives of the newly annexed provinces in the centre. Only with some sleight of hand over procedural technicalities did he then succeed in staving off Garibaldi's urgent request for a full-scale debate over Nice. Parliamentary consent would be required eventually, but he needed to wait until after the plebiscites had taken place, because Parliament would then have little option but to endorse the overwhelming popular vote that he was determined to secure.

Nevertheless many critical voices were raised over what was happening. Some people quoted statements he had once made against the alienation of national territory; others quoted his promise about never treating Parliament as a rubber stamp; and another criticism denounced the improper use of government pressure on voters in the plebiscites, because an obviously selective censorship was being imposed on local newspapers that opposed cession. Rattazzi contended that surrendering the Italian region of Nice was a negation of the very principle of nationality on which the *risorgimento* was based, and others supported Fanti's contention that with France in command of the Alps, the country would be militarily indefensible. A further argument was simply that the cession was unnecessary, since even without it France could not at this late stage have prevented Piedmontese annexation of Tuscany.

The most damaging criticism was that the results of the plebiscite were patently fraudulent. The vote was taken in the presence of French soldiers after the Piedmontese authorities had virtually withdrawn, despite Cavour's promise that he would not permit this. In many districts there were no tickets available for voting 'no', though a determined voter could without difficulty procure many 'yes' tickets to place in the urns; consequently some areas showed more than a hundred per cent of the registered voters opting for France, and in only five of the eighty villages round Nice were any negative votes recorded. Cavour may have been correct in thinking that most people in Savoy genuinely wanted to be French, but some doubts remained, and one neutral observer present during the vote told Nassau William Senior that he estimated ninety-five per cent were privately in favour of remaining Italian.

Cavour was embarrassed when replying to the many objections to what he was doing. In guarded phrases he had to say that the cession, however unwelcome, was demanded by France as a condition for the annexation of central Italy, and he furthermore tried to maintain that he had in no sense acted unconstitutionally – though this was the opposite of what he confessed in private. When asked to permit a parliamentary commission to be present to supervize the freedom of the plebiscite, he had to refuse because Napoleon would not have allowed it. He could not tell the deputies that he had privately made the strongest protests to the Emperor about the way the affair was being handled; nor did they know that he was sufficiently disconcerted to be almost on the point of resignation.

With his fairly safe majority, Cavour could lose the argument and still win the vote in Parliament. Nevertheless his reputation as diplomat and parliamentarian was damaged when eventually the surrender of Nice and Savoy came before the *camera* for final confirmation. Hudson reported after the debate that the Prime Minister had 'rendered himself odious to a very large proportion of the deputies'. Daniel thought that public opinion had turned against him. By causing a final breach with Rattazzi and Garibaldi, the patriotic front was radically divided at a moment when unity was needed more than ever before. Some among Cavour's admirers had to agree that his negotiating skills and political resourcefulness had not been shown at their best.

Possibly he never fully appreciated how much damage was done by disingenuousness and occasional mendacity to the reputation for being high-principled and honourable which he had sought in other countries. Nor did he realize how much the Swiss would resent his disregard of their special treaty rights in neutralized Savoy. The permanent neutrality of northern Savoy had been guaranteed by the powers of Europe in 1815, and Cavour admitted that since Piedmont had obligations to those guarantors and especially to the Swiss, he had a duty to make certain that the rights of others were not impaired if sovereignty was surrendered. Nevertheless he failed to ensure that the French took over these obligations, and did not seem much worried by the fact; indeed he said he was surprised that the Swiss were so upset. His friend de la Rive called this a cynical disregard of a weak country, Switzerland, and a regrettable obsequiousness to the strong empire of France.

What critics called cynicism and obsequiousness, Cavour considered a matter of straightforward expediency, and in making such a calculation he could no longer afford half-measures. He now persuaded Parliament to approve the Treaty of Zürich with its bizarre acceptance of 'peace and perpetual friendship' with Austria; but in private told people that he still had every intention of launching war against the Austrians to win Venice. So long as this national enemy held Venetia, he knew that Piedmont would not be able to return to playing the balance of power and alternating between a French and Austrian alliance. Such an alternation had been highly profitable in the past and might be again in the future. Though he would require French help to obtain Venice, he already foresaw the day when he would seek an Austrian alliance to fight against France.

The sheer virtuosity of his political imagination was never shown more vividly or fancifully than when he speculated in this way about possible contingencies in the future. He was already weighing up the chances of one day joining a European coalition against France that might provide an opportunity for regaining Nice and Savoy. Alternatively, events might bring France and England together, in which case a different kind of war might ensue from which England would acquire Egypt while France took Belgium, leaving Italy to occupy Venice. Napoleon let him know that a project was under active consideration in Paris for pushing the French frontier to Antwerp and Mainz; after this news, Cavour told his colleagues that he intended to have three hundred thousand Italian soldiers ready for such an eventuality. He would in that case be able to engineer what he had vaguely hoped for in the Crimean war: the Slavs would revolt, backed by Russia; the Hungarians and Roumanians would revolt against Vienna; the two empires of Austria and Turkey would crumble; and an enlarged Kingdom of Italy would be created as the by-product of a general holocaust.

CHAPTER 19

Sicily
April – July 1860

What occurred in practice was something less grandiose: not a continental revolution, nor even a war to acquire Venice, but a miniature revolution in Sicily that Cavour would have preferred to avoid. From his distant exile in London, Mazzini had been looking hopefully to southern Italy and especially Sicily, seeing this as the most likely place for a truly popular initiative to prove to the outside world that Italians could act for themselves without having to depend on foreign assistance or manipulating the balance of power. Here were two personalities and two policies in confrontation. Mazzini distrusted Cavour as too subservient to imperial France and too much opposed to popular movements of any kind; Cavour looked on Mazzini as a republican and social revolutionary, indeed as 'the greatest enemy of Italy' and someone whose alliance the government would have to repudiate whenever it was offered.

Victor Emanuel, on the other hand, was not in principle averse to allying with republicans if that turned out to be the way to achieve a strong and united nation; and the monarch used to say, perhaps seriously, that he was ready to step down from the throne and become the loyal citizen of a united Italian republic. In March 1860, Mazzini likewise confirmed once again that he would accept the monarchy if such a régime was the general wish and if it proved to be the best way to unite the nation; his immediate proposal was that a revolution in Sicily might be the next step towards the political unification of Italy.

This offer received scant attention in government circles in Turin where Mazzini had a justified reputation for hare-brained schemes that invariably seemed to fail. Cavour was in any case determined to minimize the element of popular revolution, and saw the *risorgimento* as something that so far as possible should be imposed and controlled from above. His own preference was for concentrating on northern and central Italy, leaving Naples and Sicily for a future generation to sort out. Indeed, any revolution in the south would weaken his diplomatic position. He knew that the French had been planning to withdraw the troops they had kept in Rome since 1849; such a withdrawal would leave Piedmont with an unchallengeable authority over most of central Italy, but it would hardly happen if a revolution in southern Italy put the Pope's security at risk. Only at the end of March, when rumours of a Sicilian rising began to circulate, did he realize that he might become involved and be forced to intervene 'in the name of order and authority'.

A small and disorganized revolution broke out early in April at Palermo. To all appearances it was under Mazzini's direct inspiration, and for the next month conflicting reports made its success or failure impossible to predict. Garibaldi asked the King for a brigade of regular soldiers that he could take to Sicily in support of the insurgents, but Cavour could not tolerate such a move and to counteract it invited General Ribotti to resign from the Piedmontese army and lead a very different kind of expedition which the government would supervise and provide with arms. Nothing came of either proposal because they were both far too dangerous an involvement for the government. Instead a note was sent to King Francesco on 15 April, urging him to grant a constitution in Sicily and Naples. Cavour pointed out in this note that the Bourbon sovereign, who was Victor Emanuel's cousin, could in that way block the revolution and obtain the requisite credentials to join Piedmont in a dual dominion over Italy.

The following day, the Piedmontese Prime Minister arrived in Florence with a hundred members of Parliament to celebrate the annexation of Tuscany. He had never before been so far south. On the journey he was quite unexpectedly attacked by his sovereign over the sacrifice of Nice and the failure to acquire Ancona and a larger area of the Papal States. Their quarrel became even sharper once both were lodged together in the Pitti Palace in Florence, and it was especially upsetting to observe the royal favours shown to Ricasoli who was now clearly a rival. Cavour was so disconcerted that he pleaded a headache and did not attend the celebrations prepared for the visitors; he remarked that if anyone else but the King had insulted him so crudely, that person would immediately have been challenged to a duel. His secretary Artom found him pale, almost in tears, and on the point of returning prematurely to Turin. Realizing that his departure might be misinterpreted, Cavour agreed reluctantly to remain for two days, but said he could no longer bear the boorishness and crass ingratitude of a monarch for whom he had done so much.

His indignation was justified, though it may be guessed that contributory factors were his own bad temper, lack of tact and manifest contempt for the courtiers among whom on this occasion he was forced to live. The King was possibly jealous that the crowds in Florence – as they had in Milan some weeks earlier – showed as much enthusiasm for the minister as for the monarch. Victor Emanuel, as Hudson noted, always objected to the way Cavour used to preach and talk down at him, and their mutual dislike could hardly fail to be sharpened by the uncustomary personal juxtaposition of these days. Another foreign diplomat, Henry d'Ideville, who became friendly with Cavour at this period, was similarly astonished to observe the minister speaking to the head of state with a brusque condescension as if to a child who could not be trusted with the details of high policy.

On his way back home, a deeply depressed Prime Minister stopped briefly in Pisa, where the *Camposanto* with its funereal frescoes provoked him to macabre thoughts of death. Passing through Genoa he revisited the house that had been his home in happier times. On returning to Turin he talked sadly and disparagingly to Massari about the national character in the light of what he had learnt in Tuscany about the real Italians whom he was now meeting for the first time.

This disconsolate mood had its origin in the political and personal conflict he encountered in Florence. The King clearly disliked all the present ministers except Fanti, and was hoping to appoint a new government under either Rattazzi or Ricasoli. Cavour said he would give way to the latter and in that case would be positively pleased to resign, but while there was any chance of Rattazzi succeeding he would do his utmost to stay in power; he added, however, that from now onwards he would endure no relations with Victor Emanuel except those imposed by official duties.

His chief worry at the end of April was how to stop a small group of volunteers from assembling at Genoa and sailing to support the Sicilian revolutionaries. He had briefly, if unenthusiastically, considered arming a controlled expedition under Ribotti, but to help an irregular volunteer force would be politically dangerous and compromising. A subscription under Garibaldi's patronage had recently collected plenty of guns, some of them the very latest model rifles, and the government had agreed to store these in a police barracks. Garibaldi's agents had two months earlier been given assurances of having free access to this armoury, but suddenly met every kind of resistance, and finally in a secret decision the Cabinet was unanimous in refusing to let the guns out of store. The ministers did not want to help Garibaldi; their problem was how to avoid the odium of opposing him too openly.

Cavour wrote on 27 April that he had never been a in a more difficult situation, and hence for two important weeks he let events take their own course with a minimum of interference or direction. He still needed to get a vote in Parliament legitimizing the cession of Nice and Savoy – the final vote was not taken until 10 June – and this made it desirable to avoid any action that might further weaken a coalition which was in some danger of collapse. He knew that in any real emergency he could use the army to prevent Garibaldi going to Sicily, but employing force would antagonize the *italianissimi* in the National Society and would certainly threaten his majority in Parliament; quite apart from which, it would also imperil the supplementary elections on 6 and 10 May when sixty of the seats in the *camera* were due to be filled. He was fully aware of the fact that public opinion was deserting him and being drawn towards the more glamorous Garibaldi. This radical leader had by now been mortally affronted by the surrender of his home town of Nice and, as Cavour admitted, would become a serious danger inside Piedmont if the army used force to stop the expedition sailing.

Early in May, the French ambassador found the Prime Minister in another mood of profound depression, quite unable to act decisively. The same day, the British Foreign Minister heard a rumour that Cavour might fall from power and said he was pleased to hear it. Even the Minister of War, General Fanti, was threatening to resign and bring the government down. Fanti not only agreed with Garibaldi in disapproving of the cession of Nice, but now discovered that the French insisted on bringing the frontier even closer to Turin than Cavour had said. The army leaders were further disturbed that many soldiers, against Garibaldi's published wishes, were deserting to join the volunteers, and an urgent demand had to be made to take severe action against these deserters before some regiments disintegrated altogether. The gaols were said to be so full of captured soldiers that there was no remaining room for ordinary prisoners.

Another reason why Cavour's powers of decision were momentarily paralysed was his strong suspicion that Victor Emanuel was secretly encouraging Garibaldi. On 1 May the Prime Minister travelled to meet the King at Bologna in the hope of stopping this underhand intrigue, only to learn that a few hours before his arrival there had been further discussions about replacing the government. Evidently Victor Emanuel still had it in mind to appoint other ministers who, being less beholden to France, could act with more independence and initiative.

These many complications help to explain why Garibaldi and his 'Thousand' were allowed to embark for Sicily on 6 May, the same day as the elections. Cavour had done what he could to dissuade them, partly because he thought that what he called this 'mad enterprise' was bound to fail, but much more because their action was in direct opposition to his own policy of alliance with anti-revolutionary France. He told the Prussian envoy in Turin that their sailing was almost the worst thing that could have happened, yet added that he was afraid of falling from power if he acted to stop them.

Only later, after Garibaldi had astonished the world by winning against all the odds in Sicily, was the story disseminated that Cavour had all along given secret assistance and encouragement. In reality serious help was sent only some weeks later when, after Garibaldi had shown he could win, the moderates in Turin needed to control and exploit such a wholly unexpected success. But on 6 May the volunteers were not allowed to take their own good rifles; they sailed with a thousand rusty, smooth-bore, converted flintlocks, most of which could be used for nothing more than bayonet charges; and – apparently because defrauded by private suppliers – they left with no ammunition at all.

According to Cavour's colleague, Lanza, this ambiguous and hesitant attitude reflected a lack of courage and straightforwardness on the part of the government, and Prince Napoleon agreed that on grounds of expediency as well as morality, the volunteers should either have been stopped or else wholeheartedly helped. By refusing requests for assistance, Cavour made the breach with Garibaldi wider at a moment when some degree of at least partial cooperation was required. Worse still, whether the expedition succeeded or failed, the government was bound to be in difficulties either way, because they had incurred the discredit of being thought to abet revolution at the same time as they failed to help that revolution succeed. In so doing, for the next four months Cavour let the initiative of the Italian movement escape out of his own hands into those of another potentially dangerous rival.

One partial explanation of his hesitancy was that he had very little contact with Garibaldi during two vital weeks. Indeed he was not sure whether the expedition was bound for Sicily or for an invasion of the Papal States – which in his view would have been a major disaster. His main contact with the volunteers was through La Farina who was increasingly distrusted by them, and from whose National Society many of Garibaldi's friends had by now resigned on the grounds that it was a mere instrument of officialdom and altogether too hostile to revolutionary action. La Farina provided the thousand rusty guns, but admitted that he had plenty of other better arms and ammunition that he refused to give them. Moreover, on 11 May he issued an order that members of the Society must try to stop any further movement of volunteers. This order was in fact a precise statement of government policy.

When the elections were over and when other countries protested against the sailing of the 'Thousand', Cavour decided to take more positive action against them. Once Garibaldi was at sea, and knowing that being short of coal and arms he might land in Sardinia to take on supplies, Cavour sent an order that he and his men should in that case be arrested. Shortly afterwards a further order was sent to Admiral Persano that the navy should try to intercept them anywhere outside Sicilian waters, and that all expeditions to reinforce them were to be prevented at all costs: these last words 'at all costs' were underlined.

On 14 May, Cavour made a further attempt to regain control over events when he suggested that France and England might intervene and mediate between the Sicilian rebels and the Neapolitan Bourbons before the revolution had gone too far. The English government, however, saw no reason to help someone they now regarded as a 'catspaw' of France. Indeed, Russell referred to Cavour as this 'prefect of the department of the Po' who was probably acting on orders from Paris. But the French were almost equally mistrustful, since the Piedmontese were going far beyond what had been agreed at Plombières and Villafranca. Cavour tried to make the British believe that Napoleon was threatening to occupy Florence and Bologna by force, and certainly the French formally protested that the Piedmontese 'were making dangerous use of the independence that they owe to us'.

Meanwhile Garibaldi eluded the Piedmontese and Neapolitan navies and did not land in Sardinia. He reached Sicily at the small port of Marsala after picking up arms and ammunition during a brief stop on the Tuscan coast, and at Calatafimi on 15 May won a small-scale but brilliant and in fact decisive engagement. The Neapolitans had thirty thousand soldiers available in Sicily and under good leadership could easily have beaten such an ill-armed force of irregulars, but they over-confidently committed too small a force to this battle and were outmanoeuvred. Garibaldi's victory was sufficient to win the enthusiastic support of many Sicilians who had been reluctant to commit themselves until they could see good chances of a successful rebellion against Naples. The victorious general assumed dictatorial powers, under which he appointed a provisional government to rule in Victor Emanuel's name until Sicily could join a united Italy.

Pushing on without delay to the capital city, Palermo, the invaders again routed the opposition by even more masterly tactics, and within a matter of days the whole island was in full revolt. An outside observer, Friedrich Engels, writing in a New York paper, called this brief campaign one of the most astonishing military enterprises of the century. Its political results were equally dramatic, because at last there was further clear evidence in the eyes of the world that the movement for Italian liberation had a spontaneous momentum of its own: it was no longer dependent on diplomatic subterfuge, or on foreign armies or on attempts to start another major European war.

Cavour reached much the same conclusion and quickly adapted to a new situation with the intention of dethroning the Bourbons before this voluntary army of irregulars was too successful on its own. In the past he had tried to make people believe that he had a horror of revolutionary activity and of breaking international law, but by 18 May was wondering if he could secretly send help to Garibaldi without being compromised. On 21 May he spoke excitedly of attacking Austria and of possibly being in Rome by Christmas. A few days later, while he continued to promise the Bourbons in Naples that he would have no truck with revolution and was 'totally opposed' to the 'usurper' Garibaldi, he was planning to undermine their dynasty. The first step was an attempt to bribe some of the Neapolitan senior officers to change sides, promising them money and promotion in the Piedmontese armed services if they could prepare the way for a *pronunciamento*. At the same time he studied the possibility of displacing Garibaldi and annexing Sicily outright; and another possibility was to play on insular feelings of independence by offering to resuscitate the ancient Sicilian Parliament that had been abolished in 1849.

Once again he turned for help and counsel to the National Society, which under La Farina's influence had moved away from Manin's independent position and was now virtually a government agency. La Farina as a Sicilian could give advice that was badly needed. Cavour confessed to knowing far more about England than southern Italy – he once told Parliament that he thought Sicilians spoke Arabic. On 3 June he decided to send La Farina to Sicily with secret instructions and plenty of money to halt the revolution and take the government out of Garibaldi's hands so that the island could be quickly annexed to Piedmont. The choice of person was a strange one for such a delicate mission, and it was at once seen as a deliberate move to bully the revolutionary movement into submission. La Farina was intemperate, tactless, even slightly fanatical, and the selection of such an instrument made Hudson comment that Cavour 'has not the gift of putting round men into round holes'.

Garibaldi had arranged that one of his chief lieutenants, Giacomo Medici, should remain behind in Genoa to train a second and larger expedition. This force was ready to leave by 20 May and might have arrived in time for the attack on Palermo, but Cavour at first forbade any reinforcements to leave. A small group of sixty volunteers succeeded in reaching Palermo, but not until a week after that town had been captured, and Medici continued to protest that Garibaldi had calculated on receiving far more substantial reinforcements at once. Eventually, once La Farina was ready to carry out his *coup*, the three thousand men of this second expedition were equipped with arms and transport, largely at government expense, though Cavour continued to promise the Neapolitans that he was still giving no assistance to the revolution. As a result of these delays, Medici's expedition did not reach Palermo until 21 June, just in time to prepare for the final assault on Messina.

The ministers in Turin continued to have mixed feelings about the whole operation and their position was far from easy. Garibaldi was a man whose great prestige throughout Europe it was important to preserve and utilize, yet who had political ideas of his own and refused to be dictated to. He was surrounding himself in Sicily with some reliable conservatives, but also with radicals such as Francesco Crispi over whom the government in Turin could have little influence. Admiral Persano was therefore ordered to play a double game from his flagship in Palermo harbour: namely, to keep on good terms with the revolutionary government but also to work secretly alongside La Farina to deprive Garibaldi of effective political power. Persano's attempt to bribe some of the Neapolitan naval officers eventually failed when the crews refused to support the projected mutiny. But he did succeed in persuading an unsuspecting Garibaldi to choose a Piedmontese naval officer to command his miniature revolutionary navy, and Cavour arranged that this man should surreptitiously appoint other Piedmontese officers to individual ships where they would be ready to defect and turn against the dictator when the time came for La Farina to act.

The government in Turin was meanwhile being strongly pressed by Napoleon to reach some agreement with the Bourbon dynasty in Naples before the Sicilian revolution had time to spread to the mainland. The young King Francesco tried to avert the threat of revolution by following advice from Turin to grant a constitution, which he did on 25 June. Once again he was told by Cavour that their two countries should form an alliance and work together towards Italian independence. At the same time, however, the Piedmontese envoy in Naples, Villamarina, was secretly instructed to work in an opposite direction to make such an alliance impossible. Cavour was, quite justifiably, ready to operate a number of alternative policies as he waited to see how events developed.

At this moment, by what seems to have been a regrettable mistake, two Piedmontese police agents arrived mysteriously in Sicily. Giacomo Griscelli and Pasquale Totti were also in the pay of Napoleon, King Francesco and probably the Pope, as well as of Cavour himself. They were a thoroughly disreputable pair and possibly hoped to be paid also by Garibaldi. When they were apprehended and confessed that they had been sent by the Neapolitans to murder Garibaldi, and when on top of this their simultaneous employment by Cavour became known, they were summarily expelled from the island. Garibaldi was infuriated to find such questionable individuals claiming to be in Sicily on clandestine but official business. On 7 July, in his anger, he also expelled La Farina who had been creating all manner of difficulties in an attempt to take over the government of the island. There was little chance after this for Cavour to re-establish good relations. Back in Turin, an embittered La Farina tried to excuse his failure by spreading the false story that Garibaldi was secretly working with Mazzini and aiming at civil war. Cavour believed this improbable story, or at least acted as though he did, and the results were unfortunate.

Events in Sicily thus opened a much bigger rift between the two most important people in the Italian national movement; but, in compensation, Cavour by the end of June was developing a new and more positive policy as he sensed that public opinion was changing and that he must follow it. Recognizing that even some of the more moderate liberals were beginning to accept Italian unification as at last possible – and perhaps even necessary – he admitted that he could no longer afford to let Garibaldi keep a monopoly on what was suddenly turning out to be an exciting idea.

There were, of course, some dissidents who on realistic grounds continued to entertain doubts about unification. When Villamarina reported improbably on 3 July that there was an almost unanimous wish among Neapolitans to be annexed by Piedmont, Azeglio commented that no one who knew Naples would think for a moment that more than five per cent of the population could have any such desire. Likewise, Francesco Ferrara told Cavour that even if some of his fellow Sicilians might be coming round to accept annexation to Piedmont, this would be merely because it was their one chance to break free from Naples, and he prophesied that unless events were handled with the greatest delicacy, Sicily as a province of a united Italy might be as intractable and indigestible as it had been for the Bourbons of Naples.

Cavour did not think that this warning deserved so much as a reply. He quite unexpectedly found himself to be in a stronger position as a result of Garibaldi's success, because the Bourbons would soon be faced with a simple choice between either letting Sicily have its freedom or refusing to make concessions: either way their dynasty could hardly survive. He agreed to begin formal negotiations with them for an alliance, but was determined to move slowly and only make proposals that they could with difficulty accept. Negotiations, even if insincere, would provide an insurance against the possibility that Garibaldi's volunteers might yet be defeated. In addition, negotiations would win time during which he could try once again to persuade or force the provisional government at Palermo to surrender Sicily to Piedmont. But there was one drawback in being seen to negotiate with the self-same anti-national government that Garibaldi was engaged in fighting, because it lost him a good deal of credibility and support among most of the patriots.

Garibaldi was perplexed by it, and could only assume that Cavour's attempt to annex Sicily was designed to stop any use of the island as a base for launching an attack against Naples. He was therefore all the more determined not to surrender Sicily so long as he might need such a base. The activities of Griscelli and La Farina, coming on top of the delay to Medici's expedition, and now this attempt by Turin to negotiate with Naples, confirmed his belief that Cavour was more anxious to halt than help the revolution. Another batch of reinforcements was allowed to leave Genoa early in July, but by 10 July Cavour was becoming increasingly afraid that the volunteers might soon be in a position to invade the Neapolitan mainland, and on the twelfth he sent to ask the English government to help prevent anything so dangerous. He also took the courageous decision of putting a stop to any further expeditions of volunteers from Piedmontese territory. He wrote on the eighteenth that the time had not yet arrived to break publicly with Garibaldi, but that it was imperative to make one further serious attempt to take the initiative out of the hands of the revolutionaries before they were too successful.

CHAPTER 20

Naples
August – November 1860

One possible, if hazardous, way for Cavour's moderate liberals to resume control of the national movement was by starting their own 'moderate revolution' in Naples before the volunteer army could cross the Straits of Messina; and by the middle of July a plan was being prepared. A large amount of money was taken secretly to Naples for the purpose of bribing soldiers, ministers and dissident members of King Francesco's family. A dozen trusted agents were also sent there, though the operation was badly co-ordinated and they were sometimes working at cross-purposes. The Piedmontese ambassador, Villa-marina, was put in general charge of quietly preparing this movement, and he reported with excessive optimism to Turin that he would find no great difficulty in overthrowing the Bourbons. Admiral Persano was instructed to do what he could to delay Garibaldi's crossing of the Straits while the details and timing of this *coup* were settled. Either Persano or Villamarina would then proclaim himself dictator and annex Naples to Piedmont.

Cavour was realistic and generous in acknowledging his debt to the volunteer army in Sicily for their amazing military success, and above all for proving to outside observers that Italians were ready to sacrifice their lives for freedom and nationhood. Garibaldi was his political opponent and had a different concept of the *risorgimento*, yet consider-ations of gratitude as well as of expediency led Cavour to proceed with caution before he challenged these devoted patriots too openly, especially as they were showing their good will by continuing to introduce Piedmontese legislation into Sicily. As Nigra was told early in August, the government could if necessary and at any moment win a parliamentary vote against Garibaldi's brand of populist and radical politics, but public opinion throughout Europe would strongly disapprove of an open split. Cavour knew by now that he had made one bad mistake in sending La Farina to undermine Garibaldi's position in Sicily. The success of the 'Thousand' suggested that perhaps a second mistake was not to have helped them more. A third and possibly fatal mistake would be a failure to recognize that these revolutionaries, despite the embarrassment they caused, 'had done the greatest possible service by giving Italy a new self-confidence', since national unification had been brought within the bounds of practical possibility by their quite unexpected victories.

But gratitude could not be allowed to obscure the fact that the revolutionary general had 'at all costs' to be stopped before his success and reputation became too great; his conquest of the large kingdom of Naples would be 'deplorable'. If necessary, as Cavour told the Prussian ambassador on 16 July, the volunteers might have to be halted at the point of a gun, and confirmation was sent to Ricasoli that every possible means would be employed to stop them succeeding. It was sad enough to have been obliged to accept Lombardy as a gift from Napoleon in 1859. It would be doubly demeaning to receive southern Italy as a gift from a self-made freelance guerrilla, especially as Naples was the largest town in all Italy and the capital of a country with twice the population of Piedmont. If Garibaldi became dictator of Naples as well as Sicily, he would govern as large an area as did Cavour himself; 'he would be absolute master of the situation, and Victor Emanuel would lose almost all his prestige by becoming for most Italians little more than Garibaldi's friend'. This is what Cavour wrote, but perhaps he was even more afraid of something very different: namely that the King in alliance with a victorious Garibaldi would become too strong. In other words, the King might appoint an alternative government under Rattazzi, or try once again to break free from all parliamentary restraints.

On 10 August, as Cavour celebrated his fiftieth and last birthday, he wondered again if stirring up another European war might help to recapture the initiative. He made the strange remark that even a military defeat at the hands of Austria would be preferable to seeing Garibaldi score yet another success; but, with perhaps excessive optimism, he did not expect to be beaten in such a war 'because whenever our soldiers have been truly eager for combat they have always defeated the Austrians', and such a victory would help to eclipse the achievements of the volunteers. He again imagined that there would be no great difficulty in dragging the French into a war. The Italians could, he thought, defeat Austria by themselves; but Napoleon could help by attacking the German Confederation on the Rhine, and hostilities would then be on a scale large enough to provide the opportunity for a comprehensive realignment of frontiers in favour of France and Piedmont.

This ambitious and not very realistic project had to be put aside temporarily when, on 19 August, Garibaldi's army carried out the hazardous operation of landing in Calabria after once again evading the Neapolitan fleet. There was one incidental disaster when the bigger of their two transport ships ran aground on a shoal, since the Piedmontese navy had orders to keep well out of sight and refuse any request for assistance – though an official report soon tried to explain that Persano had done his best to help them. Everything now depended on whether Cavour could anticipate the volunteers by starting his own revolution in Naples, and again he was confident of success. Persano's frigates were already anchored in the Bay of Naples with soldiers hidden under hatches ready to disembark as soon as the revolt began. Quantities of arms had also been secretly landed at various points along the coast. The Piedmontese ambassador was merely waiting for the right moment to give the signal for revolt.

When he did, almost inexplicably once again nothing happened. The revolution was a complete fiasco, for the Neapolitans understandably preferred to remain uncommitted and wait for Garibaldi to arrive. Cavour blamed them for what he called their disgusting and spineless inactivity, while his friends on the spot blamed his bad organization and his failure to send them enough support or clear directives. A lot of money and resources had been wasted with nothing gained; indeed a great deal had been lost by giving Garibaldi further proof that the Piedmontese were trying to hinder rather than help him. Cavour did his best to cover up what had happened and put into circulation a very different story: he thus sent a personal message to the victorious general saying that, despite appearances, the government had complete confidence in him and was anxious for the two of them to work together in harmony. On 7 September, Garibaldi entered Naples with a small advance guard, correctly judging that the large Bourbonist garrison in the city was by now too demoralized to fire a shot. A provisional administration was then set up with himself as a dictator governing in the name of Victor Emanuel, who, for the first time, was hailed as 'King of Italy', and the Piedmontese constitution was published.

In Turin, policy had to be adjusted quickly after this brilliant but highly inopportune success. Cavour's first assumption, so he told the Swiss envoy in Turin, was that Garibaldi would invade the Papal States within a week, in which case it was likely that the French would once again propose their own solution of restricting papal sovereignty merely to the city of Rome with a corridor to the sea: otherwise the four thousand French troops in Rome would surely by now have been reinforced. He may well have guessed that Brofferio and the King were privately in touch with Garibaldi and possibly advising the volunteers to invade papal territory. But such an attack, successful or unsucessful, would involve a head-on challenge for the leadership in Italy. There was also an acute danger of armed conflict between Garibaldi and the French troops in Rome, and that would be a disaster: it would certainly shatter the alliance with Napoleon which was the main plank in Cavour's foreign policy.

To avert this prospect, he was already preparing one of the boldest strokes of his career by carrying out Mazzini's favourite scheme of invading the Papal States from the north. He had been annoyed early in August when Ricasoli urgently advised such an invasion, but Garibaldi's defeat of the Neapolitan army had since then removed one major obstacle. The plan was to persuade Napoleon to permit Piedmontese forces to cross the northern papal frontier into Umbria, and the pretext would be that this alone would contain Garibaldi's influence and stop the volunteers attacking Rome from the south.

On 26 August the Cabinet approved this plan and sent Farini to inform Napoleon, who made no objection provided that it was carried into effect quickly, successfully, and without suggesting any connivance by France; but the Emperor stressed the need for some kind of preliminary revolution to take place in the Papal States so as to provide a plausible excuse and make it appear to be a war of liberation rather than of aggression. Cavour already had this in mind. Selected agitators were at once sent over the papal frontier to start such a revolt, well provided with money, guns and 'Orsini bombs'. On 3 September an order then went out from the National Society that the provinces of Umbria and the Marche should commence a general uprising and demand Piedmontese help. There was some urgency, because a much more radical movement had already begun to set up provisional governments in the extreme south of the Papal States ahead of Garibaldi's invasion. An ultimatum from Turin was then sent to Pius IX at the same time as the volunteer army entered Naples. This ultimatum protested in the name of humanity against any attempt by the Pope's soldiers to suppress the revolution, and demanded that the papal army be disbanded since it posed a grave threat to the tranquillity of the peninsula.

Once again there were various hitches. First, the plan was allowed to leak out, perhaps deliberately so as to implicate the Emperor in what was afoot: the project was known in London at the end of August, and was a topic of conversation in Rome and Turin several days before 8 September when the insurrection was timed to begin. Secondly, the ultimatum by mischance did not reach the papal government until late on the tenth and the reply to it was not received in Turin before the thirteenth, two days after the Piedmontese had launched their attack. Thirdly, the popular revolution organised by La Farina and his friends turned out to be deplorably inadequate: clearly it had been much too hastily prepared and by people who had a very fearful and amateurish idea about revolutionary action. Most local adherents of the National Society apparently preferred to wait until the invading troops arrived; no doubt they remembered that they had similarly been asked to revolt in June 1859, only to be left in the lurch when Cavour was unable to support them.

Napoleon was greatly embarrassed and felt obliged to distance himself from what was happening by withdrawing his ambassador from Turin and sending more troops to defend the Pope from any attack on the town of Rome. He protested to Turin that he had been placed in an impossible position by the failure of the revolution and the lack of any credible excuse for the war. He also complained at the clumsiness of an ultimatum that talked of humanity and tranquillity when trying to justify manifest aggression. The Emperor was not greatly worried about violation of international law, but he had expected something much better organized, and was especially annoyed that the Piedmontese were spreading stories about him being in full agreement with what they had done. Even liberal Catholics in France were protesting at the 'piratical' policy of Turin in killing innocent people for no better reason than national aggrandisement; some of them called Cavour far more blameworthy than Garibaldi, because the Piedmontese were hypocritical enough to claim that they were fighting the Pope to restore a higher morality and the true interests of the Church.

Protests were also received from other foreign governments, notably Spain, Portugal and Bavaria, for whom the use of armed force against the Pope was an unthinkable enormity. The Russians broke off diplomatic contact after protesting that international relations would become impossible if countries started invading each other without provocation and without even declaring war. The Prussians similarly protested that a frank declaration of war would have been less dishonourable than the insincerity of relying on such an obviously mock revolution.

Much the same criticism was heard inside Piedmont itself, for instance from the former Prime Ministers Lamarmora and Azeglio, and also from Marquis Alfieri and Count Sclopis, the two most prominent senators. Hitherto the Piedmontese had been able to appeal to European public opinion by accusing Austria of inhumanity, bad faith and breaches of international law, but Azeglio pointed out that these accusations would now seem a mere pretence; on the contrary, the same accusations would henceforward be levelled against the Italians themselves, and hence the moral justification of the *risorgimento* would no longer look so persuasive to public opinion in Europe. Nor was this merely a matter of morality, because the confidence and support coming from foreigners was one of Italy's most effective practical assets.

Cavour admitted that his plans had gone wrong, but the main point had been gained because the initiative had been recaptured from the revolutionaries, and the momentum, once recovered, had to be retained even at the risk of civil war. In Naples, for instance, he ordered Admiral Persano to land the *bersaglieri* from his ships so as to seize the Neapolitan fortresses and navy before Garibaldi could do so, and he must have been puzzled to learn that Garibaldi had already made a gift of these forts and vessels to Persano in a friendly and indeed quite gratuitous action that more than doubled the size of the Piedmontese navy at a stroke. A second minor embarrassment was a further appeal for concord made by Mazzini, who reminded everyone that the republicans in the previous few months had loyally if unenthusiastically accepted the Piedmontese monarchy as the best hope of success for the patriotic movement. Mazzini urged that divisions among the patriots should disappear in the last crucial phase of their common struggle for national unification, but this olive branch from the republicans had to be rejected by the politicians in Turin and had to be kept from public knowledge as far as possible. So long as French support was needed, Mazzini's opposition remained far more useful than his cooperation.

Another untoward event was Garibaldi's inclusion of pro-Piedmontese moderates in his provisional government at Naples. Cavour expressed regret at this because, especially after the French protest at the invasion of Umbria, official policy had to be directed all the more at subduing the volunteers rather than working with them. The excuse he had given to Paris for the invasion was that Piedmont had to 'combat the influence of Garibaldi' and 'prevent the revolution extending into northern Italy'; hence any hint of fraternization must be rigidly excluded.

Garibaldi was momentarily delighted to hear about Cavour's invasion of the Papal States, and only on second thoughts saw that it was probably directed against himself. Though too innocent a politician to understand all the difficulties of the Turin government, his instinctive assumption was that he was being cast in the role of an enemy to be fought and beaten. Probably he did not understand that Victor Emanuel was playing a dangerously devious game of simultaneously trying to keep in with both wings of the national movement; and when Garibaldi on 11 September asked for the dismissal of Cavour, this was because he had been led to believe that such a request was what the King might want. But the latter had to reply that 'for the moment' a change of government would be impossible (the words 'for the moment' were prudently omitted when a copy of the King's reply was sent to Cavour). After the almost unanimous opposition in Europe to the invasion of Umbria, the monarch could not afford to get rid of an expert pilot, at least until the storm subsided. Nor would his regal dignity survive intact if he were seen to be changing his Prime Minister in response to public demand from the revolutionaries. Indeed, on 5 September, Victor Emanuel sent private word to the Bourbon King Francesco with the advice to launch one more attack on the volunteer army in the hope of defeating and then hanging Garibaldi.

Cavour at once realized the advantage to be gained if this hitherto half-concealed conflict came out into the open. On 8 September he offered to resign, but this was in the secure knowledge that once Piedmont was at war with the Pope, he was a necessary man and the King would have no alternative but to confirm him in office. If Cavour's policy against the Garibaldians had hitherto failed, it was because he had been forced to compete with the revolutionaries on their own ground where their skills were more effective, but in an open fight at diplomatic and parliamentary level he would hold all of the trump cards.

For example, Garibaldi was now caricatured in Turin as a populist dictator who had little use for parliamentary government and must be an enemy of liberal values. It was stressed that as governor of Sicily he had given clear indications of penalizing the rich to aid the poor, and hence was a social danger. Though not a republican in the normal sense of the word, he at least represented a political challenge to the Piedmontese establishment, as could be deduced from the fact that Cattaneo and the outlawed Mazzini were both permitted by him to live unmolested in Naples. An extravagant scare was even raised that the volunteer army might be intending to invade Piedmont itself, which was in fact almost the reverse of the truth. It was rather Cavour who knowledgeably ran the risk of civil war by sending troops to the south, and who said more than once that he would not flinch from such a catastrophe: indeed he specifically empowered his army command to 'hurl the Garibaldians into the sea' if they refused to surrender.

The invading troops from the north had first to overrun papal territory before they could reach the Neapolitan frontier, but this took only three weeks because the Pope had a scratch international army that was greatly outnumbered. The Piedmontese commander, General Cialdini, issued a provocative proclamation referring to this papal army as hired and cowardly assassins heedless of the laws of war; but he himself was none too scrupulous in his use of terroristic means, since his orders were to win quickly and decisively so that the regular army could 'throw into the shade the prestige that a series of lucky accidents has bestowed on Garibaldi'. Furnished with plenty of money, he offered to double the wages of any papal soldier who agreed to desert and change sides. When Cialdini on 18 September decisively beat the Pope's men in a small engagement at Castelfidardo, Massari expressed the delight felt in Turin at what was a victory at one remove against Garibaldi himself. On 29 September the first main objective was attained when the town of Ancona was relentlessly, and to all appearance unnecessarily, bombarded into submission. From Ancona, Naples was only a few days' march.

Simultaneously, plans were revived in Turin for starting another European war in conjunction with a general uprising of the subject nationalities inside the Austrian and Turkish empires. The long-term objective was to drive the Austrians out of Venice, but a more immediately urgent motive was said to be that of helping to save Italy from internal revolution. Not only would war against Austria have the incidental effect of recapturing prestige for the regular generals and the King, but Garibaldi and his dangerous followers could be removed from the scene by sending them to take part in this Balkan uprising – so getting rid of more than one enemy at a time, wrote the Prince di Carignano to Cavour.

Within hours of deciding to attack the Papal States, the government invited Lajos Kossuth and other Hungarian revolutionaries to Turin. The plan was to provide them with fifty thousand rifles and facilities for making Hungarian uniforms, while an American machine would be used for printing false banknotes. Nearly half a million *lire* was also produced for them out of two departmental budgets after the accounts had been manipulated to conceal its provenance. The extent of this support would have startled Garibaldi had he known and been able to compare it with the thousand dilapidated muskets and ten thousand *lire* he had received from the National Society for his expedition to Sicily five months earlier. It might also have surprised Mazzini, whose simplistic belief in revolutionary action was so often scorned by Cavour, yet whose unrealistic and utopian schemes were never on quite this scale. Cavour told Abraham Tourte that the Austrians would be powerless against a concerted revolt by the various subject nationalities in the Balkans, though this was an illusion and in practice the Serbs, Croats, Hungarians and Roumanians showed almost as much distrust of each other as of Vienna.

Two officials from the Foreign Office in Turin were put in charge of planning a revolution across the whole of eastern Europe from Poland to Greece. This general insurrection was timed to take place in the spring of 1861. Cavour's imagination was fired as he pondered various possible developments. A revolt in Poland might help to keep Russia in check – because he had changed his mind again and said he feared the 'horrible danger' of Russian influence spreading into the Baltic and Mediterranean. Another objective would be to extend the influence of catholicism against the Orthodox clergy in the southern Balkans. Possibly the Greeks could be encouraged to recreate a new Byzantine empire, and one day this might enable the 'Latin races' in Greece, Italy and Spain to reacquire their former predominance in the Mediterranean and Levant. Alternatively it might be more useful if the Greek nation was dismembered, in which case Austria might be persuaded to surrender Venice in return for being allowed to annex northern Greece and obtain an outlet to the Aegean at Salonica.

Another possible development open to exploitation was the unification of Germany, and the Prussians were light-heartedly informed that Cavour would be prepared to offer them his services once he had finished with Italy – the word 'finished' aroused some wry amusement in Berlin. His optimistic belief was that a united Germany would be 'the best if not the only guarantee of world peace', especially as their two countries were destined to be 'the joint coping stones of the new Europe'. At one moment he persuaded himself that liberal ideas were each year becoming more deeply entrenched in Germany, though he was less sure about patriotism among the various German states and eventually concluded that without better leadership they would take fifty years over unification, whereas the Italians needed only three . At another moment he said in Hudson's hearing, 'I wish I was Prime Minister of the Kingdom of Prussia; I would soon put liberty in the shade'.

Preoccupied with the complexities of diplomacy, Cavour did not have sufficient time to consider the difficulties of dealing with Garibaldi in Naples; he simply thought his best hope was for a direct confrontation as soon as possible. When he instructed the army to invade Neapolitan territory he again warned it to expect armed resistance from what he referred to as 'the Garibaldian hordes'. Public opinion was now warned that Garibaldi was a secret republican with whom no compromise was possible, and to prove this a fabricated document was circulated in Turin purporting to give solid evidence that the revolutionary leader was preparing to resist the Piedmontese invasion by force of arms.

The truth was quite different, for Garibaldi was if anything an exaggerated monarchist, and had already shown his good will by spontaneously handing over the Bourbon navy and fortresses into the care of Admiral Persano. Far from contemplating resistance, Garibaldi's instruction was that the northern army be welcomed as brothers-in-arms who would act in concert to harry the retreating troops of King Francesco. It was in Turin, not Naples, that the prospect of military cooperation between conservatives and revolutionaries was viewed with alarm. As late as 6 October, Cavour tried to pretend to the Bourbon King, with whom he continued very surprisingly to maintain diplomatic relations, that Piedmont had no quarrel with the dynasty which Garibaldi had just defeated. The intention in Turin was rather to disarm and supplant Garibaldi's régime in Naples. Agents sent from the north were already trying to undermine the provisional government in that city, and Cavour's supporters in Palermo reported that they had everything ready by 18 September for an armed *pronunciamento* against Garibaldi's administration in Sicily.

On 3 October, after appointing Carignano to act as regent, the King arrived in Ancona to take command of the advance on Naples. The Prime Minister at first intended to join the army on this march, but the painful memory of earlier quarrels with his sovereign gave him pause, and no doubt he preferred to avoid the embarrassment of meeting Garibaldi face to face. Victor Emanuel thought that, as a conciliatory gesture to the volunteers, it would be useful to appoint Rattazzi as civilian Governor of Naples and Valerio to the same post in Sicily, but Cavour was in no mood for reconciliation and threatened to resign. Instead he insisted on Farini and Fanti accompanying the invasion as the King's chief advisers; two men who, since they were known to be among Garibaldi's greatest personal enemies, could be counted on to show no weakness or leniency. A number of Cavour's friends warned him against such a provocative step, but he replied that the choice was deliberate so as to ensure that there would be no compromises and no half-measures.

He had no intention of being deterred by those who offered different advice. However, the unexpected and very uncomfortable information arrived from Naples and Palermo that, quite contrary to what he had been told by La Farina and others, Garibaldi enjoyed in southern Italy an immense popularity which it would be absurd not to utilize – and even more absurd to combat if that could possibly be avoided. Others reminded him that the volunteers deserved better after defeating a much larger army and conquering half of Italy; moreover they had shown no sign of wanting to create an Italian republic but had consistently governed in the King's name. A further warning came from England that if Garibaldi were treated badly after such a series of astonishing victories, the Italian cause would be discredited everywhere.

Cavour was nevertheless adamant, because he had reason to think that any sign of compromise might threaten the French alliance and his own position at the head of government. He advanced the unconvincing argument that the volunteers would be of no further use as a fighting army; also that Garibaldi himself was no longer a serious political force but on the contrary had lost moral support in Italy; and indeed that only the arrival of regular Piedmontese soldiers would save the volunteers from catastrophic defeat at the hands of the Bourbon army.

Bolstering himself with these dubious premises, Cavour again ordered General Fanti to prepare to use force if necessary against the forty to fifty thousand men in Garibaldi's army. If really necessary – to quote his own words which were subsequently deleted from the published text – they might have to be 'exterminated to the last man'. If, on the other hand, the volunteers behaved well and made no further trouble, he would prefer to avoid being taxed with ingratitude, and so opposed Fanti's recommendation that they be sent home at once with a simple gratuity.

It would create a very bad impression if the victorious volunteers were simply discarded, especially as some of the defeated Bourbon troops were already being incorporated into the Piedmontese army. Yet this very important problem was not easily soluble, and in practice Cavour preferred to leave its solution largely to others. He merely gave his own opinion that a few of Garibaldi's more politically reliable senior officers could certainly be used, but preferably not too many, while the ex-dictator should be sent back to his island home of Caprera with a generous annual pension and the gift of a steam yacht for his private use.

What encouraged Cavour to take such a firm line was that at last, on 2 October, Parliament met again in Turin after a long recess and provided him with just the backing he needed if he was going to stand up to Victor Emanuel, Garibaldi and his own army officers. There was hardly any opposition on the right, because the clericals abstained from voting in elections and the deputies from Savoy were now excluded from Parliament. The urgency of the moment allowed him to initiate a debate before the *camera* was properly constituted – something he had refused to allow in April when Garibaldi tried to raise the equally urgent matter of Nice. What he now asked of Parliament was authority for the annexation of Naples and Sicily if these two regions voted for it by universal suffrage. Annexation, he told the deputies, was needed in order to stop the diffusion of revolutionary sentiments. He conceded that the conquest of the south had been due to action outside his control or direction, but rightly insisted that Garibaldi's success would have been impossible without the policy pursued in Piedmont since 1848. He also tried to argue that he had not provoked the 'profound division' that existed between himself and Garibaldi; but now that it had come into the light of day he asked the deputies to back him, and they did so by an almost unanimous vote.

A few days later, speaking in the senate where ecclesiastical interests found much stronger support, Cavour turned to justification of his invasion of the Papal States. In reply to those who said that the Pope had committed no act of provocation that could conceivably excuse an invasion, he admitted that in normal times the invasion might have been considered wrong, 'but our aim is holy and this will perhaps justify any irregularity in the means we have employed.' He had felt obliged to restore what he called legality and morality against the 'hateful yoke' of the Pope, whose former subjects were said by him to be overjoyed at the change of régime.

With great courage he then shocked many of his listeners by asserting that Rome must one day become the capital of Italy. Turin would be too near the new frontier between Italy and France, while to choose Florence or Naples would cause too much jealousy elsewhere. Manin, Mazzini and Garibaldi had all said that Rome alone would be generally acceptable as the national capital, though in adopting their view Cavour knew he was challenging the loyalty of many Catholics and conservatives as well as those Piedmontese municipalists who looked on the *risorgimento* as a movement to establish the dominance of Turin. Six weeks earlier he had pretended to the French that his excuse for invading Umbria had been to save Rome for the Pope. But after the huge vote of confidence in the *camera* he could afford to be bolder and more honest. Not only did he now want to annex Rome, but he felt strong enough to call on the papacy to change some of its fundamental dogmas, to accept liberalism and freedom of conscience, and to 'reconcile itself with the basic principles of modern society'; but above all it must surrender the Holy City and the Pope's last claims to territorial sovereignty.

Parliament met for only a few sessions in October and was then closed during most of the next four months. Ricasoli and Fanti were two leading politicians who would have liked Cavour to set Parliament aside altogether by establishing a formalized royal dictatorship to carry out the final stages of unification. Others were nevertheless frightened by memories of how in 1859 the King had been given dictatorial powers and used them to exclude his ministers from effective authority. Cavour in fact had few misgivings about acting dictatorially in practice, yet at the same time was genuinely anxious to be seen as a moderate liberal who, unlike Garibaldi, abhorred the very notion of dictatorship. He needed Parliament because the *camera* was the greatest source of his personal strength. Nevertheless in private he repeatedly exhorted Farini to apply martial law in governing the south, because a *de facto* dictatorship was unquestionably needed there, though the word and the fact should preferably be mentioned only in private correspondence.

On 9 October, before leaving Ancona, Farini issued a proclamation in the King's name that seemed to be quite unnecessarily provocative: it announced that the northern army was coming to Naples not to accept the fruits of Garibaldi's achievement, but rather to terminate an unsavoury revolution and purge the country of Mazzini and his followers. Garibaldi for his part had sent a very different message, because on the contrary he welcomed the imminent arrival of the royal forces and asked for joint action against the Bourbon army that still held out in Capua and Gaeta. Farini merely commented that this friendly message must be insincere. Piedmont had not technically declared war against the Bourbons, and in any case had no intention of allowing the volunteers a further military role. Farini's primary intention was quite different: all traces of what he called Garibaldi's thoroughly unpopular régime and what Cavour referred to as 'the Garibaldian disease' must be swept away, if necessary by military action.

The northern army, when it crossed into Neapolitan territory in mid-October, found that many of the peasants took arms on behalf of their former legitimate sovereign against a destructive foreign invasion that they could not be expected to understand. General Cialdini affected surprise and reacted by summary execution of 'brigands' and 'traitors' and civilians who tried to defend their property. He was prepared to treat captured Bourbon soldiers and uniformed mercenaries as prisoners, but anyone else who dared to resist had to be shot even if they surrendered. Although Cavour proudly claimed that 'never was war fought with greater generosity and magnanimity', a good deal of offence was taken in other countries as well as in Italy over the unfortunate methods employed in this civil war, and the memory was to be a painful burden on the future.

In the early summer Garibaldi, despite what La Farina pretended, had been far more eager than Cavour for the whole of the south to be united with northern Italy. At first Garibaldi's ministers hoped that the union would be decided by the deliberation of elected assemblies in Naples and Sicily, but the government in Turin vetoed this because they preferred a simple 'yes' or 'no' plebiscite and justifiably feared that an assembly might lay down unwelcome conditions for annexation. Cavour knew, however, that he needed to appease the strong feelings in favour of regional autonomy, and hence promised southerners, as he had already promised the Tuscans, to introduce 'a system of wide administrative devolution' if only they accepted annexation by the north. Garibaldi accepted this offer and agreed to hold a plebiscite, though to avoid the humiliating word 'annexation' he chose a different formula which was strongly disliked in Turin: the vote would be on whether to join 'Italy one and indivisible under our constitutional sovereign Victor Emanuel'.

The King's immediate reaction was delight that he could incorporate the south without having to use force against too many of his future subjects. He delayed his march southwards until after 21 October, the date when plebiscites were held in Naples and Sicily. Despite conditions of near anarchy and civil war in some areas, the vote was managed well enough to give the by now familiar ninety-nine per cent in favour of joining a united Italy, and Cavour was insistent that, despite Garibaldi's unfortunate formula, this had to mean 'annexation' of the south by the north. Five days later, King and Dictator met. Victor Emanuel was at least polite and shook hands, but Farini and Fanti refused to do so and pointedly affected to take no notice of the man they despised and viewed as an enemy. Despite what legend pretends, this meeting near Teano was not a particularly happy encounter. The thirty thousand or more soldiers remaining under Garibaldi's command were abruptly informed that their military collaboration was no longer wanted since the regulars were quite capable on their own of bringing the war to a speedy end – a supposition that soon turned out to be excessively and even naïvely optimistic.

CHAPTER 21

Consolidating the Union
1860 – 61

During the second half of October a rumour circulated that the Austrians, profiting from the Piedmontese army's absence in the south, would take their chance to recapture Lombardy, and this rumour became stronger during the few days after 22 October when the ruling sovereigns of Austria, Prussia and Russia met at Warsaw. Cavour reaffirmed his belief that any invasion could be repelled, because he continued to maintain that the Austrian empire was internally divided and no longer strong enough to win a major war. But he was nevertheless relieved to receive assurances from France and England that Franz Joseph had no intention of repeating the mistake of April 1859 by starting further hostilities.

Most opportune of all was a public announcement on 27 October by Lord John Russell, stating more forcefully than any foreign government had done that the population of Italy must be allowed to form a united nation if they so wished. Nothing could have been more timely, and Cavour was seen with tears in his eyes as he read such a welcome pronouncement. He had condemned the English for being egoists when they criticized his continual agitation for war, but now they alone in Europe expressly welcomed what had happened in Naples. In another note, Russell condemned the governments of Francesco and the Pope for having been tyrannical, corrupt and thoroughly demoralizing to their subjects: if Austria ever tried to restore such discredited régimes, Italy would receive active and no longer merely moral support from London.

The retreating Bourbon army was meanwhile preparing to make a last stand north of Naples. Garibaldi refused to bombard an inhabited town, no doubt remembering the pejorative appellation of 'Bomba' accorded by the whole of Europe to the Bourbon King Ferdinando for what he had done at Messina and Naples in 1849. But Victor Emanuel, who badly needed the prestige of a quick military success, ordered that the city of Capua be shelled into submission just like Ancona, and explained that there was no point in worrying about humanitarian considerations. Garibaldi refused to watch what he called a barbarous spectacle of slaughter among a civilian population. He was further upset to learn how these northerners justified their refusal of his continued help by deprecating his military ability and calling his success pure luck. Obviously there was a plan for the prestige of this revolutionary general to be diminished so that the regular generals should appear in a better light. Cavour made an unconvincing and strangely ungenerous comment when he tried to persuade a French visitor that if the Bourbons were not yet finally defeated, it was for some obscure reason Garibaldi's fault.

What to do with the ex-dictator was a problem. One suggestion by Lord Palmerston was that, since one of Garibaldi's earlier vocations had been that of a naval commander in South America, he should be put in charge of the Italian navy; another suggestion was that he be sent as an ambassador to South America where his reputation was very high; and Admiral Persano thought that his enormous popularity among southerners should be harnessed by appointing him nominal Governor of Naples. But Cavour preferred him safely pensioned off with money, titles and gifts. On 7 November the King formally accepted from Garibaldi's hand the sovereignty of Naples. But Farini, who had to be present as Cavour's *alter ego* on this occasion, again took pride in looking the other way and refusing to address a single word to the man who had conquered half of Italy on the King's behalf. Garibaldi then sailed for Caprera after scorning offers of rank and reward; his departure was accorded a formal salute by the guns of the British fleet, but Persano's ships were ordered to remain silent.

Cavour was torn between the dual and conflicting necessities of seeming generous while in practice being politically unyielding, and the second of these had to take precedence. Three or four times during the next month he threatened to resign rather than allow any political concession to his radical opponents. When Victor Emanuel made the imaginative and reconciling suggestion of offering Mazzini an amnesty – an offer supported by Ricasoli as well as Giuseppe Verdi and other

237

moderates who remembered Mazzini as the inspiration and guiding light of their youth – Cavour persuaded the Cabinet to refuse categorically. Likewise, when the King went too far in promising to retain the rank of those among Garibaldi's officers who wanted to join the regular army, an abrupt reminder was sent that ministers had still not addressed themselves to this delicate and divisive problem.

Advice came from half a dozen of his closest advisers that the Prime Minister ought to visit Naples and see the difficulties for himself. Garibaldi said he would much rather have dealt with him than with Farini. Everyone knew that Cavour had already accompanied the King to all the other principal towns in the newly annexed regions, but he now refused to do the same in Naples or Palermo, saying that he and Victor Emanuel would only quarrel as they had quarrelled often before. He explained that as a subject he was willing to sacrifice his possessions and his life for the monarch as a symbol of national unity, 'but as a man I ask a sole favour, to be allowed to stay as far away from him as possible'. His predecessor Azeglio once said much the same in very similar words.

Cavour already had far too much to do in Turin where he was in charge of four ministerial departments, but his refusal to go south, however understandable, was the more unfortunate in that he was much too far away to judge what the situation required, yet could not afford to let people on the spot decide for themselves. In any case Farini and Victor Emanuel were entirely out of their depth in such unfamiliar surroundings where great political tact was required, and after a week they had to admit that their new régime was turning out to be 'an unheard-of fiasco'. Whereas Garibaldi had won the trust and co-operation of many southerners by his good nature and honest concern for their welfare, the new Piedmontese administration chose to impose an authoritarian and military rule over a population that they all too clearly disliked and treated often with open contempt. Farini indignantly reported that the inhabitants of the countryside were utterly inferior to those of what he called 'Italian Italy' in the north. He referred to them as primitive barbarians, compared with whom the African bedouin seemed the very flower of civilization; and the phrase 'ferocious bedouin' was also used to describe Sicilians by Cavour's first viceroy in Palermo. When the King boasted that a single Piedmontese regiment would be sufficient to keep such *canaille* and riff-raff in subjection, Cavour repeated his approval of using martial law and armed might 'to force unity on the weakest and most corrupt region of Italy' – another remark that was prudently cut out of Luigi Chiala's edition of his letters.

Looking back, it now seems that this attitude derived from a number of illusions. Any belief in the effectiveness of armed force to control the south, let alone arrogant talk of a single regiment being sufficient, was questioned by others from the outset. Then there was the almost racialist notion, unfortunately disseminated in Piedmont by Poerio and other Neapolitan exiles, that southerners were incorrigibly lazy and corrupt: Massari, himself born in the extreme south, reported from Naples that the place was an Augean stable where 'corruption and immorality' made government impossible and which only 'a thorough dose of Piedmontese morality' would cleanse. Another illusion derived from the plebiscite, because the voting figures were taken to signify that everyone was freely asking for annexation by the north, whereas Farini on his arrival could barely find a hundred out of seven million people who knew what such a union meant and truly wanted it – Dr Pantaleoni, another friend of Cavour, put the figure at fewer than twenty. The awesome possibility was raised that the plebiscite might have been something quite different: a personal vote of confidence in the dreaded and despised Garibaldi.

Another misconception was Cavour's belief that Sicily and Naples were potentially the richest instead of two of the poorest provinces of Italy, and indeed that they needed only efficient government and 'Piedmontese morality' to become the garden of Italy and a flourishing centre of prosperous industry. There was irony in the fact that the backwardness of the south was said to be a temporary fact due to Bourbon misgovernment; interested parties later tried to blame it on Garibaldi's misrule and mismanagement, in other words something that could easily be corrected. Even in December 1860, when Cavour saw misgovernment to be no better under Piedmontese administration, he still deluded himself that the difficulties would disappear 'by magic' when the last enemy stronghold of Gaeta was captured and the Bourbons accepted defeat. He was handicapped by the fact that almost no one in the north knew much about the south or had any inkling of its underlying structural problems. He used to talk in the same not very realistic vein of the 'gigantic' improvements about to descend on the island of Sardinia under the administration of Turin – though after a century and a half there were surprisingly few improvements to boast about in that misunderstood and neglected region.

Eventually Cavour realized that his choice of Farini to govern Naples had been a grave error, and others of his own party called it an almost fatal blunder. Policy had been based on the assumption that Garibaldi was hated so much that a new conservative administration would be received with delight. But the British government was informed by one of Cavour's friends in Naples that Farini's 'feverish activity to model everything on the Piedmontese pattern' was arousing enormous local opposition; indeed 'he is utterly unfit for the task he has to perform and is hated by everybody except a small circle round him.' In Turin, on the contrary, the main fear was that Farini might make too many concessions to local autonomist sentiment. Whichever view was correct, opposition in Naples was such that the quoted price of government stock fell by one third in a few weeks. There was extravagant talk of begging Garibaldi to return, and even of drawing up a petition to the rest of Europe against the 'horrors' of Piedmontese rule.

One measure adopted by Farini to meet local criticism was to appoint a consultative body of Neapolitans to advise him about local needs. But Cavour had no patience with such a concession to popular opinion in what was a corrupt society. Better a civil war, he said, than the irreparable catastrophe that might follow any such symptom of weakness or irresolution. Piedmontese laws had to be imposed on Naples, by force if need be, and certainly without discussion at local level. Firm decisions were needed and quickly, and he added that if anyone were able to say that Garibaldi had governed Naples better than the moderate liberals of Piedmont, 'we shall be ruined'.

If Farini at Naples was a mistake, even more ill-advised was Cavour's choice of La Farina to be the chief administrator of Sicily: not only were both these men known to be bitter personal enemies of Garibaldi, but there can be no doubt that this was a main reason why they were selected. Many people, moderates as well as radicals, pointed out that La Farina's return to Sicily could be guaranteed to cause discord, quite apart from the fact that he had not the least experience of government. Victor Emanuel, who had shown at Villafranca that he sometimes possessed more equanimity and common sense than the Prime Minister, tried to veto the appointment, but Cavour forced it through by another threat of resignation. On arriving at Palermo in December, La Farina proceeded to arrest some of his opponents as well as to dismiss senior police officers and civil servants appointed by the previous régime, but within days was so unpopular that he took to his heels leaving a disorganized and demoralized administration behind him. Reports were soon reaching Turin about an overwhelming dislike in Sicily of anything that could be called Piedmontese.

These difficulties in southern Italy meant that hopes of another military campaign against Austria – which Cavour in November said might be desirable 'for reasons of internal order' – had to be abandoned. Cavour was intercepting some of the French and English diplomatic communications that passed through Turin, but none the less found the policy of Napoleon so enigmatic and contradictory that no firm plans for the next war could yet be made. At the end of November the Emperor reassured one Italian official that he was still intending to fight against the Germans for the Rhine frontier, but also told the English that he strongly disapproved of Cavour fighting against the Bourbons, nor did he think that southern Italy would long remain united with the north. Even when talking to the Austrians, Napoleon referred to Cavour's policy in the south as misguided, and he reassured the deposed King Francesco that the Bourbon government had justice and law on its side in resisting 'Piedmontese aggression'.

Feeling he was without much support in Europe except from England, Cavour had to tell General Lamarmora on 16 November that their hoped-for European war must be put off for two years at least. But by this time it was too late to stop five shiploads of rifles and cannon already sent to Roumania for distribution to various unauthenticated, or indeed possibly imaginary, groups of revolutionaries. The cargoes were listed as grain and coffee. On 22 November, two of these ships reached Galatz on the Danube, but by an unfortunate error the three thousand crates of coffee were clearly marked as having been packed in the royal arsenals of Turin and Genoa. Three Piedmontese consular officials urgently set to work painting out these compromising signs, but were too late because an Austrian warship had been tracking the operation. Protests were soon pouring in from Turkey and other European governments.

Cavour continued through January 1861 to pledge his word of honour that he knew nothing about this gun-running, and made an official protest at Constantinople when the three other vessels were impounded by the Turks. But this further piece of bluff did not improve his reputation abroad. Queen Victoria fulminated against the 'piratical and filibustering proceedings' of 'this really bad, unscrupulous Sardinian government', and a note from the Foreign Office in London cynically wondered 'what lie Cavour will palm off on Hudson' to explain what had been going on.

The lie, when it emerged, cannot have caused much surprise: it was to put all the blame on Garibaldi, a convenient if innocent scapegoat, and Piedmontese ambassadors were instructed to spread the story that Garibaldi owned these arms and was irresponsibly seeking to employ them for a revolution of his own making in eastern Europe. Here was another useful opportunity to deflate the dangerously high esteem enjoyed abroad by the ex-dictator of Naples. But the story was not believed, and Russell was confirmed in his belief that Cavour could no longer be trusted to tell the truth about anything.

The Prussian government was similarly incredulous. Lamarmora, who went on a bridge-building mission to Berlin in January 1861, found some intellectuals who sympathized with Italy, but officials in general saw much to criticize. Public opinion in Germany, so Lamarmora reported, was inclined to put Cavour on a par with Mazzini because of the revolutionary and sometimes ruthless methods he employed. To correct such an impression, Cavour tried once again through Lamarmora to convince the Prussians that he secretly thought of them rather than the French as his 'natural ally'. He even invented the excuse that he had invaded the south so as to stop Napoleon putting a French-controlled puppet on the throne of Naples; and he confirmed that the time would come when he no longer needed to depend on Paris, at which point his sympathies and calculation of national interest would draw Italians towards their natural ally in Berlin.

His anxiety to convey this impression was understandable, but protestations about deserting the French alliance were not easily credited. Nor had he sufficiently taken into account that although Prussia might be in rivalry with Austria for domination in Germany, she also needed Austrian support as a check on France and Russia; for which reason Italy, with her determination to break up the Austrian empire, was still likely to be seen in Berlin as a potential enemy rather than an ally. Since Trieste and the Adriatic were vital commercial links along the southern route into central Europe, military opinion in Prussia was unanimous in considering the Austrian possession of

Venice to be necessary for the defence of the whole German Confederation.

This was one reason why Cavour decided that the acquisition of Rome had to take precedence over another war to win Venice. The last months of his life were therefore devoted to a good deal of complicated diplomacy with the papacy, his aim being to undermine and destroy the last relics of the Pope's temporal power. This, he thought, would be the culminating triumph of the *risorgimento* and would rank 'among the most glorious and fruitful achievements in the whole of human history'. A preliminary and indispensable step would be to secure the withdrawal of the French garrison which for ten years had been guarding Rome. Napoleon had for some time been eager to repatriate these soldiers 'as quickly as possible'. For this reason the French urged Cavour to try his hardest to win the Pope's confidence by a policy of conciliation, and at one point Prince Napoleon suggested a straight barter of Rome in exchange for giving Pius ix either Elba or the island of Sardinia.

Cavour on the other hand was sure that time was on his side, and was determined not to give the Vatican any impression that he was in a hurry to reach an agreement or indeed that he had much to offer by way of compromise. He thought that the Pope could be coerced into giving way, and hence insisted on immediately introducing the anticlerical laws of Piedmont into the newly annexed territories, even in parts of the Papal States that he had recently captured. Moreover he wanted this done without discussion and before the elected representatives of those regions could raise any doubts in the Turin Parliament. He intended to negotiate with the Pope, but from strength not weakness, and only after he had forcibly carried out what he called a revolution in the relations between Church and State.

The existing concordats with Rome were thus unilaterally and without consultation abolished in Naples, Tuscany and Lombardy. Cardinal Corsi was arrested for 'showing lack of respect to the King', and other bishops were put in prison on relatively trifling accusations of refusing to co-operate. Church property was seized on a grand scale, because Cavour still believed that 'the leprosy of monasticism' was a principal cause of economic backwardness. Seven hundred monasteries were eventually dissolved in the former papal territories of the

Marche and Umbria, over a thousand in southern Italy, and more than twenty thousand monks and friars were dispossessed on the grounds that the state could not afford so many idle hands. In the long run much land was thereby brought into more profitable production, to the delight of rich landowners who had agitated for just such a reform and now found themselves happily situated in a buyers' market; but others called it a spoliation by the wealthy at the expense of the poor. And one of the contingent causes of southern unrest was that this wholesale redistribution of land was not accompanied by a policy of agrarian reform such as had been so often discussed or even promised in the past. When the 'common lands' were enclosed by their new owners, there were widespread agrarian riots as the peasants retaliated by occupying land to which they knew that they had a legal right.

Since Parliament was not in session, this social revolution was carried out by executive action before there was time to mount any organized protest and before there could be adequate discussion in the press. Cavour was sure that the convincing arguments were all on his side. On the other hand, not having to defend his actions in debate, he did not appreciate the degree of offence given to Catholics who were trying to be good patriots; nor how useful it would have been to make more concessions so as to secure the allegiance of parish priests; nor how damaging was the effect on poor communities who depended on the religious houses for charity or for a livelihood. In some backward areas, according to the Piedmontese aristocrat he sent to govern Sicily, monks and friars acted as 'the advisers, the doctors, the lawyers, and even as the newspaper of every family', so that to dispossess them in such a hurry was for many people a major disaster.

These brusque and not very considerate actions hardly made a promising start to the harmonious negotiations with Rome that Napoleon was eager to see. Another point of discord was Cavour's attempt to modify the clause of the constitution that declared catholicism to be the official state religion. Here, too, he underrated the intractability as well as the strength of the Church. In July 1855 by the allocution *Nemo vestrum*, Pius IX had confirmed that catholicism should be the sole state religion; in *Ad apostolicae* and other official pronouncements he justified the temporal power as ordained by Christ himself to be an indispensable guarantee of papal independence; and

Acerbissimum pronounced that Cavour's attempt at separating State from Church was an indefensible error.

Cavour used to admit that he was not versed in canon law, but over the years had developed ideas very different from those of the Vatican. He had learnt in France and Switzerland about an ideal 'free church in a free state'. He had liked the toleration of different religious opinions that could be found in England and Scotland, and admired the separation of Church and State in the United States. As there seemed to be more and more of a worldwide consensus on this point, he assumed as self-evident that the Church could only gain from accepting liberalism, 'modern civilization' and a divorce between politics and religion; hence there was no immediate need to make further concessions.

But it was utopian to imagine that Pius IX would ever agree, and the future was to show that a complete separation of Church from State would be impossible to achieve. Cavour had not studied the matter sufficiently to be entirely clear what his favourite idea of a free Church could or ought to mean; nor, despite his formal assurances, was he prepared to allow churchmen as much liberty as he claimed for statesmen. He intended, for instance, to impose a reduction in the number of dioceses from two hundred and fifty to eighty; also to retain a veto in the hands of the government over the Pope's choice of bishops; and even to claim for Italy a right to veto any choice made by the cardinals when the time came to elect a new Pope.

Pius told Odo Russell that he was proud to call himself 'an Italian at heart' who loved his country, and boasted of it as 'harbouring more talent, mind and energy than any nation in the world'. If the Pope opposed the territorial unification of the peninsula, one reason he gave was that these qualities of intellect and character would eventually make a united Italy into 'the first of the great powers of the world', and hence too strong for her own good or for world peace. In January 1861, Pius nevertheless authorized his Secretary of State, Cardinal Antonelli, to begin informal talks with Cavour's two negotiators, Dr Pantaleoni and Padre Passaglia, and was sufficiently accommodating to inform Antonelli that the temporal power might just possibly be negotiable.

Cavour did not have a particularly high regard for the Pope's intellectual competence and was sure that the papalists were defending a lost cause. He therefore tried to insist that they must first yield in principle over the surrender of temporal sovereignty. He asked for, and received, French approval to begin negotiations on this point, though he was warned in Paris that he was being far too optimistic. Brilliant diplomat that he was, he might conceivably have become more conciliatory later and been able to strike an acceptable bargain had these preliminary talks gone well. But his negotiators were neither well chosen nor well briefed. Subsequently he sent two more representatives to Rome, but they were not working in common harness and made the discussions more difficult by resenting each other's presence.

Pantaleoni, who as a fashionable medical practitioner had a long and close experience of the papal court, advised that some bribery of junior officials would be necessary, though it is impossible to discover if the money sent for this purpose was used profitably. On hearing that Cardinal Antonelli might personally be open to an offer, Cavour agreed to suggest a solatium of three million papal *scudi* to this one man, in other words over fifteen million *lire*, which was nearly a thousand times the salary of a government minister. In addition he agreed to indemnify Antonelli's numerous relatives and condone the corrupt practices exercised by this family in the civic administration of Rome. He referred to what he was proposing as 'the less attractive part of our enterprise'; yet the other party apparently accepted it as providing at least a preliminary basis for discussion.

The agreement he hoped for was to be allowed to annex Rome, including if possible the area later known as the Vatican City; in return for which the state, in addition to guaranteeing certain territorial immunities, would pay the Pope an annual income of two million *lire* and the College of Cardinals another million – in other words about one per cent of the state budget. He was confident of success, especially after being told that a number of cardinals, estimated at between six and ten, had been won over to favour his proposal. He even hoped that six weeks might be sufficient for the whole matter to be concluded. But Antonelli was depending on complete secrecy and suddenly changed tack when his officials intercepted a letter mentioning the enormous sum of money intended for himself. Pius was equally annoyed when he discovered that the Piedmontese government was too confident to be flexible. When there was no abatement of the secularizing measures against the Church in Naples and Umbria, the Pope took this as evidence of Cavour's 'bad faith and duplicity', and decided that there was little point in further discussion with someone so insensitive and disingenuous. Finally a papal encyclical, *Iamdudum cernimus*, formally repudiated any possibility that catholicism could ever 'come to terms with progress, liberalism and modern civilisation', and Pantaleoni was summarily expelled from Rome.

Cavour still put on a bold face, arguing that such obduracy would merely isolate the papacy and make a final solution all the easier to obtain. He dropped a sardonic remark about the Pope soon becoming more malleable 'in an interval between his epileptic fits'. But in truth there was no ground for optimism. It was unfortunate that with all his other preoccupations he had been unable to supervize the negotiations more closely, and Pantaleoni protested at having been left without instructions for weeks at a time. When his various negotiators were seen to be proceeding along different paths, this merely confirmed a general belief in Rome that the Turin government was devious and untrustworthy.

CHAPTER 22

Centralization or Decentralization?

One main reason for Cavour's confidence at the beginning of 1861 was his determination to recall Parliament as soon as elections could take place in the south. Victor Emanuel would much rather have continued with his own kind of uninhibited personal rule, and Napoleon agreed with Ricasoli that the problems of the south could be settled only by the continued use of dictatorial powers. But Cavour saw Parliament as his 'safety anchor' and acknowledged that he always had reason to feel vulnerable when the *camera* was not in session. If there had to be a clash with the clerical right or the Garibaldian left, or indeed with the King himself, it was better to choose the favourable ground of a public debate where he had all his opponents at a disadvantage. The imminent prospect of further parliamentary battles put him in what he called, using the English phrase, 'high spirits'.

Elections could not by law be held until the end of January, which meant that Parliament could meet only in the second half of February, and indeed that would be possible only if some technicalities in the regulations were disregarded. In the intervening weeks there was a great deal to be done. An unwilling Costantino Nigra was sent to replace a thoroughly discredited and by now seriously ill Farini in Naples, where enthusiasm for unification had diminished catastrophically. Many reports were being received of anarchy spreading through the Neapolitan countryside, and there were protests against arbitrary arrests, against the eviction of recalcitrant magistrates, and against the illegal deportation of political opponents to Sardinia. Cavour chose Nigra as someone he could trust to study the problems of Naples at first hand and recommend a more reconciling or at least a more effective policy. Many southerners were demanding some degree of regional autonomy, as they had been repeatedly and authoritatively

248

promised; it was therefore important to investigate whether this would be practicable and whether or how far Naples would need special treatment.

Cavour had always been a theoretical champion of decentralization and local self-government, but although he said he would like to change the centralized prefectorial system that Piedmont had inherited from Napoleon I, he lacked the leisure to study the alternatives. It is also probable that his self-confidence and unwillingness to trust others deterred him from putting into serious practice his avowed preference for devolution of power, and on a number of occasions he had already been accused in Parliament of centralizing the administration too rigidly in Turin at the expense of Genoa and Sardinia. Believing that rivalries and jealousies between towns and provinces were a principal cause of Italy's troubles, he knew that he had to move carefully before relinquishing governmental power to local authorities.

The speed of unification in 1859–61 presented him with this problem in an acute form, because he suddenly had to devise a system of administration that could be applied to the whole of Italy. If only there had been time to make a study of the different regions, each might have been found to possess some laws or institutions that could be profitably adopted by the others. However, the pace of events and the urgent need for a least a provisional settlement compelled ministers to treat the nation as an extension of Piedmont: in other words to assume that the laws and traditions of the old kingdom, even if some were defective, should be taken as a general norm.

This helps to explain why, late in 1859 while Cavour was out of office, Piedmontese legislation had been hurriedly introduced under emergency powers into Lombardy and Emilia. Naturally there was almost at once a reaction in both regions against 'Piedmontization', and it was pointed out that the plebiscite which authorized the annexation of Lombardy had been specifically conditional on the holding of a constituent assembly to determine a new constitution. This condition had been forgotten or at least was now ignored. The consequent indignation in Lombardy not only helped Cavour back into power in January 1860, but subsequently convinced him that to offer some degree of regional autonomy might be an attractive inducement to other regions not yet annexed. He once said for example (and presumably believed) that the Ministry of Education ought to be abolished outright because no uniform system of education could be applied everywhere in a country whose component regions were at such different stages of development. This was the kind of thinking that persuaded him during 1860 to allow two of his Ministers of the Interior, Farini and Marco Minghetti – both of them non-Piedmontese from central Italy – to investigate and propose a scheme of regional devolution. The general principle was unanimously approved by the Cabinet.

While discussion of this major reform continued, Cavour had confirmed in April 1860 that he would permit, temporarily at least, a degree of autonomy in Tuscany, as he had already promised before the Tuscan revolution of April 1859. In part he did this because Napoleon's support was needed, and the French not only disliked the outright annexation of Tuscany but would be far more ready to accept a federal or quasi-federal Italy, in other words one based on distinct regions. In part he was moved by Ricasoli who made a strong plea for the Piedmontese *statuto* to be modified before being applied in Florence. Ricasoli nurtured a strong resentment against Cavour's apparently authoritarian attitude and against the idea of absorption by Piedmont. The Tuscan Governor's initial attitude was that the old regional capitals, Florence, Milan and Bologna, ought to preserve some degree of autonomy. Otherwise, he said, 'the stupid pedants and repugnant bureaucrats of Turin may force us into another revolution to throw off a yoke more hateful than that of Austria, because such people do not understand that we want to be Italians with an Italian soul, not automatons like them'.

Sicily was another region with a long tradition of autonomist sentiment developed during centuries of foreign rule, and some Sicilian moderates expressed the fear that under Turin their island might become another neglected area like Sardinia. Cavour's former colleague, the Sicilian economist Ferrara, had already warned that a policy of straight unconditional annexation might alienate feelings of sympathy for a united Italy. A region with no tradition of military conscription could not suddenly be subjected to it without causing trouble. To introduce all at once a new language, completely new codes of law, a different educational system, new coins and a new system of weights and measures would be asking too much. The public debt in Sicily per head was less than a quarter of that in Piedmont, and a sudden equalization in the burden of debt and taxation would be seen as another injustice that could only provoke opposition.

Such considerations would have been in Cavour's mind when, on a number of occasions during 1860, he held out the attractive offer that after annexation Sicilians could expect from Piedmont 'a very large degree of administrative decentralisation' with at least some of their ancient privileges kept intact. He told them it was his wish to grant 'real self-government' to individual regions, and he and Victor Emanuel both made vague references to the possibility that Sicily might be allowed to keep its own elected assembly with some powers of legislation. No promises were made, but Cavour's Sicilian friends were encouraged by him to give special publicity to such statements so as to win local support for annexation, and some people were therefore encouraged to believe that an affirmative vote in the plebiscite would be conditional on both Sicily and Naples being allowed to regain 'real self-government' with some of their old laws and institutions.

Cattaneo and Ferrara, on the other hand, assumed that Cavour was merely being deceitful in a calculated attempt to win votes, and it is true that although the Prime Minister continued to speak approvingly of regional self-government and put it forward to be discussed by a parliamentary commission, he never went out of his way to push it politically or make it an issue of confidence. The secretary of the commission thought that his contribution to their private discussions indicated that in fact he did not favour the idea. In any case, by the end of 1860 the example of Ricasoli's independence and extravagance in Tuscany was another warning against letting decentralization go too far in the direction of regional autonomy.

Whatever his theoretical preference, Cavour decided after the plebiscites of October 1860 that Piedmontese laws should be arbitrarily imposed on Naples and Sicily. There was no time to waste in trying to obtain from Parliament the necessary powers to sanction this decision, nor time to investigate whether the laws of other regions might in some respects be preferable, nor how far local conditions made uniformity of treatment inadvisable. The courageous order was given that Piedmontese legal codes had to be introduced at once and entire before Parliament could question this act of centralization: in fact, not by accident, the relevant royal decree was hurriedly published the very day before Parliament was due to assemble. In the final few hours before Parliament met, fifty-three decree-laws were rushed into print in

Naples, altering the whole administrative structure of the south before this immense revolution could be discussed in the press or by local representatives in the legislature.

Of course many objections were at once raised, but they were either overruled or buried. When southerners argued that the jury system would not work in a different and still semi-feudal milieu characterized by mafia intimidation and general illiteracy, the obviously false answer came that juries worked perfectly well in Sardinia. When some of the deputies protested that the government had been given no authority to impose the Piedmontese legal codes on the whole country, the minister replied that there could be no rigid observance of legality during a revolution. Specific instructions were sent to appoint Piedmontese civil servants in Naples and to take no account of local objections, while the administration was furthermore told to disregard the strong opposition of the committees of Sicilians and Neapolitans that had been appointed to give advice on this and kindred matters.

When the new Parliament finally assembled on 18 February 1861, Cavour found himself with another comfortable majority for what he told Poerio was the 'fight against Garibaldism'. Until almost the last moment he had been in some doubt about the election result, especially since the great majority of deputies would be from regions with no parliamentary tradition. But official pressure and electoral manipulation was used on a substantial scale, and fortunately for Cavour all good Catholics were discouraged from voting, in protest at official policy. On a very narrow franchise, in which only about one and a half per cent of the population voted, candidates backed by government patronage and by local authorities had a strong advantage, while the restricted suffrage helped to elect conservatives who stood against the threat of social or political revolution. To make doubly sure, in the days before the election Cavour gave orders for wide publicity to be given once again to the government's commitment to regional self-government.

By the appointment of Rattazzi as Speaker of the lower house the Prime Minister successfuly neutralized the man whose criticisms were most to be feared. But these two leading liberals in the country, though their friends made further attempts to reconcile them, were now refusing to speak to each other. This was the more unfortunate in that a number of other prominent politicians turned down the offer of a ministerial post, and Cavour had the greatest difficulty in finding representatives of other regions whom he thought suitable for the Cabinet. Victor Emanuel, seeing this as another opportunity to replace Cavour, privately asked Ricasoli to consider accepting the premiership, and apparently Rattazzi received a similar offer; but they knew better than to indulge this regal whim, and both were ready to admit that only one man had the ability, experience and parliamentary support needed to unite the new nation.

Cavour decided before Parliament met that the royal title ought to remain 'Victor Emanuel II', though others would have preferred 'Victor Emanuel I' to show that the Kingdom of Italy was a new nation and not merely a continuation or extension of the former 'Kingdom of Sardinia, Cyprus and Jerusalem'. Ricasoli protested that keeping the old title was yet another example of 'Piedmontization' and of Cavour's high-handedness; he thought it degrading to other regions who thought of themselves not as 'annexed' to Piedmont but as part of an altogether new kingdom for which they had voted. Cavour, however, under pressure from the royal palace, insisted on 'annexation' and argued that a change of title would dishonour the King by making him seem a new ruler holding his office merely by virtue of popular plebiscites, rather than as a hereditary monarch by grace of God.

A more disturbing parliamentary controversy was over the rapidly worsening condition of Naples. The Prime Minister had warned that the liberals would not be forgiven if, with all their resources and experience, they governed the south less well than Garibaldi had with almost no resources whatever. But by trying to diminish the latter's reputation in Naples, Cavour weakened one of the most powerful myths behind the new sense of national unity. He had assumed that conditions in the south would at once be improved when Crispi, Depretis and Garibaldi's other ministers had departed and been replaced by northerners with their traditions of freedom, efficiency and morality; but he eventually had to admit that to solve the 'southern question' and harmonize north and south was quite as difficult as defeating Austria.

The Prime Minister and his new proconsul, Nigra, were soon as unpopular in Naples as Farini had been. The local finances were in complete disarray and getting worse, which was precisely the criticism that Cavour had made of Garibaldi's administration. Prices, reported the English consul, rose in a few months by sixty per cent – much more for some commodities. The abolition of protective duties by up to eighty per cent in a single day, however desirable it may have seemed to the theorists of free trade, favoured imports from the north but damaged some of the hitherto protected industries in the south. Some people called this a deliberate piece of discrimination so as to make national unification more palatable to northerners. The number of bureaucrats in Naples continued to grow instead of diminish, with no obvious sign of increased efficiency. Moreover, the power of under-world racketeers seems to have increased after Nigra's appointment of administrators notoriously involved with the *camorra* – another criticism that had been made against Garibaldi. The officials sent from Piedmont to set things to rights found themselves powerless and could not so much as understand the local language. Massari and other southerners reported to Parliament that law and order had broken down absolutely, so that not only Garibaldi but the ex-King Francesco were being thought of by some people with nostalgia.

Cavour had never met any remotely similar problem before. Sincere though he was in his belief in liberty, he had to accept the advice of local military commanders that repression, martial law and even executions without trial would be necessary. More and more troops had to be sent to the south to deal with 'brigands', who were sometimes simple malefactors but were often loyal subjects of the deposed Bourbons, or Catholics outraged by a policy of despoliation and secularization carried out by the freemason Nigra.

After receiving Cavour's instructions to act with the maximum severity, General Della Rocca ordered that no time be wasted in taking prisoners because 'brigands' deserved only summary execution and the imperative need was to 'inculcate terror'. General Pinelli in February authorized his soldiers to be pitiless in 'purifying the countryside by fire and the sword' against 'the hired assassins of the Vicar not of Christ but of Satan'. Pinelli was censured for this tactless order, but Crispi stated in Parliament that such repressive action was not an effective answer to disaffection; it would merely be a further stimulus to a widespread movement of political reaction. The Austrians were also able to assert that the convenient word 'brigand-age' was merely a euphemism for civil war. They pointed out that this terrible conflict in southern Italy required more troops than had been used in the national war of 1859, and hence that Cavour was being hypocritical when he protested against the aggressiveness and repression of Austrian policy; nor could he claim to be leading a people united in a desire for freedom and nationality.

Comment inside Italy was necessarily muted, because the facts were not generally known and those who knew were averse to exposing this failure to outside eyes. Cavour was most unhappy about it, and Rattazzi and Lamarmora privately agreed with Victor Emanuel that the need to take the initiative out of Garibaldi's hands had forced Piedmont into what now looked like a premature annexation of Naples. Azeglio concluded once again that if only Cavour had had time to learn more about the rest of Italy he would surely have acted with more caution. According to Azeglio, the union with Naples was 'like going to bed with someone suffering from smallpox', and if the south could only with the greatest difficulty be held down by half of the Italian army, he concluded that there must have been some mistake in the plebiscites. The principle that justified the *risorgimento* was the right to self-determination; hence, if Neapolitans did not after all want to join the other regions, Azeglio wondered whether they should not be allowed their freedom to secede. Many other northerners, without going so far as to mention secession, were almost equally disillusioned. 'It is a misfortune for this country', wrote the Swiss representative in Turin on 4 June 1861, 'that the Piedmontese are hardly regarded by others as being real Italians and in general show little interest in being considered as such, especially now that they have come in contact with Neapolitans and Sicilians whose customs and culture are so different from those in northern Italy.'

CHAPTER 23

Problems in Parliament
1861

At the end of 1860 Garibaldi returned to his home on the lonely island of Caprera. His activities and visitors were closely scrutinized from a gunboat placed at his disposal, whose officers had orders to give warning to Turin of the least sign of further military preparations on his part. From Caprera he issued a public appeal for national concord and called for an active policy of recruitment so that half a million soldiers would soon be ready for another war to capture Venice from Austria. Cavour feared that secret encouragement for this dangerous idea was coming from the royal palace, but promised the French that no further initiative by the volunteers would be permitted. If necessary, he said, force would be used to stop it, and meanwhile a mollifying message was sent to Caprera early in 1861 pleading for no precipitate action until the government saw better chances of success.

The radicals in Parliament were in part propitiated by being privately informed that Cavour still intended to annex Venice and Rome during his lifetime. This was the limit of his immediate territorial ambitions. Though he believed that Malta and Istria and possibly also the Swiss Canton Ticino were ideally part of Italy, these areas were to be left as a problem for future generations to solve. The South Tyrol was in a similar category, and Lamarmora perhaps represented current belief in Turin when he made the strange claim that only an insignificant number of people spoke German south of the Alps. Valerio, taking too literally one of Cavour's private statements, once spoke publicly of Trieste and Dalmatia being objectives of Italian policy, but the Prime Minister quickly published an official denial. All that could be permitted, he told Valerio, was to 'sow in order that our children may reap' in the 'not too distant future': any premature talk of acquiring Trieste would alienate the German Confederation and other countries whose friendship was needed.

Cavour knew that he must not risk making enemies in northern Europe by public talk of turning the Adriatic into 'an Italian lake'. But when foreign statesmen asked him for a specific repudiation of further warlike plans, he had to explain that any public statement would merely 'put a weapon into the hands of Garibaldi and the reds'; the rest of Europe would therefore have to remain content with a private undertaking that he was doing all he could to prevent war. With half the available soldiers tied up in Naples, quite apart from the enormous difficulty of applying Piedmontese laws about conscription to a recalcitrant population in central and southern Italy, he could not hope to put the army on a war footing until the spring of 1862; by which time, according to what he gave an astonished Hudson to understand, he thought that France might be ready to help him by launching another European war for the conquest of Belgium.

With this in mind, General Fanti the Minister of War began to plan a major reorganization of the army in January 1861, only to run into strong criticism in Parliament from General Lamarmora and others who thought that the German rather than the French army might be a better model to copy. Cavour loyally stood by Fanti, though privately he told people that Lamarmora's criticisms were substantially justified. Disturbing information had been received that Napoleon and the French General Staff thought Fanti to be an incompetent, but this minister had backing from the King and therefore could not be dropped without provoking a political crisis.

The issue of army reform came before Parliament in a dramatic debate on 23 March, during which Cavour made clear that the reorganization of the armed forces was in his opinion the most urgent of all the problems facing the country. But when Lamarmora's alternative policy was supported from the benches of the left, notably by Brofferio and Crispi, the government sensed political danger. During the debate one of Garibaldi's ex-generals let fall a remark suggesting that Cavour had made considerable difficulties for the volunteer army during the conquest of Sicily, and also that French permission for the invasion of Umbria had been obtained on the plea of thus bringing Garibaldi's victories to an end. Both remarks were true, but the Speaker, Rattazzi, in the interests of national solidarity called them 'impossible and false' and hence ruled them out of order. Cavour was sure that most of the deputies had, like himself, been largely convinced by Lamarmora's arguments, but this unfortunate incident compelled him to rally his majority behind government policy, though at some cost to the cause of army reform.

Another aspect of policy in which, as Cavour had to admit, Fanti was desperately ineffective was dealing with the soldiers of the former Bourbon army and Garibaldi's volunteers. Some of the Bourbon senior officers had been admitted at once into the new Italian army, preference being given necessarily but perhaps unfortunately to those who had deserted to join the Piedmontese in the summer of 1860. Most of the rank and file were left to disband, and sixty thousand unemployed ex-soldiers added greatly to the problem of 'brigandage' in the south. But Cavour backed Fanti in preferring to conscript new younger soldiers in Naples rather than face the problem of admitting veterans from an enemy force who had obeyed their oath of allegiance rather than desert.

Many of the fifty thousand volunteers who claimed to have fought under Garibaldi's command had gone home when the fighting came to an end. Most of the other junior ranks were given six months' pay and disbanded, because few of them were prepared to sign on as regulars for a fixed term of years. The most difficult problem was the inflated number of seven thousand officers that Garibaldi had appointed, especially as a good number of them had seen no fighting, or very little, and could hardly expect to keep their rank in competition with seasoned products of the military academy in Turin.

Garibaldi understood this difficulty, but was resentful that the senior army officers were so strongly prejudiced against all volunteers that they continued to treat them with manifest contempt. It seemed wrong to him that more favourable treatment was accorded to regular Neapolitan soldiers who had recently been fighting against the Piedmontese. Cavour in part sympathized with Garibaldi's resentment; yet the man was an overmighty subject 'who combines the petulance of a soldier of fortune with the profound dissimulation of a savage' (another observation omitted from Cavour's published letters); such an unruly person could not be allowed to continue acting as though he were a power in the land. It was humiliating to be told that everyone in Paris and London thought of this guerrilla leader as personifying Italian patriotism and as holding in his hand the key to European peace or war. Victor Emanuel was equally indignant when Garibaldi publicly criticized the monarchy for being too much under Cavour's thumb and for not acting to reach an equitable settlement. Rattazzi went twice to see Garibaldi, but failed to prevent him from bringing these fundamental differences to general attention in a parliamentary debate.

On 18 April there was a tragic confrontation when Garibaldi appeared in his incongruous red shirt and poncho to take his seat on the extreme left of the *camera* while other redshirts packed the public galleries. He started to speak in favour of the volunteers, but lost the thread of his argument and in a moment of uncontrolled passion, to cheers from the galleries, repeated the accusation that the government in 1860 had come close to provoking civil war. He must have known that he was hopelessly at a disadvantage challenging experienced ministers in debate, and Cavour in reply was able to protest angrily if inaccurately that the possibility of civil war had never entered his mind. A tumult ensued and the debate had to be closed while tempers cooled. After it was resumed, the government had a majority of a hundred and ninety-four votes against seventy-nine, Garibaldi being among those who abstained; apparently some of the provocative words he used were then tactfully deleted from the public record.

With so many other difficulties to resolve, it was bitter for Cavour to have to endure a public encounter with the best known and most admired Italian in the world. The Prime Minister's close associates were sure that he had not been too worried about the prospect of meeting this challenge on his own ground in Parliament, but no doubt he had hoped at first for a victory in debate that would pave the way to a reconciliation. Instead the division became even more bitter when General Cialdini, with Cavour's approval, sent Garibaldi a note that was virtually a challenge to a duel, repeating the gratuitous and incredible accusation that Garibaldi had given an order to fire on the Piedmontese in September 1860.

Immense anger was caused by this challenge. In Naples a mob demonstration took place with the cry of 'death to Cavour and Cialdini'. In Milan and Mondovì there were attempted insurrections and some people called for a republic. Garibaldi, however, realized he had gone too far and replied to this offensive note with moderation and dignity. The King summoned the aggrieved parties to the palace to make a formal truce. Garibaldi was told that the government still intended to win Venice from Austria but not yet, and accepted this information in good faith, though he requested that more generosity be shown to those of the volunteer officers whose fate was not yet settled. He also asked Cavour to free himself from too obvious and undignified a dependence on the wishes of Napoleon; after which in a published letter he pledged his support for the final unification of the peninsula when the government decided that the time was ripe.

Another controversial debate took place over Cavour's proclamation that Rome must one day replace Turin as the national capital. Azeglio would have preferred to choose Florence; Alfieri suggested Naples; but a wide spectrum of opinion – from Ricasoli on the right to Garibaldi on the left, and especially among anticlericals – would accept nothing less than Rome, and this ambition was powerfully supported by those inside the ruling coalition who were unhappy with the spread of 'Piedmontization' from Turin. Many Catholics were of course deeply shocked by the suggestion. Cavour tried to persuade Parliament that any responsibility for the antagonism between Church and State lay with the Pope alone, who by his intransigence was provoking a fatal struggle within the Italian nation. He stressed that the current rebellion in the south could not be solved while Rome remained independent and while the papal authorities continued to send trouble-makers to stir up trouble in Naples. Perhaps he forgot that this was just what he had himself done against the Pope in Romagna and Umbria.

A number of conservatives were against raising the issue of the annexation of Rome. Lamarmora was not happy about making this essentially ecclesiastical town into the national capital. Menabrea, Sclopis, Alfieri and Casati also thought it was probably a mistake. Azeglio was one of those patriots who wanted a kingdom of northern Italy alone, and repeated that if Cavour had known southern Italy at first hand he would never have advanced beyond Umbria and the Marche. According to Azeglio, this talk of moving the capital to Rome was a mere tactic on Cavour's part, and perhaps an insincere device to recover the government's popularity by showing that ministers could outdo Mazzini and the Party of Action; it was an attempt to take people's attention off the urgent and important problem of 'how we Italians can succeed in hating each other a little less'. Azeglio was convinced that Rome, like the south, would prove a corrupting element in Italian society.

Cavour did not personally look forward to moving the government to Rome and said that he himself would prefer to stay behind in Piedmont even if it meant leaving politics altogether. But he thought the long-term objective to be necessary, indeed self-evident, and in his opinion it did not warrant discussion as a general principle however much people might differ over the means adopted. It was possible that if the papacy could after all reconcile itself to accepting liberal practice and the existence of an Italian nation, there might before long be an active Catholic majority in Parliament, in which case he would cheerfully move to the opposition benches further to the left. Although the Vatican, because of its supernatural sanction, might not be able to agree voluntarily to surrender temporal power, he still assumed that – as so often in the past – it would eventually reconcile itself to a *fait accompli*. He hoped at least that the Pope would agree to stay in Rome after losing sovereignty, and for that reason any idea of acquiring the Holy City by means of military conquest was out of the question. The papacy was 'our most splendid national institution' and must be kept in Italy if at all possible.

The primary task was to convince Napoleon to help or at least not to hinder, and Cavour therefore went to the extent of consulting Paris about the precise words he ought to use in Parliament, because only if the French could be persuaded to withdraw their protection from Rome would the Pope accept defeat. Though the Emperor had not wanted a completely united Italy, he needed to keep the new nation an ally of France and not of England. He was therefore one of the few Frenchmen who had in general been sympathetic to Cavour's policy. Many were openly hostile. Guizot for example, and the Count de Montalembert, were bitterly critical as they watched the liberals in Turin take over Mazzini's policy but without what they agreed was Mazzini's honesty and disinterestedness. Cavour was accused by Guizot of 'democratic tyranny' and putting 'permanent revolution in place of law'; while according to Montalembert he would go down in history as another of the barbarian invaders, as a vandal who cynically tore up treaties and callously sent people to die for an illiberal cause.

In the middle of April, Napoleon put up a new and very interesting proposal for discussion. Under this suggestion the French garrison in Rome would be withdrawn over the next few months. In return, Italy would allow the papacy to keep a truncated state round the city of Rome with up to five million subjects, and would also guarantee to defend it from outside attack. A broad hint also arrived from Paris that this would leave the way open for the Pope's subjects to rise in revolt one day if so minded, by which time France would have washed her hands of the whole affair.

Cavour at once realized that it was the best bargain he was likely to get and would in fact give him almost all that he wanted. He could promise with a clear conscience to protect this last relic of the temporal power against an invasion that was most unlikely to take place. He would not be obliged to defend the Pope against internal revolution, but on the contrary would feel free to intervene after a decent interval, on the plea of having to prevent this miniature Papal State from becoming a focus for revolutionary action. Privately he promised Napoleon that he would permit Rome to remain tranquil for six months once the French had withdrawn; to Garibaldi he said three months, after which anything could happen.

This arrangement, even if somewhat cynical and deceitful, would have been a great triumph and a fitting climax to Cavour's career, but by the time of his death had still not been formalized. Napoleon was worried what his Catholic subjects might say, and with good reason did not entirely trust Cavour, while he regarded other Italian politicians as even less reliable and straightforward. The Emperor privately told several Italians that the public announcement about Rome being the future capital had been a tactical error by Cavour because it made negotiations much harder, and informed his cousin that he was now becoming reluctant to conclude an agreement with someone whose indiscretions (and whose inability to deal with Naples and with Garibaldi) suggested that he could no longer be relied upon. In June 1861, Napoleon followed England and the United States in formally recognizing the existence of a new Kingdom of Italy, but he was privately telling the Austrians that Italian unification might not last and that their two countries had better be ready to act in concert with alternative plans. The Pope, even more dubious, categorically refused to recognize the existence of an Italian state based on the unilateral and 'sacrilegious usurpation' of ecclesiastical rights and property. Rome in fact remained outside the new kingdom until 1870; only in 1929 and with reluctance did the papacy acknowledge the existence of a unified Italy; while not until 1984 did it accept that catholicism should no longer be the official and exclusive state religion.

The other principal 'unredeemed' province of Italy, Venice, was annexed only in 1866, long after Cavour's death. A few weeks before he died he told Parliament that there could be no lasting peace until this region had been acquired, though 'in the present state of the continent I do not think we have the right to launch another European war'. He still suspected, however, that a Hungarian revolt might break out that would force Garibaldi to lead an expedition to the Balkans, in which case he would not only allow it to happen but, as he told Tourte, would certainly support it. Remembering how profitable had been the meeting at Plombières, he suggested to the French Foreign Minister that they should meet to discuss such an eventuality, and in particular brought up his favourite scheme of sending another consignment of arms to the Balkans.

Towards the end of May he told Kossuth that by the end of the year, or at least by the summer of 1862, Venice would probably be Italian. He had already informed one Hungarian refugee that yet another national war might be necessary in order to solidify the fusion of north and south Italy. He would not actively provoke hostilities, partly because he feared to arm the people or create too large an army, and partly because the continued existence for a short while longer of a strong Austria would give Italians a greater sense of unity. But up to the very end of his life he was still talking of a possible war breaking out, and Tourte concluded that Switzerland might before long find Italy a very uncomfortable neighbour.

Another problem left unresolved in his last few weeks of life was the decentralization of government. Despite the fact that he continued to deplore centralization as illiberal, expensive and inefficient, he had been compelled to modify these views when he saw the danger that Italy might fall apart if a uniform administrative system was not quickly imposed on the whole kingdom. He watched with sadness and a sense of disillusionment the example of the United States of America, where civil war broke out in April. His immediate reaction to the news from Fort Sumter was to say that secession by the southern states of the American union would be unfortunate, but probably could not be avoided since they constituted 'almost if not altogether' a separate nationality. Just possibly this pessimistic view reflected a similar but

CAVOUR

concealed fear about southern Italy. He certainly took events in America as a warning of what might happen if a state abdicated too many powers to its constituent regions. La Farina went further and asserted that just because they were both federal states and racially divided, the United States and Switzerland were not strictly nations at all, and would disintegrate at once if confronted by any European army.

Inside Italy a great number of pamphlets were written from a very different standpoint to argue that regional devolution was absolutely necessary in their own very heterogeneous country. Nevertheless, more and more evidence was accumulating to suggest that regional autonomy was wanted by dubious elements close to the mafia and the *camorra*, and in general by local notables who saw it as the best way to keep their patronage systems intact. Another argument against such autonomy was that the major regional capital cities, for example Naples, Florence and Palermo, regarded it as a means to preserve their not always enlightened hegemony over provinces and smaller towns that had fought against this domination for centuries. There was also one further important reason why prefects and mayors should be appointed by the central government and given wide powers, because without their active assistance Cavour knew that he would find it much harder to secure the victory of official candidates in parliamentary elections. He also had good reason to fear that his coalition might split if he pushed the idea of regional government to the extent favoured by his Minister of the Interior, Minghetti, while to grant regional autonomy to Naples might well mean handing over power either to Garibaldi's followers or to partisans of the *ancien régime*. To divide Italy into regions might thus have meant political suicide. It would at the very least have seriously weakened the political élite on which he based his power.

The Piedmontese prefectorial system was therefore imposed on other regions, despite the fact that a centralized administration was something different from what nearly all the political thinkers of the *risorgimento* would ideally have liked. This was not a carefully deliberated policy but a hurried and emergency answer to a largely unexpected problem. Nor was Parliament asked to vote on the matter. The question was given prolonged discussion in parliamentary commissions, but when some of the deputies tried to raise the issue of regional devolution in the *camera*, they were ruled out of order on the grounds that the integrity of the kingdom was too delicate and controversial a subject for debate in Parliament. La Farina advanced the not very plausible argument that no country had fewer internal divisions than Italy and that her chief requirement was to become a strong state in which any remaining regional differences would disappear.

It is easier in retrospect to understand why regional autonomy was abandoned than why the promises of purely administrative decentralization were not honoured. One result of this latter omission was a weakness in local self-government, a weakness which was deplored by Cavour himself and which others continued to identify as an effective obstacle to the development of Italian democratic practice. Parliamentary business would sometimes be jammed by debates on purely local matters so that important state affairs were inadequately discussed or not brought up at all. Some people subsequently looked back on this as a reason why nationwide parties took so long to form and why parliamentary institutions failed to work efficiently at critical moments in Italian history.

This was hardly Cavour's fault. He was a victim of the system and in large part of circumstances beyond his control. But he was equally the victim of a compulsive obsession to take upon himself too much authority in too many fields, with the result that some important decisions went by default. Italy had completed in a few months what had taken France hundreds of years, and inevitably there was insufficient time to develop an administrative structure that would have removed some of the burden from one man's shoulders. A contemporary quip described Cavour as being the minister in charge of all seven government departments, and although he said he wanted to reduce his responsibilities, in practice he was more than ever frightened of delegating or sharing power. Azeglio commented that 'he has created a complete void round himself in which he has no real collaborators, only instruments'. Ricasoli made the same point when he said that Cavour wanted servants who obeyed, not friends or assistants; and the Swiss minister in Turin was surprised to find towards the end of May that even other members of the Cabinet were still being kept in complete ignorance of major aspects of government policy.

CHAPTER 24

The End

Though the Prime Minister did his best to appear cheerful so as to give the impression that government actions were well considered and proceeding as planned, the reality was different. Regularly during these last months of life he could not sleep for worry, and he confessed to Castelli that insomnia left him no longer in full possession of his mental faculties. His chief secretary, Artom, was liable to be kept awake working until 3.00 a.m., even when the first interviews of the next day began three hours afterwards. Inevitably this took a toll on the health of both of them and on the efficiency of such a centralized administration. Rattazzi wrote on 26 April that the government seemed out of control, since evidently no one except Cavour was responsible for laying down general policy, and either decisions were not taken at all or else a decision made today might be contradicted tomorrow. La Farina a week later confirmed that Cavour had no time for internal affairs but was leaving civil servants to shift for themselves as best they could without any overall direction.

Perhaps, if the process of national unification had taken longer and been less a constant succession of surprises, Cavour might have appreciated the urgent need to share out more of the routine work; this would have left him leisure to consider longer-term policy and would have helped to train more people to fill the gap that he left at his death. Much of his enforced activity was in fact commonplace or trivial. Since a good deal of entertainment accompanied the inauguration of the new kingdom, he was obliged to arrange dinners for the new deputies and offer formal dances in the Palazzo Cavour during carnival. He had to deal personally with a strike of bakers in Turin; with protests by university students against a new scale of fees; with working out an improved wage structure in the docks at Livorno; with compensation for damage sustained by an English farmer who owned the island of Monte Cristo; even with a bad case of bullying in the naval school at Genoa. He would have liked to inspect progress in the construction of the great railway tunnel through the Mont Cenis, but to leave Turin was impossible at a time when so many other major and minor problems required his personal attention.

One full-time occupation should have been the management of Parliament, especially as eighty-five per cent of the elected deputies were without any previous experience of representative government. Nevertheless, in addition to his other duties, it still fell largely upon this one man to defend official policy each day in the *camera*, and the results were unfortunate. Two months after the opening of Parliament he had to complain that no bill of any importance had been voted. Sometimes members did not turn up in sufficient strength to form a quorum and business was brought to a halt; more usually discussions were far too long-winded, or there was an excessive preoccupation with minor procedural and local matters. In one long debate, on sick benefits for sailors of the merchant marine, Cavour had to intervene twenty times. At this rate, he commented, many years of parliamentary business would be consumed to very little effect, and the government would therefore have to legislate by the not very satisfactory and not very liberal method of royal decree.

Finance was perhaps the most difficult problem of all, and Cavour confessed that it would remain more worrying and intractable than the problem of how to win Rome and Venice. If Italy could not balance its budget, or if Italians could not produce far more and pay much higher taxes, he had to agree with Napoleon and the Russian minister Gorchakov that the country might yet disintegrate. For ten years he had deliberately overspent revenue, latterly by as much as a third, in the hope that the other provinces and later generations would gratefully service the debt. The annual deficit in 1861 was running at about four hundred million lire, which was not far short of the total revenue of all the former Italian states put together. Of the accumulated national debt, half was contributed by the former Kingdom of Sardinia, so that a special burden was bound to weigh on newly annexed and poorer regions that hitherto had been financially sheltered. Another problem was that the value of imports remained almost twice that of exports for the whole kingdom.

Several years earlier, Cavour had had to reduce his work-load by giving up the Ministry of Finance, but in 1861 he feared that he might have to take this post once again after finding that other politicians were either inexpert or reluctant to face the unpopularity attached to it. Farini, who was in private life a doctor of medicine, knew that Cavour's health would not have been able to stand the extra burden that this would impose. The job was finally accepted by Pietro Bastogi, a more than competent financier who was later involved in some very unsavoury scandals over the misappropriation of public funds. Bastogi accepted only on condition that he could continue with his many private business affairs, and this meant that the Prime Minister, on top of everything else, had to do some of the work in this most demanding of all departments.

Before he became obviously ill, Cavour's friends and colleagues realized that he was losing his touch. Nigra and Lanza found him more remote, more irritable and excitable, more prone to unexpected and unreasonable bouts of temper. Castelli discovered that Rattazzi still could not understand why Cavour had severed their old friendship, and Lamarmora was once again gratuitously insulted by his former friend and admirer. Valerio and La Farina noted a sadness and withdrawal into himself that made him unlike the cheerful high-spirited companion they had once known and revered. Increasingly he gave the impression of wanting to put off decisions and avoid discussion, as though he lacked the energy to work out complicated solutions and dominate the two houses as he had been wont; and it was unprecedented when he had to be reproached by the Speaker for interrupting other members of Parliament too frequently.

Not surprisingly there was a good deal of impatience with his performance. Ricasoli thought that although Cavour's position was in no immediate danger the government could no longer be sure of its parliamentary majority, while public opinion outside Parliament was also turning against him. Abraham Tourte was another who thought that the government might fall at any moment, and was told by Cavour himself that Ricasoli alone could in that case claim the succession. Sir James Hudson took note of a general dissatisfaction with the conduct of affairs and a lack of confidence in the government's ability to weather the storm. Hudson wrote, surprisingly for such a devoted friend, that 'although Cavour is admired and feared and followed, he is not loved', and confirmed that there was a perceptible move towards Ricasoli as a possible successor.

The King was obviously waiting for just such a move. Victor Emanuel told Hudson in June 1861 that despite Cavour's very considerable qualities as a politician, 'I often doubted whether he were a safe guide'; 'his great statesmanship was at times most hazardous to the state', and possibly Italy would have done as well 'with less labour and without alarming all Europe'. At the minister's last Cabinet meeting, held under Victor Emanuel's presidency in the palace, the sounds of another furious altercation between King and Premier could be heard through the double doors, and both were subsequently seen red in the face with anger.

Cavour had a strong physical constitution, but suffered from two recurrent illnesses. One was said to be gout or 'sciatic gout', which also afflicted his father and brother: sometimes this yielded to homeopathic treatment, or 'magnetism', or to the application of chestnut oil. The other illness must have been malaria. Among the symptoms that still worried him from time to time were violent stomach cramps and 'internal inflammation', accompanied by intermittent fever and occasionally mild derlirium. Possibly relevant is that his naturally ruddy complexion gave way in later life to a general yellowing of the skin. He remained badly overweight, and a young member of the diplomatic service who knew him in these last years remembered chiefly that 'he used to eat a great deal'.

During four days in the previous November, Cavour was in bed with vertigo, fever and delirium. The following month he was again taken with a sudden colic, but it passed after being bled twice. In mid May 1861 he registered a slight fever at Leri where he had gone to escape the heat of Turin, and this was in the dangerous period when the fields were flooded for the new rice crop. Foreigners were warned in contemporary guide books against sleeping anywhere near the rice fields, but Cavour had his own very different ideas on this subject. On 26 May he was visited in Turin by Salmour who was alarmed to find that the whites of his eyes were yellow and his skin had a deathly pallor. He confessed to feeling unwell, and ascribed his poor health to the rift with Rattazzi and his passage of arms with Garibaldi in Parliament.

In each of the next three days there were busy parliamentary sessions, during which he intervened on a dozen occasions. Edward Dicey was in the gallery and noticed that he was unusually nervous and restless. Massari was worried that he showed himself to be intolerant of contradiction, while La Farina observed him in the *camera* holding his head in his hands in a mood of grave dejection. He was again in a black humour when on the twenty-ninth he visited his mistress Bianca Ronzani in the house above Turin that he had provided for her. That evening he suffered what was called 'one of his usual attacks of blood to the head' with fever and violent abdominal pains. Waking his servant about midnight he said he feared an apoplectic attack. His family doctor, Rossi, was called urgently and bled him twice on request, and the next day twice more. Cavour told his niece that he specifically asked for this particular treatment since without it he would have been forced to keep to his bed for two weeks, and he could not afford the time. On the thirty-first he felt cured and held a Cabinet meeting in his apartment.

The use of leeches and the cupping-glass was still fashionable among the more successful physicians of Turin, who adhered to the 'anti-phlogistic' treatment of using blood-letting as a febrifuge. Some of the younger doctors, however (among them Farini and Pantaleoni), had come round to the very different ideas current in northern Europe, which considered bleeding too debilitating a remedy. Cavour did not have much faith in doctors and regularly treated himself by resort to his phlebotomist, even for a sore throat or for exhaustion: he was convinced that this was rendered necessary by his 'surplus of blood'. Unfortunately Farini, who had treated him successfully in the past and warned him against 'heroic remedies', was away from Turin and arrived too late. Farini had done research on the malarial fevers that were common in his home province of Ravenna and might well have made a more salutary diagnosis.

Cavour's personal doctor was uncertain, and this may help to explain why no death certificate was ever issued. Several newspapers gave out that he was suffering from a mysterious disease for which science still had no name. Some people, including Lanza who was also a medical practitioner, said it was typhoid, while other reports called it either encephalitis, enteritis or simply 'cerebral congestion'. There were also fantastic rumours of poison administered by Signora Ronzani, who was said to have been paid for this service by the Emperor Napoleon. The Jesuits preferred to say that the illness must be divine retribution for a sinful life.

Late on 31 May the fever returned with renewed symptoms of

delirium, and a fifth bleeding was ordered. During the next three days Cavour's conversation was constantly wandering. He talked almost always of politics, but in an inconsequential manner that others found hard to follow. He asked for a copy of the history of the first Napoleon by Thiers, but discovered that he was unable to read. Alarmed at this inability to think or concentrate, he said his head was swimming and only being bled yet again would restore his mental balance. Dr Rossi gave way as usual to this demand, but only by considerable pressure on the veins could one or two ounces of black and coagulated blood be obtained.

As these remedies proved ineffective, Dr Maffoni was called upon for a second opinion, and a consultation was sought with Professor Riberi, the court physician who had tended Charles Albert in Oporto twelve years earlier. There were those who blamed Riberi for the death of Victor Emanuel's brother after he was bled no less than eleven times. Riberi diagnosed Cavour's sickness as an inflammation at the base of the brain produced by high blood pressure and a hereditary pre-disposition to gout, ascribing the immediate attack to mental strain complicated by the patient's inability to release the tension or give vent to his feelings.

In Maffoni's estimate, on the other hand, the more serious symptom was that of a tertian fever for which bleeding was in his view not recommended, and it was decided to administer liquid quinine which for many years had been known as a remedy for the disease that later took the clinical name of malaria. Used earlier it might have been effective, but Cavour always hated taking quinine and on this occasion in his weakened state it merely caused repeated vomiting. In his disordered mental condition he insisted at one point on leaving his bed, and there resulted a further minor haemorrhage from one of the incisions that would not heal.

On the evening of 4 June, Cavour on Riberi's instructions took his first nourishment in four days – some soup and a glass of claret – but everyone could see that he was desperately ill. He was visited by the King, to whom he spoke of his obsessive concern for the Neapolitans; they were greatly talented, he said, but might need years of education in liberty before their region was purged of its corruption and could become, as it should be, the richest province of Italy. The King begged Riberi to try one more bloodletting to clear the brain, and even suggested taking it from the jugular vein; to which Riberi replied that the pulse was too weak but he might try some hours later.

The next day, after Cavour's family became desperate, a message was sent to Fra Giacomo da Poirino, the curate deputizing for the local parish priest who had been expelled from his benefice by the government. Padre Giacomo, who belonged to one of the mendicant orders that Cavour had denounced as thoroughly useless and harmful, had promised some years earlier that he would disregard the Prime Minister's excommunication and assist him with the last rites. Tradition in Turin allowed everyone to accompany the viaticum, and a crowd bearing torches moved in procession from the parish church to the Palazzo Cavour. An announcement was made that Cavour had confessed, received absolution, and had particularly asked that the papers should report that he was dying a good Catholic. All night long, many people remained in the streets outside his window. Early on the sixth, in the same house where he had been born, Cavour died peacefully after receiving extreme unction in the presence of his family, the ministers and Sir James Hudson.

Fra Giacomo had earlier asked for and received special authority from the Pope to absolve someone excommunicated who was at the point of death, and Cardinal Antonelli's first reaction was pleasure that Cavour had died with the comforts of religion. But this was on the mistaken assumption that the dying man had first retracted his many errors and made at least verbal reparation for the evil he had done to the Church. When the charitable friar explained that no reparation had been requested, the news was greeted in orthodox circles with disbelief, regret and even outrage. The *Civiltà Cattolica*, a publication of the Jesuits, denied the validity of the last rites if given to anyone anathematized by the Pope himself; in any case, absolution could not be granted to someone delirious who was unable to confess freely. The unfortunate priest was summoned to Rome for punishment and in a personal interview was reprimanded by the Pope for being a cause of grave scandal. Suspended from priestly duties and emoluments, he was subsequently given a small pension by the government, but died many years later in obscurity and penury, despite the fact that his tactful behaviour in 1861 had saved Church and State from a clash that would not lightly have been forgotten.

The day after Cavour's death, Turin was silent, shops were shut and no carriages were seen in the streets. The parliamentary record mentions the indescribable emotion as many deputies wept after Rattazzi gave the news of what he called a national disaster, and sessions of the *camera* were then suspended for three days. *L'Opinione*, the newspaper closest to Cavour, lamented the passing of a person whose authority and prestige had achieved much that would otherwise have been impossible; his powerful mind had put all those near him into the shade. Giuseppe Torelli spoke of 'the Achilles of our Iliad'. Giuseppe Verdi had already called him 'the Prometheus of our national movement'.

Even among those Italian liberals who criticized some of his actions there was a sense of irreplaceable loss. Rattazzi publicly testified to his towering genius. Lamarmora in private said that Cavour's 'grave defects' and overbearing *prepotenza* were entirely outweighed by his extraordinary courage and intellectual gifts. Azeglio, who did not always think highly of Cavour's character and sometimes referred to him as an ambitious and unprincipled adventurer, now wept for 'poor Camille', a great man who perhaps died at the best moment for his reputation before the problems of the new Italy overwhelmed him. Azeglio feared that the 'moral unity' of the country had been damaged by some of the discreditable means that had been used, but accepted that moralistic judgements were insufficient and might well differ from the judgement of history.

Foreigners had equally mixed views but most of them were far more favourable than critical. Foreign politicians were worried by what would happen now that this guiding and moderating hand had been removed. The Austrian Foreign Minister expressed his sadness at the death of such a man and feared that it might precipitate a new crisis in Italy. In Berlin, prices on the stock exchange fell immediately in apprehension that the revolutionaries might now have no one able to control them.

In Paris, Napoleon was similarly concerned whether 'without the coachman the horses may bolt and refuse to re-enter their stable', and he at once broke off his negotiations over the withdrawal of French soldiers from Rome. The Emperor of the French had been helped by Piedmontese policy in his own ambitious schemes, and in return had given more help than any other European statesman to the *risorgimento*, but he also sensed the frailty of a movement that had tried to do so much so quickly. What Thouvenel, the French Foreign Minister, singled out for praise in retrospect was the way Cavour had tried to take account of popular wishes without giving in to them too much. The immediate comment made by the French *chargé d'affaires* at Turin was that Cavour had been a great fighter but not a great builder: Italian unification was still an 'incomplete scaffolding', and regrettably the dead minister had left behind him no expert politicians, no trained assistants and no 'settled system' for his successors to follow.

At Westminster, the Catholics in Parliament shocked most other members by sharply criticizing a man who had violated every law, human and divine. Lord Acton, the Catholic historian, wrote of Cavour's life as 'a triumph of unscrupulous statesmanship' directed more to the greatness of the State than to popular liberty; a true liberal would not have tainted the noble idea of Italian unity by resort to illiberal means. Another man who, while praising his 'almost unrivalled union of subtlety and vigour', judged him to have been 'utterly unscrupulous' was Disraeli.

On the other hand the *Quarterly Review* called him 'the most remarkable man of our generation, and his influence will probably be felt longer and more widely than that of any living being'. *The Economist* agreed that he was 'the foremost statesman in Europe', whose combination of audacity, tact and cool calculation had been equalled by no one in the whole course of English history. Palmerston had already given him a supreme accolade as 'one of the most distinguished patriots who have adorned the history of any country'. To Hudson he was 'in private life the warmest, most constant and most genial of friends'. Palmerston, Russell and the Prince Consort spoke for public opinion in London when they deplored the irreparable bereavement that Italy had sustained.

How great was that loss could best be described by relating the history of the next ten years. Cavour's former colleagues succeeded him in turn as Prime Minister – Ricasoli, Rattazzi, Farini, Minghetti, Lamarmora and Lanza. These were the people whom Ferrari and De Sanctis belittled as 'the generals of Alexander'. All claimed to follow Cavour's policy. All were honourable men, and much in each was to be admired. But none of them lasted very long; none had the vision, the courage, the strength of character possessed by their predecessor, nor his financial experience and acumen. Not one of them had his ability to manage Parliament, nor his fertility of expedient in foreign policy, nor the sheer virtuosity in every branch of the political arts which Cavour exercised, and with which he put his inimitable stamp on the most glorious decade in modern Italian history.

Bibliographical Note

There have been two substantial biographies of Cavour written in English: one of them by A. J. Whyte in two volumes, *The Early Life and Letters of Cavour, 1810–1848* (Oxford, 1925), and *The Political Life and Letters of Cavour* (Oxford, 1930); the other by W. R. Thayer, also in two volumes, *The Life and Times of Cavour* (Boston, 1911). The most convincing and comprehensive character study of Cavour was published by one of his younger friends from Switzerland, William de la Rive, and appeared in English as *Reminiscences of the Life and Character of Count Cavour* (London, 1862). Two other accounts by contemporary authors with first-hand information are R. Dicey, *Cavour: a Memoir* (Cambridge, 1861) and C. de Mazade, *The Life of Count Cavour* (London, 1877).

Documentary material available in English includes one important translated work by Cavour himself, *Considerations on the Present State and Future Prospects of Ireland* (London, 1845); a different version appeared later as *Thoughts on Ireland, its Present and its Future* (London, 1868). One of Cavour's fiercest and most eloquent opponents, A. Brofferio, published a short essay in an English translation, *The Career and Policy of Count Cavour* (London, 1861). A great deal of the diplomatic correspondence between London and Turin can be found in English, notably in *Le Relazioni Diplomatiche fra la Gran Bretagna e il Regno di Sardegna, 1848–60* (7 vols, eds F. Curato and G. Giarrizzo, Rome, 1961–68). Useful but of less direct relevance are *The Roman Question: Extracts from the Despatches of Odo Russell from Rome, 1858–1870* (ed. N. Blakiston, London, 1962); H. R. Marraro, *American Opinion on the Unification of Italy* (New York, 1932); and, in greater detail, *L'Unificazione Italiana vista dai Diplomatici Statunitensi* (4 vols, ed. H. R. Marraro, Rome, 1871).

Two recent outline-histories of the general period by English historians are Stuart Woolf, *A History of Italy, 1700–1860* (London, 1979), and H. Hearder, *Italy in the Age of the Risorgimento, 1790–1870* (London, 1983). Among earlier, more specialized but highly readable books are W. K. Hancock, *Ricasoli and the Risorgimento in Tuscany* (London, 1926), and two volumes by G. M. Trevelyan:

Garibaldi and the Thousand (London, 1909), and *Garibaldi and the Making of Italy* (London, 1911). Later publications include an important study of the National Society by R. Grew, *A Sterner Plan for Italian Unity* (Princeton, 1963); also, in translation, A. C. Jemolo, *Church and State in Italy, 1850–1950* (Oxford, 1960); D. Beales, *England and Italy, 1859–60* (London, 1961); Brigitta Eimer, *Cavour and Swedish Politics* (Lund, 1978); R. Marshall, *Massimo d'Azeglio, an Artist in Politics* (London, 1966). The best current biography of one of Cavour's chief opponents is J. Ridley's *Garibaldi* (London, 1974).

Detailed documentation and references for facts and opinions in this present volume can be found in D. Mack Smith, *The Making of Italy, 1796–1870* (New York and London, 1968); *Victor Emanuel, Cavour and the Risorgimento* (New York and Oxford, 1971); *Cavour and Garibaldi, 1860* (Cambridge, 1954). Other short collections of relevant documents are D. Beales, *The Risorgimento and the Unification of Italy* (new edn, London, 1981); *The Unification of Italy, 1859–1861: Cavour, Mazzini, or Garibaldi* (ed. C. F. Delzell, New York, 1965); *Cavour and the Unification of Italy* (ed. Massimo Salvadori, Princeton, 1961); *Plombières: Secret Diplomacy and the Rebirth of Italy* (ed. Mack Walker, New York and London, 1968).

The basic sources for any biography of Cavour are his own writings, most of which have been published in the original French. A full edition of his personal correspondence is in process of being edited and has so far reached the year 1851 in seven volumes: this is the comprehensive *Epistolario* (ed. C. Pischedda, N. Nada and R. Roccia, Bologna and Florence, 1962–83). Letters from the period after 1856 are to be found, less complete and organized awkwardly by subject rather than chronology, in the *Carteggi di Camillo Cavour* (15 vols, Bologna, 1926–54), and particular mention should be made of the indispensable index to these volumes by Professor Pischedda (Bologna, 1961). Letters for the intervening period 1852–55 must be sought in earlier and somewhat bowdlerized publications, notably *di Camillo Cavour: Lettere Edite ed Inedite* (6 vols, ed. L Chiala, Turin, 1884–7); also *C. Cavour: Nouvelles Lettres Inédites* (ed. A. Bert, Turin, 1889); *Nuove Lettere Inedite del Conte Camillo di Cavour* (ed. E. Mayor, Turin, 1895); and *Una Silloge di Lettere del Risorgimento* (ed. C. Bollea, Turin, 1919). In addition there is *Camillo Cavour: Lettere d'Amore* (ed. M. Avetta, Turin, 1956).

Cavour's parliamentary speeches are easily consultable in the *Discorsi Parlamentari* (15 vols, ed. A. Omodeo, L. Russo and A. Saitta, Florence, 1932–73). His early essays, notebooks and casual writings are to be found in *Tutti gli Scritti di Camillo Cavour* (4 vols, ed. C. Pischedda and G. Talamo, Turin, 1975–78).

Essential for Cavour's early life is the *Diario Inedito con Note Autobiografiche del*

Conte di Cavour (ed. D. Berti, Rome, 1888). For the period 1847–50, a copy of his newspaper *Il Risorgimento* is in the Lilly Library of Indiana University. Many of his diplomatic documents can be found only in *Storia Documentata della Diplomazia Europea in Italia dall'Anno 1814 all'Anno 1861* (vols 7–8, ed. N. Bianchi, Turin, 1870).

A number of contemporaries who knew Cavour well have left particularly interesting accounts of his life. Apart from de la Rive and Mazade mentioned above in their English translations, there is that of G. Massari, *Il Conte di Cavour: Ricordi Biografici* (Turin, 1872), and Massari's *Diario dalle Cento Voci, 1858–1860* (ed. E. Morelli, Rocca S. Casciano, 1959): this latter, in particular, is the most precise and interesting account we possess of the years 1858–60. Another personal and detailed contribution is that of one of his closest associates in journalism and politics, *Il Conte di Cavour: Ricordi di Michelangelo Castelli* (ed. L. Chiala, Turin, 1886; enlarged edition 1888), and *Carteggio Politico di Michelangelo Castelli* (2 vols, ed. L Chiala, Turin, 1890). A further tribute was published by his secretary, I. Artom, in an introduction to *Oeuvre Parlementaire du Comte de Cavour* (ed. I. Artom and A. Blanc, Paris, 1862), with further important details in *L'Opera del Senatore I. Artom nel Risorgimento* (ed. E. Artom, Bologna, 1906). Also of interest for its personal comments is H. d'Ideville, *Journal d'un Diplomate en Italie, 1859–1862* (2 vols, Paris, 1872).

Among more recent studies, four authors stand out as having provided a new direction to research and given it new documentation. The first, with a particular interest in Cavour's religious convictions, was F. Ruffini, *La Giovinezza di Cavour* (2 vols, Turin, 1912), and his *Ultimi Studi sul Conte di Cavour* (Bari, 1936). Another, who first made use of the French national archives, was P. Matter, *Cavour et L'Unité Italienne* (3 vols, Paris, 1925). A third outstanding study of Cavour's parliamentary career was the unfinished work by A. Omodeo, *L'Opera Politica del Conte di Cavour* (2 vols., Florence, 1940), though the author was unaccountably denied access to Cavour's private papers at Santena. These papers have now been catalogued by G. Silengo, *L'Archivio Cavour: Inventario* (3 vols, Santena, 1974), and have been intelligently used by R. Romeo, whose *Cavour e il Suo Tempo* is due to have its fourth and final volume published in the course of 1984: this constitutes, as its title explains, less a biography than a wide-ranging history of the period, dealing in particular with the diplomatic context and economic background. Romeo's conclusions differ in many respects from my own, but this is an important work and is likely to remain the most exhaustive study we shall possess on the subject for some time to come.

For anyone intending to pursue the subject in detail, indispensable documentary material will be found, apart from the unpublished papers on foreign affairs in the archives of the main European countries, in the *Atti Parlamentari* of the legislature in Turin, both the *Discussioni* and the *Documenti* of both houses. Mention must also be made of *Le Relazioni Diplomatiche fra L'Austria e il Regno di Sardegna* (3rd series, vols 3–4, ed. F. Valsecchi, Rome, 1963); and *La Questione Italiana dalle Annessioni al Regno d'Italia nei Rapporti fra la Francia e L'Europa* (4 vols, ed. A. Saitta, Rome, 1968); and *Le Relazioni Diplomatiche tra la Gran Bretagna ed il Regno di Sardegna, 1852–1856* (2 vols, ed. F. Curato, Turin, 1956); and *Die Auswärtige Politik Preussens, 1858–71* (vols 1–3, ed. C. Friese, Berlin, 1933–39).

Sources dealing with other principal characters include *Le Lettere di Vittorio Emanuele II* (2 vols, ed. F. Cognasso, Turin, 1966); *Pio IX e Vittorio Emanuele dal loro Carteggio Privato, 1848–61* (3 vols, ed. P. Pietro Pirri, Rome 1944–61); G. Mazzini, *Scritti Editi ed Inediti* (106 vols, Imola, 1906–73); F. Sclopis, *Diario Segreto, 1859–1878* (ed. P. Pietro Pirri, Turin, 1959); *Epistolario di Giuseppe La Farina* (2 vols, ed. A. Franchi, Milan, 1869); *Giacomo Dina e L'Opera sua nelle Vicende del Risorgimento Italiano* (3 vols, ed. L. Chiala, Turin, 1898); *Carteggio di Michele Amari* (3 vols, ed. A. d'Ancona, Turin, 1896); *Le Carte di Giovanni Lanza* (vols 1–2, Turin, 1935–36); *Memorie di Giorgio Pallavicino* (3 vols, Turin, 1882–95); *Daniele Manin e Giorgio Pallavicino: Epistolario Politico, 1855–1857* (ed. B. E. Maineri, Milan, 1878); G. Asproni, *Diario Politico* (vols 1–3, eds B. J. Anedda and C. Sole, Milan, 1974–80); *Giacomo Durando: Episodi Diplomatici del Risorgimento Italiano dal 1856 al 1863* (ed. C. Durando, Turin, 1901).

A number of important documentary collections have been published dealing with members of the Azeglio family. Two of the more interesting concern Emanuele d'Azeglio who was Piedmontese minister in London – *Carteggi e Documenti Diplomatici Inediti di E. d'Azeglio* (2 vols, ed. A. Colombo, Turin, 1920). For a commentary on events by his mother there is Constance d'Azeglio, *Souvenirs Historiques* (Turin, 1884). For Emanuele's uncle we have a volume by E. Rendu, *L'Italie de 1847 à 1865: Correspondance Politique de Massimo d'Azeglio* (Paris, 1867); also *Lettere di Massimo d'Azeglio a Giuseppe Torelli* (ed. C. Paoli, Milan, 1870); *Lettere di Massimo d'Azeglio a sua Moglie Luisa Blondel* (ed. G. Carcano, Milan, 1870); *Lettere Inedite di Massimo d'Azeglio al Marchese Emanuele d'Azeglio* (ed. N. Bianchi, Turin, 1883); *La Politica di Massimo d'Azeglio dal 1848 al 1859: Documenti in Continuazione alle sue Lettere al Marchese Emanuele d'Azeglio* (ed. N. Bianchi, Turin, 1884; and some of the censored passages can be consulted in the originals which are in the University Library, Cambridge); *Massimo d'Azeglio e Diomede Pantaleoni: Carteggio Inedito* (ed. G. Faldella, Turin, 1888). Most important of all is *Massimo d'Azeglio: Scritti e Discorsi Politici* (3 vols, ed. M. de Rubris, Florence, 1938).

It may be helpful to mention some of the many additional books that deal with individual problems or successive periods in Cavour's life. For his earlier years we have D. Berti, *Il Conte di Cavour avanti il 1848* (originally published in 1886, but reissued in 1945 at Milan with an introduction by F. Bolgiani); and an essay on his schooldays in G. Falco, *Pagine Sparse di Storia e di Vita* (Milan, 1960). For his views on economics and his place in economic history there is P. Guichonnet, *Cavour Agronomo e Uomo d'Affari* (Milan, 1961); A. Dunand-Henry, *Les Doctrines et la Politique Economique du Comte de Cavour* (Paris, 1902); F. Arese, *Cavour e le Strade Ferrate* (Milan, 1953); *C. Cavour: Scritti di Economia* (ed. F. Sirugo, Milan, 1962); G. Guderzo, *Finanza e Politica in Piemonte alle Soglie del Decennio Cavouriano* (Santena, 1973); *Cavour Agricoltore: Lettere Inedite* (ed. E. Visconti, Florence, 1913); *Lettere di Giacinto Corio a Camillo Cavour, 1843–1855* (ed. A. Rogge, Santena, 1980).

For the period 1848–57 important references can be found in *Ricordi Politici di Giuseppe Torelli* (ed. C. Paoli, Milan, 1873); *Ricordi di Ercole Ricotti* (ed. A. Manno, Turin, 1886); M. Ricci, *Ritratti e Profili Politici e Letterari* (Florence, 1882); L. Chiala, *Une Page d'Histoire du Gouvernement Représentatif en Piémont* (Turin, 1858); G. Gonni, *Cavour Ministro della Marina* (Bologna, 1926); A. Brofferio, *Fisionomie Parlamentari* (Turin, 1853); *Diario Politico di Margherita Provana di Collegno, 1852–1856* (ed. A. Malvezzi, Milan, 1926). Three excellent studies published more recently are E. di Nolfo, *Europa e Italia nel 1855–1856* (Rome, 1967); F. Valsecchi, *L'Europa e il Risorgimento: l'Alleanza di Crimea* (Florence, 1968); and C. Pischedda, *Problemi dell'Unificazione Italiana* (Modena, 1963). Useful essays are contained in *Miscellanea Cavouriana* (ed. Fondazione 'Camillo Cavour', Turin, 1964).

For the last years of Cavour's life there is a vast literature to consult. Among the more important volumes, the war of 1859 is treated in P. Pieri, *Storia Militare del Risorgimento* (Turin, 1962), and abundant documentation is given in four volumes of *La Guerra del 1859 per L'Indipendenza d'Italia* (ed. Comando del Corpo di Stato Maggiore, Rome, 1910). For the annexation of central Italy and the surrender of Savoy: Luc Monnier, *L'Annexion de la Savoie à la France et la Politique Suisse* (Geneva, 1932); R. Avezou, *La Savoie depuis les Réformes de Charles Albert jusqu'à l'Annexion à la France* (Chambéry, 1934); U. Marcelli, *Cavour Diplomatico dal Congresso di Parigi a Villafranca* (Bologna, 1961); G. del Bono, *Cavour e Napoleone III: le Annessioni dell'Italia Centrale, 1859–60* (Turin, 1941); R. Ugolini, *Cavour e Napoleone III nell'Italia Centrale* (Rome, 1973).

Relations with the papal government are discussed in L. M. Case, *Franco-Italian Relations, 1860–1865: the Roman Question and the Convention of September* (Philadelphia, 1932); M. Tedeschi, *Cavour e la Questione Romana, 1860–1861* (Milan, 1978); M. de Leonardis, *L'Inghilterra e la Questione Romana, 1859–1870* (Milan, 1980); E. Passerin d'Entrèves, *L'Ultima Battaglia Politica di Cavour: i Problemi dell'Unificazione Italiana* (Turin, 1956); *Il Carteggio Antonelli-Sacconi, 1858–1860* (ed. M. Gabriele, Rome, 1962); M. Mazziotti, *Il Conte di*

Cavour e il suo Confessore (Bologna, 1915).

For the period 1860–61, with particular reference to internal political controversies, mention should be made of A. Petracchi, *Le Origini dell'Ordinamento Comunale e Provinciale Italiano* (Venice, 1962); N. Raponi, *Politica e Amministrazione in Lombardia agli Esordi dell'Unità* (Milan, 1967); C. di Persano, *Diario Privato-Politico-Militare nella Campagna Navale degli Anni 1860–1861* (4 vols, Florence, 1869–71); F. Petruccelli della Gattina, *I Moribondi del Palazzo Carignano* (Milan, 1862); G. Stefani, *Cavour e la Venezia Giulia* (Florence, 1955); A. Tamborra, *Cavour e i Balcani* (Turin, 1958); I. Nazzari-Micheli, *Cavour e Garibaldi nel 1860: Cronistoria Documentata* (Rome, 1911); F. Brancato, *La Dittatura Garibaldina nel Mezzogiorno e in Sicilia* (Trapani, 1965); A. Scirocco, *Governo e Paese nel Mezzogiorno nella Crisi dell' Unificazione, 1860–61* (Milan, 1963).

Index